Writing Places

Other readers featured in the "Longman Topics" series include:

A Longman Topics Reader

Writing Places

PAULA MATHIEU
Boston College

GEORGE GRATTAN
Boston College

TIM LINDGREN
Boston College

STACI SHULTZ
Boston College

PEARSON
Longman

New York   San Francisco   Boston
London   Toronto   Sydney   Tokyo   Singapore   Madrid
Mexico City   Munich   Paris   Cape Town   Hong Kong   Montreal

Publisher: Joseph Opiela
Marketing Manager: Alexandra Smith
Senior Supplements Editor: Donna Campion
Production Manager: Joseph Vella
Project Coordination, Text Design, and Electronic Page Makeup:
    GGS Book Services, Atlantic Highlands
Cover Designer/Manager: Wendy Ann Fredericks
Cover Photo: © Deborah Davis/Photo Edit
Manufacturing Buyer Manager: Mary Fischer
Printer and Binder: Courier Corp.—Westford
Cover Printer: Coral Graphics Services

For permission to use copyrighted material, grateful
acknowledgment is made to the copyright holders on
pp. 253–254, which are hereby made part of this copyright page.

Library of Congress Cataloging-in-Publication Data

Writing places / edited by Paula Mathieu . . . [et al.].
    p. cm. — (Longman topics)
    ISBN 0-321-31685-1
  1. Readers—Geography. 2. Geography—Problems, exercises, etc.
3. English language—Rhetoric—Problems, exercises, etc. 4. Report
writing—Problems, exercises, etc. 5. College readers. I. Mathieu,
Paula. II. Longman topics.

PE1127.G4W76 2005
808'.0427—dc22

                                                    2005043597

Please visit us at http://www.ablongman.com

ISBN 0-321-31685-1

  2 3 4 5 6 7 8 9 10—CRW—08 07 06

CONTENTS

TOPICAL CONTENTS

Travel, Leisure, and Exploration

Technology and Place

Global Places, Local Places

WHY DOES PLACE MATTER?

Writing Places invites students to develop writing skills through an inquiry into places from their past, present, and future. The act of *place writing* involves researching and writing about familiar locales as well as new ones via a range of inquiry methods and writing genres. This anthology combines an eclectic range of place-based essays written by professional writers, community members, and college students whose work spans geographic areas across the United States and beyond—from Maine to Hawaii, Florida to Washington, North Dakota to Venezuela. We feel the range of writers from professional to student is important, not as a model/antimodel approach, but because it presents place writing from people of different ages and locations, at different places in their own lives and in their development as writers. All of the essays were chosen as positive examples of writers seeking to engage a place important to them. Taken together, the essays showcase a variety of methods for inquiring into and researching places—from observation, interviewing, and memoir to library and Web-based research. For each reading, *Writing Places* offers questions and activities to encourage students' own explorations of local places. The book concludes with a toolkit of skills and exercises geared to helping students observe, remember, explore, record, research, and write.

WRITING PLACES . . .
allows students to learn important writing
and academic skills . . .

Asking students to examine and write about a place—whether a familiar haunt from the past or a new locale on a campus, in a city, or in the wild—invokes questions and issues that are simultaneously personal, social, and academic. How students initially remember or respond to a given place depends on their individual identities and life experiences; but that impression can also be formed, changed, or challenged by the broader social context of the place itself, its history, and changing dynamics. Observing, listening, interviewing, researching the past and present, and placing oneself within larger social structures and ongoing civic debates are all skills gained from encountering places as a writing student. As students become attentive observers and participants in a variety of places, they also practice the writing skills critical to academic success.

in ways that provoke innovative and engaging essays . . .

In any writing classroom the simple question, "Where are you from?" can evoke an impossibly rich variety of locales, stories, and histories in response. As a teacher, when you encourage students to write about places, you will likely receive essays on topics that are wide-ranging, specific and, best of all, interesting to read. Place writing allows students to bring their personal histories and experience to bear while encountering new places and developing new academic skills. When asking students to write about and attend to places, you can teach skills important to academic success—including careful observation, critical thinking, and accurate recording—while encouraging students to explore questions important to the places from their pasts, the changing places around them today, and their individual and collective future places in the world.

in a spirit of personal, cultural, and academic inquiry . . .

Writing Places assumes that students learn writing most organically when engaged in relevant, intellectual inquiries. Working from that assumption, we have organized this book around three simple, yet essential questions: Where are we from? Where are we? Where are we going? Learning from our pasts, attending to present places, and imagining and working toward better futures are all hallmarks of conscientious students and mindful citizens. *Writing Places* underscores the role writing can play in thinking through and debating issues of personal and social importance. Additional possibilities for inquiry—centered on topics such as technology, food production, the environment, and globalization—are offered in our topical table of contents.

in a small, inexpensive book that can be used flexibly, in a variety of courses, in a variety of ways.

We, the four editors of this collection, each come to the topic of place writing from different geographic starting points and different intellectual motivations—including cultural studies, environmental studies, technological concerns, and pedagogical interests—and as such, we do not teach the same writing classes in the same way. At the same time, we do not like to ask students to buy large, expensive readers for one short semester. Our goal has been to offer a collection that is concise but flexible. *Writing Places* compiles a range of student and professional essays that can be used in a variety of classes with various inquiries from which to choose and design a relevant place-writing course. Because the needs of writing instructors and students differ, we also include a chapter entitled "Tools for Getting Places," a collection of exercises and resources for helping students learn to observe, to interview, and to research local places.

ACKNOWLEDGMENTS

The creation of *Writing Places* involved collaborations that extended well beyond the four authors and our editor, and we wish to give our thanks to all those who helped us.

We first wish to thank the Boston College faculty and students of the First-Year Writing program who continue to generate such dynamic discussions of place-based writing. Thanks to Lad Tobin and his unwavering commitment to student writing and his enthusiastic support of our individual and collective pursuits within composition studies. We particularly thank our own students, and especially the BC student authors included in this volume: Andrea Casassa, Gian-Karlo Casimiro, Virginia Di Tata, Mathew Dudley, Robin Dunn, Sonny Fabbri, Emily Keane, Shawn McGrath, Matthew O'Connor, and Kimberly Wheaton. Along with student author Erin Komada of St. John's University, these writers earned our considerable appreciation and respect for their diligence and goodwill during the editing process.

Thanks to our editor at Longman, Joe Opiela, for encouraging this project. Thanks also to his editorial assistant, Eden Kram, for helping us keep track of all the details.

Thanks to the writers and editors at the *Journal of Ordinary Thought* for presenting such important, ongoing examples of "ordinary" people writing about the places around them. We especially appreciate Carrie Spitler and Annie Knepler for their essential assistance and advice throughout the project. Special thanks also goes to Jennifer Marlow at *Orion Magazine* for permissions assistance above and beyond the call of duty.

Derek Owens, your work in place-based and sustainable composition continues to inspire us; we thank you for opening the door into this world and for supplying such wonderful examples. Similarly deserving of our gratitude are the many members of the Association for the Study of Literature and Environment (ASLE) who have contributed to our thinking on these issues through conference papers, online conversations, and personal contacts in ways too numerous and varied to list here.

Thanks to the staff (and listening patrons) of Cafénation in Brighton, Massachusetts, our own clean, well-caffeinated place in which much of the work of this book occurred. Thanks also to Alex Tsouvalas for installing a wireless Internet network that made our work easier and to Judy Plank for her kind assistance with the manuscript.

Mary Benard, the fifth member of this team, helped us not only with our many permissions needs but also with the details that unnerved us at every turn, and deserves our warmest thanks.

Finally, thanks to all our friends and family, who generously shared their own thoughts on place and identity and who now know more about place-based studies than they ever thought they would.

PAULA MATHIEU
GEORGE GRATTAN
TIM LINDGREN
STACI SHULTZ

TO THE STUDENT

ORIENTING TO A PLACE

At most colleges and universities, orientation introduces students like yourself to a new campus. This introductory period may involve dry lectures from administrators about financial aid and course registration, stacks of brightly colored handouts describing all the services and activities on campus, and enthusiastic orientation leaders organizing social events to ease the awkwardness of meeting new people.

While orientation is designed to introduce you to a new place, the actual process of orienting yourself occurs over a longer period as you take classes, build friendships, and learn to work and study in this new environment. Knowledge of places, however, comes not only through time spent *in* them but also through attention paid *to* them. When we talk about attending to place, we refer to the meanings that we create in spaces ("place = space + meaning" is one common description of this dynamic), what we sometimes refer to as one's "sense of place." We believe that mindfulness about places—critical thinking, close observation, and personal reflection—can help us better understand ourselves and our environment while we also hone the very skills necessary for academic success.

Writing About Place

Now that we have introduced the topic of academic success, you may be wondering what the concept of place has to do with writing. Writing can help create a sense of place because writing is a fundamental way of making meaning, not just a way of getting a grade for a class or "expressing" innermost feelings. Since we often don't know what we think until we write it down, writing plays an important role in constructing a sense of place. At the same time, as we explore places, we learn to attend to details and value the complexity and dynamic nature of the everyday—skills important for any writer. Put simply, writing helps us understand places, and paying attention to places helps us become better writers.

For this reason, this book is organized around three guiding questions: Where are we from? Where are we? Where are we going? These may seem like simple questions but in fact figuring out our relationships to various places is a lifelong process.

When writing in academic settings, we are often encouraged to think critically about how our identities are shaped by racial backgrounds, social classes, and gender and sexual identities. But *place* is often overlooked as a useful category for exploring who we are and what shapes us. Places are so fundamental—we cannot imagine life without them—yet, we often take them for granted so that they recede into the background, like the scenery in a play. We focus on the actors, not on the set.

When we turn our attention to place, however, it can become a central character and we learn to relate to it on a deeper level. This increased attention may occur because the places we know well undergo change, or because we encounter new places, or because we simply decide to be more mindful of places in general.

Writing makes sense only when it is put into a meaningful context; taking a quote out of context often leads to misinterpretation or confusion. Similarly, our lives only make sense when we understand our sense of place in a broader context: both the physical make-up of that place—buildings, trees, roads, size, weather, concrete—and the shared social meanings associated with that place before we ever get there.

But it is not necessary to be a geography or engineering major in order to explore cultural and physical contexts; every discipline has something to contribute to the conversation, and in fact, we cannot fully understand where we are unless we can draw on diverse areas of knowledge. As you can tell by the topical table of contents in this book, there are numerous directions from which you can approach the topic of place, regardless of whether your major is business or biology, political science or computer science, art or agriculture.

Cultivating a critical sense of place does matter. If you are not able to do this, there is a good chance someone else will do it for you—advertisers who want you to buy their products or stay in their hotels, developers who want to change the neighborhood around you whether or not you agree to it, or companies who want to dump toxic waste near your house despite its impact on your health. For this reason, the writers in this collection tend to ask hard questions about place: Who has the power to change places? Whose interests do these changes serve? How do places affect our health? How do the choices we make in local places affect the health of those in other countries? When does a place become unjust?

In addition to reading about these writers' places and considering some of their questions, you will also go out and explore some places from *your* past, present, and possible futures. In doing so, you will develop important writing and research skills that will serve you throughout your academic career and beyond. And by research, we mean many things: surfing the Internet and properly citing books and articles from the library are important forms of *secondary research*, but you will also practice skills of *primary research*—for instance, conducting your own interviews or carefully recording observations.

Writing in a college or university setting is a way to start some important conversations that you will continue, whether you return to the neighborhood you grew up in or move to another continent. In this book, you will encounter a group of writers engaged in this process at various stages of their lives, and their essays invite you to join in the conversation with your own writing. Whether written by other students your age or by professional writers with more experience, these essays offer positive examples of different approaches to exploring your sense of place, approaches that will vary widely based on your geographic location, your stage in school, and your unique life experiences. As you start writing about place, we hope you will find you are more interested in these topics than in traditional writing assignments and that the writing you produce matters more to you and the audiences for whom you write.

PAULA MATHIEU
GEORGE GRATTAN
TIM LINDGREN
STACI SHULTZ

CHAPTER 1

Where Are We From?

Where are you from? It is a question you have likely asked—and answered—a thousand times, especially when meeting new people or traveling to unfamiliar places. We all rely on this seemingly simple question because it reveals crucial information about other people's histories and identities. But how often do you pose this question to yourself? How thoughtfully do you regard the places of your past? If who you are is bound up with the places you're from, it seems worthwhile to investigate those places of your past and how they have helped to define you.

Pausing to consider where you are from seems particularly relevant when journeying from one place to another. For instance, you have likely begun considering the places you are from, even unconsciously, during your transition from high school to college. Here are a few questions for you to answer as you begin to reflect more deeply on where you are from:

- Would you describe your hometown as urban, suburban, rural, rapidly changing, or relatively stable?
- Were you raised in the same state or country where you were born?
- What meaning does your home state or country have for you?
- Does your family still live in the same house or apartment where you grew up? What is the first place that comes to mind when you think of "home"?
- How many cities or states or countries have you lived in? Which ones, if any, feel like "home"?
- How would you describe the street on which you grew up? What would a visitor notice first?

- What places beyond your home were consistently important to you (your grandparents' house, a neighborhood gathering place, a secret spot for you and your friends)?
- What public or semipublic spaces in your hometown or neighborhood were important to you or seemed to define the place (a park, store, school, church, community center)?
- Was there a place that was important to you (a park, store, or vacant lot) that is no longer there today and is now something else? How do you feel about the new place?
- Did your family travel, move around much, or have places they vacationed regularly?
- What was the population of your hometown twenty years ago?
- How might you describe the street where you grew up in terms of economics, traffic patterns, and neighbor relations? Did people take public transportation or drive to work? Did they hang out on the sidewalks and talk or have gated yards? How did your street differ from others in your town, city, or state?

The contributing authors in this chapter have addressed many of these questions. Their essays vary in style and purpose: some are persuasive, some are celebratory, and some are more critical as they examine the traditions, families, communities, and landscapes that have helped to shape identities. What becomes clear is that the authors share a similar goal: discovering the often complex and symbolic meanings attached to the notion of place. For example, Gian-Karlo Casimiro's essay ("Get Off at 161st and Transfer to the Truth") reads like an ode to the Bronx in which he at once celebrates the diversity of his hometown and attempts to dispel outsiders' negative perceptions of it. Tim Lindgren argues against Hollywood's depiction of Fargo, North Dakota, while struggling to determine his own relationship with the city ("On Being from *Fargo*"). Virginia Di Tata examines her developing sense of self and place as she moves from one country to another and then back again ("A Bridge Between Two Cultures"). Whether writing about specific physical landmarks or more general cultural landscapes, the reflections of these writers often fluctuate—from pride to despair to joy and all the other sentiments the places of our past can invoke.

To write about place means to write about yourself, which means tapping into your emotions to ultimately generate writing that is meaningful to you. Writing about place can serve as a vehicle for you to persuade, describe, research, and narrate topics that are important to you. In turn, working with topics that are interesting to you will likely make your audience interested in them as well.

Like the authors in this chapter, you might find that your emotions and memories complicate how you understand yourself and the places you have encountered, which in turn makes answering the question of where you are from rather difficult. Your answer might be nuanced: "Well, I was born here but raised there," or "I am a native of there but a transplant to here," or "I consider several different places home." How you define home varies according to individual needs and associations. For instance, "home" might mean the place you vacation every year, the coffee shop where you worked during high school, another country in which you spent a brief but significant time, or wherever you are surrounded by friends or family. Chances are that your definition of home is more complicated than you might have thought.

For some of us, our home is far from where we are now; home can mean that place to which we return occasionally, only to leave again. Because we live in an increasingly mobile culture, it is possible to consider more than one place as home. On the one hand, this mobility offers the freedom to pursue opportunities in other places. Each new place represents a move from the past to the present to the future. On the other hand, this freedom can compromise our sense of stability, our rootedness in one place. No wonder, then, that our attachment to "home" seems tenuous, that just as we move from place to place the places of our past seem to change in profound ways—or perhaps *we* are the ones who change.

But it is not just the changes in ourselves that we should consider. The places of our past have pasts as well, and as we reflect, research, and write about these places we should also think about how much they change over time as well. Questions about the changes in population and traffic flow of a hometown or neighborhood reflect the change that is almost inevitable everywhere we go. Whether we define this change as progress or destruction depends on our attachment and understanding of a particular place. Over the next few years the place you call home might undergo tremendous change, whether it be to the physical landscape or socioeconomic climate. Do such changes reflect events on a national or even global level? How will these changes affect you? How will they affect your understanding of the places you inhabit now, like your university?

All college students share at least one place in common: their campus. The university setting can bring together students from various parts of a city, state, or country or even the world. But this migration to one common place can disrupt connections to home places and destabilize an ingrained sense of identity. The authors in this chapter recall places as disparate as Iowa and Venezuela and reflect on their transitions from one place to another and the disruptions that accompany their journeys. As a group, they contribute to a national and intergenerational experience of past places.

Where we are from colors our present and future experiences: It helps shape our political views, our responses to environmental concerns, and our positions on social issues. The places of our past inform our present and future sense of place, community, and self. Throughout this book we ask you to examine the places that shape who you are—and how you shape them. In this chapter, we will ask you to think specifically about where you are from and to reflect on the interplay of the physical and socioeconomic landscapes and your perceptions, memories, and identities of those places.

Mom and the Kitchen
KIMBERLY WHEATON

Kimberly Wheaton attended Phillips Exeter Academy in New Hampshire and is currently a student at Boston College. This essay comes from Wheaton's Lodge, *a longer nonfiction narrative that she wrote for a First-Year Writing Seminar. "Mom and the Kitchen" illustrates Wheaton's personal connection to her family's fishing lodge in Maine in which she was born and raised.*

◆

She looks back at me, dishcloth in one hand, spatula in the other, and finishes her sentence, ". . . but these women deserve a raise every year. I'm just worried that if we keep on going at this rate your father and I will be in debt by the time we retire!" She scratches her nose with her wrist—the only part of her forearm free of turkey grease.

"I know it's hard, Mom," I reply empathetically, "but if you ask me, I don't think they'd take another job for the world. They tell me that they appreciate everything you do for them while they clean the cabins. I mean, what other boss buys each employee a fifty-dollar gift at the end of the working season? I don't think they would even question your decision to deny them *another* raise. . . . At this point in their careers, they've probably forgotten how much they earn anyway!"

Mom considers my response but conscientiously returns to her original thought, "Oh I know, but it's a matter of being fair, and if I were in their position I would expect a larger paycheck. They are certainly worth it! I'm just getting tired," she says, as if to scold herself for dwelling on the issue of money. "It's that time of the season again."

The calendar hanging above the dinner table indicates Mom's point. It *is* that time of the season: September ninth, less than a month left until closing time. It is filled with colorful scenes drawn by guides and kitchen women who collectively agree that a countdown for the end of the season is in order. Each day a worker digs into the basket of my old markers and crayons, and carefully sketches something in his or her designated square. The traditional calendar countdown helps us all maintain optimism and a sense of humor during a time when most workers (including my parents) become frustrated with the business and its necessity for constant attention. The first drawing is made when there is one month left of work—one month until "the end of the year party" that is held in the dining room to celebrate another great season. The latest drawing is signed by Mitchell, an old fishing guide who used to hand me butterscotch candies when Mom and Dad weren't looking. His artwork exhibits a guest (whom he hopes will catch a glimpse of his clever idea) fishing, but on the end of the guest's line are the feces of the fish on his own line. I remember hearing him chuckle as he drew this after a long day out on the lake.

Mom continues to talk as soon as I look back from the calen- 5 dar. "Mr. Gwirtzman came up from his camp last night because his father keeled over in chest pains. We called an ambulance and luckily the old fella got back on his feet by the time it got here, thank goodness. It's ridiculous how long it takes the Houlton ambulance to get all the way out here to Forest City—almost an hour! I would just hate to think about what'd happen if old Mr. Gwirtzman's pain had continued. All I can say is it's been a long day following a long night." She begins to saw through the clean turkey with a loud electric knife, but pauses after three slices. "So, what's on the docket for the day, Kimbo?" she inquires, hoping to free her mind of the morning trifles involved in serving breakfast, and the wages of the kitchen crew.

My ambitions hardly compare to hers but I reply, "I might try the new kayaks out." Actually, my agenda only involves getting back to this very table to taste the butternut squash, stuffed turkey, and sugar snapped peas on the menu for tonight.

She moves from counter to counter in the large but orderly kitchen, with no more haste than brushing her teeth. While watching these mechanical movements, I ask, "Don't you get sick of this, day in and day out?" but realize immediately that my harsh reaction contradicts her daily optimism.

"I don't have time to get sick of it," she says with a smirk. "The good thing about this job is that as there is a beginning, there is also an end—but even the end wasn't as promising back when your father and I started out. I can remember going to bed with a Betty Crocker cookbook every night, trying to learn recipes so it didn't take me five times to boil an egg. Believe me, I was probably more clueless back then than you would be if you took this place over now. It took some time to get used to the cooking, the desk-work, the cleaning . . . and everything else that goes along with the job, especially when you and your sister were first born. God bless you, but I got so little sleep that I started having panic attacks! Your dad would be exhausted from guiding fisherman out in the sun all day, and so it took us every bit of strength to get up with you in the middle of the night.

"But as far as that goes, I wouldn't have missed having you girls for the world. In fact, when you started getting older, I would set aside about two hours every night to read to you—even when we had guests who wanted to talk with us in the lobby. I figured that your father could handle that part of the business on his own. I knew that if I didn't get my time in with you while I still could, it would come back to haunt me later on. That was the best part of my day, reading to you girls. I could get off my feet and away from the chaos of this place, spending time with the greatest kids in the world." She winks at me, puts the electric knife down since she has finished dressing the turkey, and washes her hands. I am always amazed at the amount of cooking she does, separately from our two cooks. She rarely sits down, unless it is at the desk to fill out fishing licenses for guests or to book reservations from phone conversations. She momentarily breaks from the action, however, when she returns to the topic of the kitchen women.

10   "They were so helpful when you girls were young. First of all, you were a lot easier to handle than your sister. It's a wonder we even decided to have another child after the way she used to cry. But you, oh you were great. During dinner, while we all sat eating around the

table, you would sleep peacefully in the center. The women may not be the most educated crew, but they sure know how to handle a baby. It was and still is great having them work here since they're like an extended family." She pauses for a moment, and I can sense her new train of thought. "But sometimes our closeness has repercussions. As you know, I'm already uncomfortable in the position of 'boss,' so it's hard to voice my mind when something needs to be done differently in the dining room or during cleaning. When a guest is unhappy, it's essential that I inform the women of what needs to be done, and I just hate instructing people who I consider to be my equals—especially those equals who helped raise my own two children! Granted, they do the job just as precisely as I would most of the time, so there is no need for excessive criticism."

I chuckle to show that I'm still listening, and she carries on. "Your father has an easier time directing the guides. If something they do is not correct, or isn't done efficiently, he will tell them straight out. Men are very different than women when it comes to constructive advice. Your father doesn't understand why I can't treat the kitchen crew like the guides, but I tell him that if I did, we wouldn't *have* a kitchen crew!"

Mom's tone becomes edgy as she speaks of Dad. I remember her telling me about how hard the fishing lodge is on a marriage. "It is a stressful job, and all of that stress falls on the little time I share with your dad." Despite hard times, though, they have managed to stay together, and now both Mom and Dad speak comically about being "too damn tired to split up."

In the summer, when the guests are taken care of, Mom is usually thinking about whether the lodge meets the guests' expectations. If the topic of business improvement arises, she will fully exhaust every possibility for change, until she cannot think aloud anymore. Usually these bursts of brainstorming end with ". . . overall I think we do a pretty good job of keeping the customers happy. And the guests love the Maine culture—even the accents and hard nature of the kitchen women. It all seems to come together from season to season, and that's why we keep coming back to work hard." Mom is in the middle of this contemplation as she washes her hands in the sink.

For a moment, I forget that I am in the kitchen with her. I revisit moments within the last week in which several guests have come up to me and complimented the lodge, the fishing, the meals, and the hospitality of the business. I reply to each comment with a "thank you," but cannot begin to take responsibility for the work behind such praise.

Guiding Questions

1. How would you describe Wheaton's mother? Why does Wheaton choose the kitchen as the backdrop for this essay?
2. How would you describe Wheaton's relationship with her mother? What moments in this narrative offer insight into this relationship?

Paths for Further Exploration

1. Write a character sketch of a friend or relative that is based on a place you associate with that person.
2. Have you ever lived and worked in the same place (or nearby)? If you have, write about that experience. If you have not, write about what you imagine that experience would be like.

The Joy of Mud

CATHERINE BLACK

Born in Nairobi, Kenya, Catherine Black went to high school in Hawaii and since then has lived in Providence, Rhode Island, Kailua, Hawaii, and San Francisco. "The Joy of Mud" first appeared in the collection ReGeneration: Telling Stories from Our Twenties. *Like many of the other authors who contributed to that collection, Black addresses the angst of twentysomethings enduring a "quarter-life crisis." She is now developing a magazine in Argentina and hopes to use her professional training in media to connect culture, place, and identity in both personal and social arenas. She plans to return to the Hawaiian Islands for good one day.*

———————— ✦ ————————

taro: an Asian tuber, the cultivation of which reached its largest scale in ancient Hawai'i.
lo'i: taro patches; traditional wetland beds in which taro was irrigated by a complex network of tributaries diverted from mountain streams.
poi: delicacy made by peeling, pressure cooking, and grinding the root (corm) of the taro plant.

A s always, it is warm outside. Another Wednesday morning in the endless summer I remember so well. With its unnerving ability to erase the passage of time, Hawai'i once again dissolves the years that separated us. Waking in the familiar soft air blowing through my louvers, I put on some old shorts and a swimsuit, wondering what Vince—my poi-pounding friend from the Wai'ane—has in store for me "up Mauka." The term normally refers to the mountains, but today seems to harbor a secret surprise. All I know is that we're headed for Waiahole Valley.

He soon scoops me up in his pickup truck and we drive north along the coast, presided over by the Windward Mountains in their wet, green glory. Entering the rolling pastures of Kahalu'u, traffic narrows into a single-file line; orchid farms and cows replace the Burger Kings and strip malls of concrete-encased Kaneohe. Vince updates me about his life on the West Side while we crack open pistachios, popping them into our mouths and tossing a trail of shells from the windows. I squint at the morning, dazzling between the boats on the bay.

Entering Waiahole Valley and parking beneath a banyan, Vince steps into the forest on a narrow footpath. Wild ginger and elephant ear break the light above us into geometric green and gold shapes. We cross one shallow stream, then another, both cold and quick around my bare feet. Vince walks ahead, his dark ponytail brushing the top of his T-shirt.

Turning a corner and descending a short, muddy slope, a wooden shack-like structure comes into view below us: smoke rising from a pit nearby, figures moving about, a large brown horse with a pale star on its forehead. The sun drips through an immense mango tree, pooling light through the smoke and creating bands of bright blue that twist like serpents into the sky. Beyond it, a breadfruit tree, some rows of papaya, and about two acres of taro patches, each divided by raised pathways of packed earth and thick grass, fresh Waiahole stream water swirling through the beds on its downhill path to the sea. The forest is a lush wall on all sides, and the mountains are crowned with clouds overhead.

I stop for a moment, stunned by the realization that this place   5
has always existed only twenty minutes from where I grew up. "OK, Cat," Vince turns to me with a grin, "are you ready to work for your lunch?"

Ten minutes later, I find myself sinking knee-deep in the lo'i, trying gingerly to stay as clean as possible. This is no easy task, since mud is in great abundance here. It's the beginning and end of taro's growth cycle and therefore, they tell me, the beginning and end of our own. Stepping into the lo'i is like stepping into a vat of chocolate syrup, only cooler, and pungent with the fresh, damp smell of nutrient-rich soil. My assigned task is to pull

out the weeds that eagerly choke taro corms before they can
mature.

At some point I forget about staying clean and grow increasingly absorbed in this wet world. Several hours pass, and I am still
bent over among silky, heart-shaped leaves that nod pleasantly at
me in the breeze, marveling at the mud as it slips smooth between
my toes, the long, hidden weeds straining against my foot soles. My
movements acquire a slow, deliberate rhythm as I travel up and
down the rows, pulling out green stems at the root, rinsing the rich
mud off, and tossing them onto the wet embankment. Taro—the
mythical ancestor of the Hawaiian people, the metaphor for family
and the ancient symbol of life—is also a glossy-leafed tuber that
thrives in mountain mud. *How nice to finally meet you,* I think, as I
pull up a fat corm and inspect its pink, root-whiskered body.

Vince is demonstrating to a group of teenagers nearby how to
cut the tuber from the stalk with a machete and save the latter for
replanting. There are probably twenty people scattered throughout the lo'i, and they all seem to know one another on that multi-
generational level that turns everyone you meet into an infinite
amalgam of cousins, aunties, and uncles. *What would it be like to
be surrounded by so much family?* I think to myself.

A flash of equilibrium and understanding penetrates me and
seems to set quietly in my muscles and bones. *So this is Hawai'i,* I
think with surprise. After sixteen years of floating on the periph-
eries of an island home I never cared for, I've snapped straight
back into its cool green heart. The combination of sweat and sur-
real scenery, the labor of cultivating food with others, the clarity
and sweetness of the stream as it weaves among us—it all combines so that just standing here, with the mud dripping down my
calves, makes me ache with a kind of goofy happiness. "I love this
place," I say out loud, and Vince, looking my way, says, "doesn't
everyone?"

10   Until that moment of seamlessness in a Waiahole taro patch,
I believed that beautiful places were meant for admiration, like
pieces of art, more than concrete grounds for participation. Bicultural and bred on mobility, I wound through a series of exotic
exhibits that led me to absorb the world with an art dealer's
distance and a teenager's ego. I watched carefully—often
marveling—but rarely engaged, and certainly didn't commit.

Born in Kenya to a Japanese mother and an American father,
I spent most of my adolescence in Hawai'i waiting impatiently to
escape. Unconsciously, I exuded a cultural and intellectual elitism
that put me out of sync with the down-to-earth humility of the

Islands. Instead of surfing, I hunted down the few coffee shops Honolulu could offer and buried myself in novels set in faraway times and places. I learned French instead of Hawai'i's pidgin English and developed a taste for European pastries instead of the slightly sour, glutinous starch of poi. Heading East for college and traveling abroad instead of home for the holidays only seemed to confirm that I meant to wear scarves in some foreign country where people drank wine instead of Bud Light. When I bid them farewell on the eve of my departure seven years ago, my friends and family assumed—as did I—that it was for good.

Ending up with my feet planted blissfully in Waiahole mud was an unexpected but ultimately necessary way for me to learn a key lesson: I had always prided myself on being rootless, yet here I was experiencing rootedness in the most literal sense of the word, and loving it in spite of myself. Dirty, sweating, and sun-burned, I felt *solid* and more connected to the living, breathing world around me than I could remember. Details exploded around me—the smell of fish smoking on the fire, the striking pattern of breadfruit leaves against the sky, the bearded taro farmers and their young followers passing along a chain of cultural knowledge that created community by continually investing it in one place. Hawai'i was more unique and foreign to me than I had ever imagined, and I felt a new embarrassment for my earlier dismissals of its so-called provincialism.

As we rinsed the freshly picked corms and steamed them for lunch, I was struck by the thought that I had helped pick this sweet, purple food and that the little girl swinging in the hammock across from me was now eating it with a huge grin on her face. It tasted so good I could only grin right back. Looking around, it was clear that most of the people around me had done this all their lives, growing up with their feet in the mud and the valley in their souls, and it dawned on me that, far from being limited, this life of continued investment in a single place was both rare and inspiring. What unified everyone gathered at the lo'i was their overwhelming love for Waiahole. They physically and figuratively planted their time and history in this taro patch every Wednesday, cultivating a sense of belonging that could only come from a deep connection to common ground. The mud itself was precious to them, and this produced a pride in their work that I suddenly longed for as well. You could taste it in the taro, which I'd always heard was the best on O'ahu.

I spent two years waiting tables at a Mexican restaurant and freelancing for a smattering of publications and nonprofit organizations in a quest to acquaint myself with the spirit of Hawai'i that I first glimpsed that day. I wrote grants for struggling nonprofits, attended countless community meetings, and learned to quiet my college-educated ego behind a willingness to listen. In the same way, I learned to recognize the quieter community of native plants and animals that also form the base note of a place and hum with its history. Climbing the misty ridgelines of O'ahu's mountain ranges, I recited their Hawaiian names, traditional uses, and mythical personalities. *Koa:* the warrior, the canoe, one of the most beautiful woods in the world, was also a tree with sickle-shaped leaves that curled its body gracefully around the ridgeline of the Ko'olaus. I met people who fought for fundamental things like land and family with a passion that put my own idealism and ideological fervor to shame. I went home and I fell in love with a place I couldn't claim for myself. This did what nothing else could until then: it humbled me.

15   I became increasingly attached to these islands, so rooted in their singularity and isolation, but I also knew I would have to leave. Perhaps because I already had one foot planted in the vast promise of continents, perhaps because I was infected with the restlessness of privilege or ambition, perhaps because I could simply never wear one of those T-shirts that proudly read "Born and Raised"—whatever the reason, my imagination released a thread that always unwound out, across the Pacific to the wider world beyond. At times, there was nothing I wanted more than the security of knowing that this was where I belonged, but I couldn't dismiss a feeling that I would later come to understand as I traveled back and forth between the Islands and the West Coast: I had always existed more on bridges than on land. Culturally, geographically, and even professionally, my identity was formed in that space between fixed points. Whether I will one day choose one or the other remains to be seen, but for the time being, I am satisfied trying to narrow the distance between them. Though I left Hawai'i in pursuit of more knowledge and experience working with the grassroots sector that I first discovered in Waiahole, I would like to believe that I am preparing myself for a time when I might return and not feel compelled to leave again. I would like to believe that I am becoming more useful to a place I could eventually call my own.

As the afternoon cools down to a deep green murmur and most people have gone home, Vince ambles up and seats himself on the bench next to me.

"So, you like working the lo'i or what?"

"Are you kidding? I can't remember the last time it felt so good to be this dirty and sore," I say, holding out my mud-encrusted fingernails for emphasis. "This is amazing," I add more quietly. "I can't believe I was clueless about it for so long."

"Does that mean you're gonna come out with us every week?" He eyes me seriously above the broad, whiskered smile. Though I know this is a moment of truth, I can't lie either.

"Vince, I aspire to be ready for this every week. But for now   20
I'll have to admit that I'm only at the beginning of a path I never expected to travel."

He raises his eyebrow. "Oh yeah? What path is that?"

My gaze moves across the patches of taro to the space where Waiahole Valley opens up to the ocean.

"Maybe it's the one that will eventually lead me home."

Guiding Questions

1. List some of the ways *taro* operates in Black's essay. In what ways does Black capture the culture of Hawaii?
2. How would you describe the tone(s) of this essay? What passages indicate Black's emotional state?
3. Black describes herself as "bicultural and bred on mobility." How does our twenty-first century global, mobile, and diverse culture affect our connections to places? Does Black appreciate or regret her detachment? What role does her economic status play in her relationship to places?
4. When Black decides to intentionally reacquaint herself with Hawaii, how does she go about it? How does each element of re-education add a layer to her sense of place?
5. With every generation, young adults have greater access to new opportunities, but the freedom to move from one place to another to pursue these opportunities can leave some twentysomethings feeling displaced, and it can ultimately lead to what has been officially recognized as the "quarterlife crisis." Have you already begun to feel this anxiety? Do you know others who are currently struggling to find their places?

Paths for Further Exploration

1. "Culturally, geographically, and even professionally, my identity was formed in that space between fixed points." Do you share Black's sentiments? Have specific places informed your identity, or have the spaces *between* those places attributed more to your sense of identity?
2. Write a researched essay that aims to reacquaint you with a once-familiar place—even one that is nearby—that you do not know very well anymore.

As you select a place to research, remember that proximity does not guarantee knowledge or awareness.

3. If you have lived many places in your life, write an essay that maps your personal geography of mobility. Which places have shaped you the most? Which do you like to visit most? Which places have negative associations for you? How do you think the experience of mobility will affect your future decisions about where to live?

A Bridge Between Two Cultures
VIRGINIA DI TATA

Virginia Di Tata is a psychology major at Boston College. She is originally from Bethesda, Maryland, and plans to attend law school after graduation. In the following essay she reflects on her move from the Washington area to Venezuela and back. The periods of culture shock she experienced helped her to learn how to exist in both worlds.

———————— ◆ ————————

It was Christmastime in 1996. I looked through the small window and saw an uneven tapestry of mountains sprinkled with thousands of lights. I clutched the journal that my classmates had written in for me to remember them by, and I felt a tear trickle down my cheek as I remembered my going-away party and my last few days at home. My father had accepted a work assignment in the capital of Venezuela for the next eighteen months, so Caracas would be my new home. I was uneasy about moving. I had spent all fourteen years of my life in Bethesda, Maryland, a suburb outside of Washington, DC. There I had attended a small, homogenous Catholic school in which I knew nearly everyone, since I had been there for nine years. I was upset that I was not going to be able to graduate middle school with all the people I had known since kindergarten. I knew that it was going to be a challenge to live in a foreign country, but that I had to make the most of it. So I slowly wiped the tear off my cheek and braced myself for landing.

As we made our way in the rattling taxicab through the still and silent night, down lonely, winding and bumpy roads, I peered out the window with curiosity. Mountains encompassed the city, and it seemed like a completely different world to me. All around us, on the mountains, stood hundreds of tiny metal shacks, one on top of the other. At the time I did not know much about the Venezuelan economy, but I was shocked and saddened to see so many people living like this in a country with such huge oil wealth. As we continued to pass dozens of other areas like this one, I became extremely depressed. The taxicab driver, after seeing the frown on my face reflected in the car's rearview mirror, asked what was wrong. To him this display of poverty was a common sight, and he mentioned how these people lived without electricity or water. I regretted bringing up the subject.

My first six months in Caracas were difficult. I could not fall asleep at night because my bed just did not feel like my own, the pastel blue walls of my room made me feel like I was in a hospital, and the heat and humidity of Caracas felt even worse than Bethesda on sticky August afternoons. A few days after arriving, and still not over the shock of how different this city was, I started the second semester of my eighth grade at the American School, where I would also complete my freshman year of high school. The school environment was nothing like the familiar atmosphere I had become used to in the United States. I had to take a long bus ride to and from school everyday, during which we passed various "barrios," or slums. My grade had about three times the number of students as back at home, and I knew no one. My classmates consisted of a heterogeneous group of people from different nationalities. The cafeteria food was totally different from the food at home—instead of hamburgers and French fries it sold "tequeños," fried dough filled with cheese, and "arepas," corn pancakes filled with meat or cheese. Everyone in my grade seemed to have known each other for years, and I was "the new girl," so no one made any effort to include me in their inside jokes and soccer games during recess. Even though there were about five other newcomers to the eighth grade, they all seemed to stick together because they had met at the orientation session that I had missed, and I was too shy and intimidated to join them. My academic courses covered topics nothing like those I had been taught at home during first semester. Science class at my new school consisted of memorizing the periodic table of the elements, something which I had never had to do in my science class back home, where we studied animals, plants, and ecosystems. And in literature class, I had arrived in the middle of *The Hobbit*, so my first few nights were spent reading for hours at a time so as to catch up to the class quickly. To make matters worse, though I knew Spanish, everything that the locals said to me sounded like gibberish—their accents differed so much from those of my family, and they spoke too fast. In other words, I was completely lost.

During those months I wrote to my friends back home constantly, and I counted down the days until I could go back. I felt that when I went back to the United States I would be able to resume where I had left off and that the bonds between my Blessed Sacrament school friends and I were unbreakable. But as time went on, e-mails from my friends grew scarce. One night, about four months into my stay in Caracas, as I sat in bed thinking about the "good old days," I came to a realization. I had no choice: either I adjusted to the new social and academic conditions which I faced, or I risked failure in both areas. The next day I pestered my mother to take me to the nearby recreation center and I joined the swim team. Already, by doing something I had always loved to do in the United States, I was feeling more at home. In the weeks after that, I became more open. I sat at the lunch table with all the native kids, and though it was hard at first, I made some Venezuelan friends and even started using the native slang, "*Oye chamo, que 'tas hacienda ahorita?* [Hey man, what're ya up to?]," which my parents did not seem to appreciate much. I began to love having a constant tan and wearing t-shirts year round, and I even developed a liking for arepas and tequeños. I was immersed in a whole new culture and starting to feel at home.

5   But my experience in Venezuela was not confined to making new friends and adapting to a different academic environment. As time passed, I became fascinated by the country's contrasts. Initially, I was impressed by its geography and its untouched natural beauty. Our apartment faced majestic mountains, palm trees, and all kinds of colorful tropical flowers—a sight to cheer me up even on my worst days. The ethnic diversity in the country never ceased to amaze me. There were people of Native American, African, and European descent, all of whom created a broad spectrum of racial diversity. It was so different from my sheltered life in Bethesda, where nearly everyone looked the same and I, as an Argentinean, just about made up the ethnic diversity in my grade. Everyday I learned more and more about this country, which I had grown to love because of all that living in it had taught me about the world and about myself. I learned about the dramatic differences within the Venezuelan social fabric, including the sharp inequalities in income distribution and the widespread poverty. I remember vividly the first time my father took me on a walk around our neighborhood. I was shocked by the difference

between the exclusive area where our building was located and the poor conditions in which people lived within a distance of no more than three blocks. I saw small children nearly nude and barefoot, street vendors with a few goods to offer trying to make a living for the day, and entire families sitting outside the shacks which were such a common sight to me by now. I was particularly struck by the smiles of the children playing soccer with cans, the kindness of the people, and the optimism with which they confronted daily life. My problems seemed so trivial in comparison to theirs, and I felt guilty about my own fears and intimidations, realizing how much greater theirs were.

My year and a half abroad was an experience that I will forever remember and that helped me prepare for my college experience, among other things. But a lot of what I learned from this experience occurred when I came back to what I had come to know as my other home. I had not breathed Bethesda air for a whole eighteen months, but as the taxicab drove up the familiar streets in my neighborhood, it felt like my eighth grade going-away party was only yesterday. A wave of old feelings rushed back to me, and I couldn't wait to hit the mall with Kara and Kate, my two best friends at Blessed Sacrament. But after a week of being back, and seeing how even my neighbors had changed in the months that we had been away, I knew that things were different. Times had changed and so had people. I had changed, too. My middle school friends and I had grown apart, ever since that going-away party. The process of having to make all new friends and adapt to a new culture was hard enough when I was in Venezuela, but at least then I had expected it. I had not anticipated this kind of adjustment when I got back to the neighborhood I had lived in for nearly fourteen years of my life. And the reality of it hurt.

When I finally did see Kara and Kate, it felt like we had never known each other. They had not seen what I had seen, they had not felt what I had felt, and they had not learned what I had learned. The awkward silences and lengthy conversations about the weather and other superficialities saddened me. But they also made me realize that it was time to move on, just as I had realized that night sitting in my bed looking at the pale blue walls (which by the way, I had grown to love) of my room, sweating and cursing the Venezuelan heat. My home away from home became a part of my past, as did the reminiscing about "the good old days" with all my "chamos." I became a bridge between these two distinct cultures, and my experiences have led me to where I am today.

Now it is springtime of 2002. I sit in my college dorm room, looking out my dorm-room window at the Boston College landscape, knowing that I will be in Bethesda in one week. I know that I will miss the late-night eating sessions and long talks about anything and everything with my college friends, and that returning to my old home may bring surprises, just as it did after my time in Venezuela. The challenge of readapting and perhaps rebuilding parts of my life that have fallen out of place over this school year will be one that I have faced before, but with the knowledge I have accumulated over the past few years I trust that I will have the capacity to successfully deal with these changes and move on.

Guiding Questions

1. Di Tata describes feeling "lost" upon her arrival in Venezuela. What are some of the major cultural differences she notes between Bethesda and Caracas?
2. Di Tata notes that much of what she learned from her experience living abroad occurred when she returned to what had become her "other" home. What did she learn upon her return to Bethesda?

Paths for Further Exploration

1. Have you ever traveled to another country? Describe the cultural differences you observed.
2. Di Tata describes the realization she came to: "I had no choice: either I adjusted to the new social and academic conditions which I faced, or I risked failure in both areas." Have you ever been faced with a similar challenge? What were some of the difficulties about transitioning from one place to the next, from one culture to another?

A History in Concrete
BLAINE HARDEN

Blaine Harden is currently a reporter for the Washington Post *and is the author of* Africa: Dispatches from a Fragile Continent *and* A River Lost: The Life and Death of the Columbia. *In "A History in Concrete," Harden recalls his—and his father's—relationship to Washington's Grand Coulee Dam, a place that sustained both father and son in different ways. The essay was first published in*

Preservation *magazine. It also appears in the collection* A Certain
Somewhere: Writers on the Places They Remember, *edited by*
Robert Wilson.

———————— ✦ ————————

Down in the bowels of Grand Coulee Dam, you can feel the
industrial-strength menace of the Columbia. The river, as it
pounds through turbines, causes an unnerving trembling at the
core of the largest chunk of concrete on the continent. Vibration
jolts up from the steel flooring, through shoes and up legs, and
lodges at the base of the spine, igniting a hot little flame of panic.
The gurgle of water creeping through seams in the dam doesn't
help.

Grand Coulee Dam won't hold still. And it does leak. Water
sluices noisily through drainage galleries that line the fourteen
miles of tunnels and walkways inside the dam. Engineers say all
dams leak, they all tremble. It is absolutely harmless, completely
normal, nothing to worry about. I don't trust engineers.

This gray monstrosity gives me the creeps. It has ever since
I was ten, when my uncle Chester took me on a dam tour, fed me
extra-hot horseradish at a scenic restaurant, and laughed until he
cried when I spat out my burger. Ever since I learned from my
father at the dinner table that this mile-wide monolith was the
rock upon which our middle-class prosperity was built. Ever
since I worked here in college and got myself fired.

The dam sits out in the middle of nowhere— the tumble-weed
coulee country of north-central Washington, a wind-swept landscape of basalt cliffs and grayish soil. Seattle is a 240-mile drive
west across the Cascade Mountains, which scrape moisture from
the sky and leave the country around the dam in a rain-shadow
desert. When construction began, *Collier's* magazine described
the dam site as so hell-like that "even snakes and lizards shun it."
For as long as I can remember, I have kept coming back to this
unhandsome land to feel the addictive tingle of being near an object that is intimidating and essential and big beyond imagining.

And it is big. The Bureau of Reclamation, which built Grand   5
Coulee in the 1930s in its crusade to turn every major Western
river into a chain of puddles between concrete plugs, loves to talk
bigness. The dam is so big, the bureau said, that its concrete
could pour a sixteen-foot-wide highway from New York City to
Seattle to Los Angeles and back to New York. So big that if it were
a cube of concrete standing on a street in Manhattan, it would be

two and a half times taller than the Empire State Building. As Franklin D. Roosevelt, who ordered the dam built, boasted, "Superlatives do not count for anything because it is so much bigger than anything ever tried before."

It was a tonic for the Great Depression and a club to whip Hitler, a first to smash the private utilities monopolies and a fountainhead for irrigated agriculture. The dam was a gloriously mixed metaphor validating the notion that God made the West so Americans could conquer it. Grand Coulee's turbines came on-line just as the United States entered World War II. It sated an unprecedented national appetite for electricity—to make, for example, aluminum for B-17 Flying Fortress aircraft at Boeing's Seattle plant and plutonium at the top-secret Hanford Atomic Works downriver. Without the dam, said Roosevelt's successor, Harry S. Truman, "it would have been almost impossible to win this war."

My hometown, Moses Lake, about an hour's drive south of the dam, owed its existence to Grand Coulee. Before the dam, the town was notable for its large jackrabbits and frequent sandstorms. It was a hard-luck town, where farmers worked until they wore themselves out, went broke, and moved away without regrets. Even the town fathers had admitted, before the dam, that Moses Lake had a certain pointlessness about it. As one chamber of commerce brochure put it, "Out of the desert a city was built. Some of the earliest homesteaders and settlers would ask, 'Why?'"

When I grew up, the answer to that question was obvious. Everyone knew that life itself—at least life as lived in our prosperous farm community, with subsidized irrigation and the nation's cheapest electricity—would be impossible without the dam.

My father, the out-of-work eldest son of a failed Montana dirt farmer, joined four thousand men who were building the dam in early 1936. Arno Harden was a broom-and-bucket man, working in the gut of the construction site. Dams rise from the bedrock of a river in a series of rectangular pours stacked like dominoes, and before each pour, laborers must tidy up, hose down, and sandblast every surface. Otherwise new concrete will not adhere, and cracks and structural weaknesses could cause the dam to fail. For fifty cents an hour, eight hours a day, six days a week, my father scooped up loose rocks and bits of wire and ensured that Grand Coulee would stand for generations.

He hated it, of course, but he did it until he had saved enough money to go to trade school and learn to be a first-class union welder. He then spent most of his working life building dams and welding at other federal projects along the Columbia. Because of the dams, my family was something other than poor, and I grew up in a handsome lakefront house with a bedroom for me and one for each of my three siblings, a new car in the driveway, and money in the bank for a private college.

The dam, though, meant far more than money to my father. It 10 had been the great adventure of his life. He lived at the construction site during six wild years when it was gluey mud in the winter, choking dust in the summer, and live music all night long. He and his brother frequented an unpainted, false-fronted saloon on B Street—a dirt road thick with cardsharps, moonshiners, pool hustlers, pickpockets, piano players, and a few women who, like everybody else, had come to town for money. An ex-con named Whitey Shannon employed fifteen dime-a-dance girls at the Silver Dollar, where the bartender, Big Jack, tossed out men who got too friendly with the ladies. A sweet-voiced crooner named Curly sang like Gene Autry, and between numbers a skinny kid shoveled dirt from the muddy boots off the dance floor. Mary Oaks, the dam's telephone operator, took calls from B Street nearly every night: "The owners would say, 'We got a dead man over here and would you call the police.' If they weren't dead, of course, they would want a doctor."

As my father explained it at the kitchen table, Grand Coulee was an undiluted good. It may have killed more salmon than any dam in history and destroyed the lives of the Colville Indians, who centered their existence around the fish. It may have launched a dam-building craze that turned America's most powerful rivers into adjustable electricity machines. But that was not what I learned at home. I once asked my father if he thought it might have been a mistake to kill all those fish, dispossess all those Indians, and throttle the river. He did not understand the question.

My first real job was at the dam. Grand Coulee was expanding in the early 1970s, and my father used his connections to get me a summer job as a union laborer. It paid the then princely sum of five dollars an hour. My labor crew cleaned up bits of wire, half-eaten pickles, wads of spat-out chewing tobacco, and whatever else might be left behind by craftsmen higher up on the wage scale. This was the same job that my father had hated in the thirties.

I was nineteen, a rising sophomore at Gonzaga University in nearby Spokane, and very impressed with myself. I told my crew how boring our jobs were and how I could not wait to get back to school. Many of the laborers were middle-aged Indians with families. They kept their mouths shut and their eyes averted from me.

Federal inspectors nosed around after our work, spotting un-picked-up wire and other crimes. They complained to a superintendent, who complained to some other boss, who complained to an unhappy man named Tex, our foreman, who then yelled at me, the loudmouthed college boy. Tex wasn't much of a talker. When he did speak, he had an almost incomprehensible west Texas twang. *Wire* came out as *war.*

15   "Git off yer ass, pick up that war," he would instruct me after complaints about our cleanup job had trickled down the chain of command. We worked swing shift, four to midnight, near the spillway. The river, swollen in the summer of 1971 with heavy snowmelt from the Canadian Rockies, rioted over the dam twenty-four hours a day in a cascade eight times the volume of Niagara Falls and twice as high. The dam's base was a bedlam of whitewater and deep-throated noise, and when Tex shouted "*war*" in my face, I could never hear him. Along with the racket, cold spray geysered up, slathering the construction site in a slippery haze slashed at night by hundreds of spotlights. The entire dam site—wrapped in the spray and yowl of the river—struck me as a death trap. At weekly safety meetings, I filled out lengthy reports on what I considered to be hazardous work practices.

    By my fourth week at the dam, Tex had had enough. He told me at the end of the shift not to come back. He mumbled something about *war* and how I spent too much time on my butt when bosses were around. I slunk away from the river, driving home to Moses Lake after midnight. I barely managed not to cry. My father had paid for the Volvo I was driving, paid the eight-hundred-dollar initiation fee that got me into the Laborers' Union, and paid for a big slice of my college education. He had been shrewd enough to work much of his life for men like Tex without getting canned.

    When I got home at 2 A.M., I left a note on the kitchen table. My father would be getting up in three hours to drive back up to Grand Coulee, where he was still a welder. The note said I was sorry for letting him down, which was true. What I did not say was that I was relieved to be away from that dam.

    Twenty-three years later, I invited my eighty-two-year-old father to ride with me up to Grand Coulee. I would buy him lunch, and he would tell me everything he could remember about the dam. Like most father-son transactions, the deal favored me. But my father welcomed any excuse to look at the dam.

    It was an abnormally hot Saturday in May. Snow in the mountains was melting, and water in the reservoir behind the dam was rising faster than the turbines could swallow. The river had to be spilled, a spectacle that only occurs once every few years. We had no idea this was happening until we drove down into the canyon that cradles the dam. Before we could see

anything, we heard the dull thunder of falling water and rushed
to the railed sidewalk overlooking the dam's spillway.

The river exploded as it fell, and the dam trembled beneath   20
our feet. We had to shout to talk. At the base of the spillway, three
hundred feet below us, the Columbia seethed, boiling up a milky
spray in the warm wind and turning a marbled green as it scuf-
fled downstream. The din from the falling river and the vibration
from the dam made my father smile. For him, it was a song from
the thirties, a snatch of dance-hall music from B Street.

Neither of us had ever said a word over the years about that
morning when I left him the note on the kitchen table, and it
didn't come up that day, either. He had come into my bedroom
before leaving for work and woken me up. He had told me it
wasn't my fault that I got fired, although he must have known
it was. He had said I was a good son.

Instead, as we stood together on that trembling dam, I told
my father that the noise, the vibration, and the height scared me.
He said it did not scare him, that it had never scared him.

Guiding Questions

1. What techniques does Harden use to create a character out of Grand Coulee Dam?
2. How would you describe the narrator's relationship to the dam?
3. Through Harden's descriptions of the dam, what do we learn about Moses Lake? About his connections to the town?
4. Harden ends his essay by noting the difference in his and his father's atti-tudes toward the dam. What does the last sentence in the essay reflect about Harden's relationship with his father?
5. Kimberly Wheaton, in her essay "Mom and the Kitchen," also connects a cer-tain place with a parent. How do Harden and Wheaton use place to connect the generations, or do they? How do these two writers compare in terms of their treatment of parents and places?

Paths for Further Exploration

1. Write a researched narrative about your hometown. Is there a specific place (building, park, monument) around which you might focus? What is the sig-nificance of that place?
2. In paragraph 4 Harden claims, "For as long as I can remember, I have kept coming back to this unhandsome land to feel the addictive tingle of being near an object that is intimidating and essential and big beyond imagining." Is there a place that inspires a similarly complicated response from you?

3. Explore a place in your hometown that has a different meaning for you than it does for someone in an older generation, and try to explain—through research, interviewing, and writing—what might account for those differences.
4. Research dams and their effects on the places where they are built. Argue whether a particular dam should be decommissioned (torn down), as are many today, taking into account the effects this would have on the local area.

On Being from *Fargo*
TIM LINDGREN

Tim Lindgren is a doctoral candidate in the English department at Boston College, where he is focusing on composition and rhetoric. His current research investigates how the process of composing with online and digital new media can affect our experiences of place. He hopes to return someday to the Midwest.

——————— ✦ ———————

Where are you from?

When this question arose at a party recently, it marked a familiar turn in conversation, the moment when I shift from new acquaintance to momentary novelty. "North Dakota," I answered, and when her eyes widened, I added, "Fargo." "Oh my God," she responded, looking up and turning away slightly to the left. Facing me again, she slowly said, "Oh . . . my God. No, really? You are from Fargo." A little taken aback by her enthusiasm, all I could muster was, "Yep, Fargo."

When she motioned to a friend and exclaimed, "He's from Fargo," I realized something I probably had known unconsciously for quite some time. Most of my life I had been from Fargo, North Dakota. Now, however, this new acquaintance made it clear that I was from *Fargo*—the Coen brothers' film—and I would just have to get used to it.

Fargo, North Dakota

Since leaving home to attend college in Chicago, I have been having conversations about where I am from. For a long time, they usually took a similar form: "Where are you from?"—"Fargo,

North Dakota."—"Really? I think you're the first person I've met who's from North Dakota." Before the 1996 Coen brothers' film, saying "North Dakota" meant I could look in my interlocutor's eyes and find a blank space on their mental maps just above South Dakota and below Canada, a tabula rasa of ignorance as pure white as the winter fields I encountered anew last time home.

As I drove on county highways north of Fargo, blowing snow blended the horizon into the clouds, erasing any sign of boundary to the white expanse of fields. In front of me snow flowed across the road, at one moment a stream of smoky white and the next moment a flock of wisps that tore and regrouped in flight, as if someone left their smoke machine in Montana and a momentous wind was blowing it low across the plains. I passed a massive pile of decaying sugar beets with steam rolling off it in thick billows that faded just as they reached the road. This pervasive whiteness became the canvas for a late afternoon sundog, a winter rainbow made by airborne ice crystals that formed a nearly complete circle, except where its bottom edge dipped just below the horizon.

A white blankness of the mind appeared each time someone   5
ventured to me, "North Dakota, isn't that where Mount Rushmore is?" It was a friendly form of ignorance that I usually found empowering. By the time I gently let them know, "No, that's South Dakota," they had already commissioned me their myth-maker, letting me shatter their misconceptions if they had them or, if they did not, create a fresh portrait of Fargo they could call their own. Show me someone from Malibu or Manhattan, and I will show you a clean canvas prepared for the brush.

It was always difficult for my new myths not to start off sounding flat. Difficult because Fargo lies in one of the flattest spots in North America, in what was 9,000 years ago the bottom of a glacial lake. To grow up in Fargo is to see the world lying down, a horizontal life with no overlooks and all sky, with no vistas but the Twelfth Street overpass or the bird's-eye view when flying into Hector International Airport. Our only mountains were the thunderheads rolling in over the plains that I watched when working out in the fields, the dark gray Rockies that we could watch until the gust-front winds blew the first drops ahead and sent us running for the pickup.

Living in Fargo is to learn to walk backwards. Someone once said that in the Chinese view of time we back into the future, facing our past as we move into the unknown of what is to come. I often backed my way through the winters of my childhood, trudging with my front side shielded from the certainty of the North wind.

In places where winters are rainy and wet, the cold will seep into your bones as you stand waiting for the train. But in Fargo, when it is 15 below with a brisk wind, the cold crashes in around you within seconds of walking out doors and drenches you within a minute. As you crunch and creak across the partially shoveled sidewalks, bodily fluids begin changing state—hair and eyelashes getting crispy, snot beginning to congeal. But this only true of some days, and of only one season, and if you learn to walk backwards, keeping warm means you forget less quickly where you have been.

So Fargo is flat and cold. The unspoken question that I often face is "Why does anyone live there?" Believe it or not, I will often answer, Fargo was once rated the most desirable city in the nation, based on factors like cost of living, pollution, education, unemployment, crime rate. Somehow the poll politely evaded the issue of the weather, but there is no doubt for me that Fargo was a fine place to grow up for all the reasons the ratings noticed. It is safe and clean, the schools are good, and the people are friendly. It is a college town with twenty-five thousand students and a lively economy, and the winter weather is nothing you can't get used to.

Have you seen the movie?

There was a time when talking about where I was from gave me opportunity to act as advocate for my hometown, to save it from the East Coast cultured despisers or the West Coast cosmopolitans. However, after 1996 that blank gaze of ignorance I once relished became a look glazed over by a thick film called *Fargo*. For more than three years after the movie hit the box office, I lacked a convincing answer for why I had failed to see the movie. Usually I claimed to dislike violent movies, but in reality, I was simply unwilling to admit that I had a rival in representing where I'm from.

10   I had become comfortable having license to create people's myth of Fargo, and now there was a movie out that usurped that role, that caricatured the natives of Minnesota and North Dakota, and did so under the title of my hometown. I have never been much of a movie critic, but since the movie *Fargo* came out, talking about where I am from has become a movie review.

So what did you think?

Now that I've seen the film, I'm willing to admit that I like it, though I always hope conversations will last long enough for me to voice a few modest criticisms. Normally I wouldn't bother, but this particular movie has made things personal. Since the Coen brothers chose to call their film *Fargo*—where I grew up—even though the movie really takes place in Minneapolis and Brainerd—near where they grew up, their attempt to represent their hometown impinges on my own effort to figure out what it means to be from mine.

The danger for the Coen brothers, like anyone who has moved away to one power center or another, is that in representing their hometown they too often land at one of two extremes—idealization or disparagement. We usually idealize when we stand to benefit from associating ourselves with something that, in hindsight, appears superior to where we now live. We malign our hometown when we have more to gain by severing any associations with what seems to be a provincial, benighted past. Avoiding either extreme is the more difficult task.

As one *Washington Post* reviewer (originally from Fargo) put it, the problems with *Fargo* can be stated simply: too much violence, too much accent, too little Fargo. If I fault the Coen brothers for anything in *Fargo*, it is for what I see as a loss of nerve. When faced with a stark white landscape populated by simpleminded yokels, they couldn't resist the urge to splatter it with blood, as if violence was their preferred antidote against the risks of an unremarkable setting. As Wes Jackson once put it, "Any fool can appreciate California; it takes real character to appreciate Kansas."

Moreover, the caricatures of the Minnesota accent at moments sound like the graceless humor of someone who has been away too long, one who knows enough to do hilarious impersonations of Minnesotans at New York parties but has lost the ability to sustain nuanced humor through an entire movie. Minnesotans do not mind being made fun of—Garrison Keillor does it every Saturday night—but they have a right to expect that someone from Minnesota will avoid letting good-natured ribbing slip into body checking.

I liked it

Despite my frustrations with the film, I have developed a fond- 15
ness for it by learning to adopt a Marge-centric perspective. I refer to Marge Gunderson, the pregnant policewoman from Brainerd who investigates the increasingly violent consequences of Jerry Lundegaard's inept machinations. Jerry, a car saleman from Minneapolis, hatches a scheme to deal with his mounting financial problems by hiring two thugs to kidnap his wife and

then to demand a ransome from his father-in-law, which he will split with criminals he has hired. A series of murders ensue at the hands of the men Jerry has hired, and it falls to Marge, the Brainerd sheriff, to investigate.

Marge is intelligent, acutely observant, and shrewdly witty. She is tough-minded in doing her job but also deeply compassionate in a brilliantly understated Minnesota way. She deals with crime when it comes her way, but her robust affirmation of the everyday makes it clear that the "malfeasance" she investigates in no way defines her life. Marge is not only the redemptive element in an otherwise bleak story, but she also compensates for the Coen brothers' loss of imaginative nerve in other aspects of the film. The excessive violence may have seemed an artistic risk, but it was not nearly as risky as having a heroine more brilliantly and triumphantly ordinary than most of us were prepared to appreciate.

I like to imagine that Marge occasionally appears in the Coen brothers' dreams, the voice of their repressed consciences, making them regret for just a moment that in representing where they were from, they may have overdone a few things: "So I hear ya made a movie about a string of murders up there in Minnesota then. Even put a guy in a wood chipper. Ya, that sure was different. Well I suppose when you've lived out East a while ya gotta throw a guy in wood chipper once in while to make the old home country seem a little more interesting. (Pause) Well, there's more ta making movies than being violent and ironic, ya know. (Pause) Don't ya know that?"

In the end, I would like to believe that at some level the Coen brothers, like me, were trying to answer the question, Where are you from? If Marge was their best attempt to represent their hometown, to tread a middle path between idealization and disparagement, I would say they did a pretty good job.

I have to admit I am still a bit sore that the movie broke up a perfectly good monopoly on representation, making my job of portraying Fargo a bit more challenging than it was before. But I suppose a little competition never hurts. If the movie does not literally represent where I am from, I am now more willing to admit that the pictures I draw of Fargo also bear the marks of my own idiosyncrasies and shortcomings. While it is true that I am originally from the geographical place called Fargo, a place with a particular landscape and a particular culture that has shaped me, it is also true that I no longer live there and I am shaped as much by the story I am writing about *being from* Fargo as by physically being there. If answering the question where I am from has made me a movie critic, it also has made me more conscious of the myths I have created since leaving home.

"A lot can happen in the middle of nowhere" is the advertising catchphrase on the rental box for *Fargo*, but the more I try to talk about where I am from, the more I have to believe that in fact quite a lot happened in Fargo before the movie came out, if for no other reason than because I grew up there and my family still lives there. And if it ever becomes "the middle of nowhere" in my imagination and in the stories I tell of it, if I ever become content either to malign or idealize it, then leaving there—being from there—has done me little good. 20

Guiding Questions

1. Lindgren writes, "By the time I gently let them know, 'No, that's South Dakota,' they had already commissioned me their myth-maker, letting me shatter their misconceptions if they had them or, if they did not, create a fresh portrait of Fargo they could call their own." How and why do we create myths about places? How would Lindgren respond to this question?

2. Examine Lindgren's rhetorical style. Is his organization around a conversation at a party effective?

3. What is at stake for Lindgren in the inaccuracies depicted in the film version of the place where he is from? Do these inaccuracies complicate his sense of identity?

Paths for Further Exploration

1. What kinds of responses do you get when you tell people where you are from? What do they assume they know about that place, and why do they assume it? Script a conversation at a party between you and a new acquaintance in which you describe where you are from. What kinds of questions might the image of your hometown elicit from outsiders? What kind of myths would you have to dismantle?

2. What does it mean to represent a place? What are the various ways in which you represent your hometown?

3. "While it is true that I am from the geographical place called Fargo, a place with a particular landscape and a particular culture that has shaped me, it also true that now I no longer live there and I am shaped as much by the story I am writing about *being from* Fargo as by physically being there. If answering the question where I am from has made me a movie critic, it has also made me more conscious of the myths I have created since leaving home." What myths have you created about where you are from? What does it mean for you to participate in this myth-making process?

4. Write about a representation of your hometown, such as a movie, a book, a Web site, or a song. In your estimation, where does it represent the place accurately? Where does it misrepresent the place? Whose experience of this place does it represent?

The Ship-Shape
DAVID SEDARIS

David Sedaris's account of the summer his family considered the merits and pitfalls of owning a summer house first appeared in the New Yorker *in 2003. He is recognized for his humorous critique of the American family, and in this essay he notes the chronic pressure families experience when it comes to owning a house—or two. Sedaris has been featured on Public Radio International's* This American Life *and is the author of several plays as well as collections of essays and short stories, including* Naked, Me Talk Pretty One Day, *and most recently* Dress Your Family in Corduroy and Denim.

◆

M y mother and I were at the dry cleaner's, standing behind a woman we had never seen. "A nice-looking woman," my mother would later say. "Well put together. Classy." The woman was dressed for the season in a light cotton shift patterned with oversize daisies. Her shoes matched the petals and her purse, which was black-and-yellow striped, hung over her shoulder, buzzing the flowers like a lazy bumblebee. She handed in her claim check, accepted her garments, and then expressed gratitude for what she considered to be fast and efficient service. "You know," she said, "people talk about Raleigh but it isn't really true, is it?"

The Korean man nodded, the way you do when you're a foreigner and understand that someone has finished a sentence. He wasn't the owner, just a helper who'd stepped in from the back, and it was clear he had no idea what she was saying.

"My sister and I are visiting from out of town," the woman said, a little louder now, and again the man nodded. "I'd love to stay awhile longer and explore, but my home, well, one of my homes is on the garden tour, so I've got to get back to Williamsburg."

I was eleven years old, yet still the statement seemed strange to me. If she'd hoped to impress the Korean, the woman had obviously wasted her breath, so who was this information for?

"My home, well, one of my homes"; by the end of the day my   5
mother and I had repeated this line no less than fifty times. The garden tour was unimportant, but the first part of her sentence brought us great pleasure. There was, as indicated by the comma, a pause between the words "home" and "well," a brief moment in which she'd decided, Oh, why not? The following word—"one"— had blown from her mouth as if propelled by a gentle breeze, and this was the difficult part. You had to get it just right or else the sentence lost its power. Falling somewhere between a self-conscious laugh and a sigh of happy confusion, the "one" afforded her statement a double meaning. To her peers it meant, "Look at me, I catch myself coming and going!" and to the less fortunate it was a way of saying, "Don't kid yourself, it's a lot of work having more than one house."

The first dozen times we tried it our voices sounded pinched and snobbish, but by midafternoon they had softened. We wanted what this woman had. Mocking her made it seem hopelessly unobtainable, and so we reverted to our natural selves.

"My home, well, one of my homes . . ." My mother said it in a rush, as if she were under pressure to be more specific. It was the same way she said, "My daughter, well, one of my daughters," but a second home was more prestigious than a second daughter, and so it didn't really work. I went in the opposite direction, exaggerating the word "one" in a way that was guaranteed to alienate my listener.

"Say it like that and people are going to be jealous," my mother said.

"Well, isn't that what we want?"

"Sort of," she said. "But mainly we want them to be happy   10
for us."

"But why should you be happy for someone who has more than you do?"

"I guess it all depends on the person," she said. "Anyway, I suppose it doesn't matter. We'll get it right eventually. When the day arrives I'm sure it'll just come to us."

And so we waited.

At some point in the mid- to late nineteen-sixties, North Carolina began referring to itself as "Variety Vacationland." The words were stamped onto license plates, and a series of television commercials reminded us that, unlike certain of our neighbors, we had both the beach and the mountains. There were those who bounced back and forth between one and the other, but most people tended to choose a landscape and stick to it. We ourselves were Beach People, Emerald Isle People, but that was mainly my mother's doing. I don't think our father would have cared whether he took a vacation or not. Being away from home left him anxious and crabby, but our mother loved the ocean. She couldn't swim, but enjoyed standing at the water's edge with a pole in her hand. It wasn't exactly what you'd call fishing, as she caught nothing and expressed neither hope nor disappointment in regard to her efforts. What she thought about while looking at the waves was a complete mystery, yet you could tell that these thoughts pleased her, and that she liked herself better while thinking them.

15   One year our father waited too late to make our reservations, and we were forced to take something on the sound. It wasn't a cottage but a run-down house, the sort of place where poor people lived. The yard was enclosed by a chain-link fence and the air was thick with the flies and mosquitoes normally blown away by the ocean breezes. Midway through the vacation a hideous woolly caterpillar fell from a tree and bit my sister Amy on the cheek. Her face swelled and discolored, and within an hour, were it not for her arms and legs, it would have been difficult to recognize her as a human. My mother drove her to the hospital, and when they returned she employed my sister as Exhibit A, pointing as if this were not her daughter but some ugly stranger forced to share our quarters. "This is what you get for waiting until the last minute," she said to our father. "No dunes, no waves, just this."

From that year on, our mother handled the reservations. We went to Emerald Isle for a week every September and were always oceanfront, a word that suggested a certain degree of entitlement. The oceanfront cottages were on stilts, which made them appear if not large, then at least imposing. Some were painted, some were sided, "Cape Cod style," with wooden shingles, and all of them had names, the cleverest being "Loafer's Paradise." The owners had cut their sign in the shape of two moccasins resting side by side. The shoes were realistically painted and the letters were bloated and listless, loitering like drunks against the soft faux leather.

"Now that's a sign," our father would say, and we would agree. There was The Skinny Dipper, Pelican's Perch, Lazy Daze, The Scotch Bonnet, Loony Dunes, the name of each house followed by the name and home town of the owner. "The Duncan Clan—Charlotte," "The Graftons—Rocky Mount," "Hal and Jean

Starling of Pinehurst": signs that essentially said, "My home, well, one of my homes."

While at the beach, we sensed more than ever that our lives were governed by luck. When we had it—when it was sunny—my sisters and I felt as if we were somehow personally responsible. We were a fortunate family, and therefore everyone around us was allowed to swim and dig in the sand. When it rained, we were unlucky, and stayed indoors to search our souls. "It'll clear after lunch," our mother would say, and we would eat carefully, using the placemats that had brought us luck in the past. When that failed, we would move on to Plan B. "Oh, Mother, you work too hard," we'd say. "Let us do the dishes. Let us sweep sand off the floor." We spoke like children in a fairy tale, hoping our goodness might lure the sun from its hiding place. "You and Father have been so kind to us. Here, let us massage your shoulders."

If by late afternoon it still hadn't cleared, my sisters and I would drop the act and turn on one another, searching for the spoiler who had brought us this misfortune. Which of us seemed the least dissatisfied? Who had curled up on a mildewed bed with a book and a glass of chocolate milk, behaving as though the rain were not such a bad thing after all? We would find this person, most often my sister Gretchen, and then we would beat her.

The summer I was twelve, a tropical storm moved up the 20 coast, leaving a sky the same mottled pewter as Gretchen's subsequent bruises, but the following year we started with luck. My father found a golf course that suited him, and for the first time in memory even he seemed to enjoy himself. Relaxing on the deck with a gin-and-tonic, surrounded by his toast-colored wife and children, he admitted that this really wasn't so bad. "I've been thinking, to hell with these rental cottages," he said. "What do you say we skip the middleman and just buy a place?"

He spoke in the same tone he used when promising ice cream. "Who's up for something sweet?" he'd ask, and we'd pile into the car, passing the Tastee-Freez and driving to the grocery store, where he'd buy a block of pus-colored ice milk reduced for quick sale. Experience had taught us not to trust him, but we wanted a beach house so badly it was impossible not to get caught up in the excitement. Even our mother fell for it.

"Do you really mean this?" she asked.

"Absolutely," he said.

The next day, they made an appointment with a real-estate agent in Morehead City. "We'll just be discussing the possibility," my mother said. "It's just a meeting, nothing more." We wanted to join them but they took only Paul, who was two years old and unfit to be left in our company. The morning meeting led to half a dozen viewings, and when they returned my mother's face was so impassive it seemed almost paralyzed. "It-was-fine," she said. "The-real-estate-agent-was-very-nice." We got the idea that she was under oath to keep something to herself, and the effort was causing her actual physical pain.

25   "It's all right," my father said. "You can tell them."

"Well, we saw this one place in particular," she told us. "Now, it's nothing to get worked up about, but . . ."

"But it's perfect," my father said. "A real beauty, just like your mother here." He came from behind and pinched her on the bottom. She laughed and swatted him with a towel and we witnessed what we would later come to recognize as the rejuvenating power of real estate. It's what fortunate couples turn to when their sex life has faded and they're too pious for affairs. A second car might bring people together for a week or two, but a second home can revitalize a marriage for up to nine months after the closing.

"Oh, Lou," my mother said. "What am I going to do with you?"

"Whatever you want, Baby," he said. "Whatever you want."

30   It was queer when people repeated their sentences, but we were willing to overlook it in exchange for a beach house. My mother was too excited to cook that night, and so we ate dinner at the Sanitary Fish Market, in Morehead City. On taking our seats I expected my father to mention inadequate insulation or corroded pipes, the dark undersides of home ownership, but instead he discussed only the positive aspects. "I don't see why we couldn't spend our Thanksgivings here. Hell, we could even come for Christmas. Hang a few lights, get some ornaments, what do you think?"

A waitress passed the table and, without saying please, I demanded another Coke. She went to fetch it and I settled back in my chair, drunk with the power of a second home. When school began my classmates would court me, hoping I might invite them for a weekend, and I would make a game of pitting them against one another. This was what a person did when people liked him for all the wrong reasons, and I would grow to be very good at it.

"What do you think, David?" my father asked. I hadn't heard the question but said that it sounded good to me. "I like it," I said. "I like it."

The following afternoon our parents took us to see the house. "Now, I don't want you to get your hopes up too high," my mother said, but it was too late for that. It was a fifteen-minute drive from one end of the island to the other, and along the way we proposed names for what we had come to think of as our cottage. I'd already given it a good deal of thought but waited a few minutes before offering my suggestion. "Are you ready?" I said. "Our sign will be the silhouette of a ship."

Nobody said anything.

"Get it?" I said. "The shape of a ship. Our house will be called   35
The Ship Shape."

"Well, you'd have to write that on the sign," my father said. "Otherwise nobody will get it."

"But if you write out the words you'll ruin the joke."

"What about The Nut Hut?" Amy said.

"Hey," my father said. "Now, there's an idea." He laughed, not realizing, I guess, that there already was a Nut Hut. We'd passed it a thousand times.

"How about something with the word 'sandpiper' in it?" my   40
mother said. "Everybody likes sandpipers, right?"

Normally I would have hated them for not recognizing my suggestion as the best, but this was clearly a special time and I didn't want to ruin it with brooding. Each of us wanted to be the one who came up with the name, and inspiration could be hiding anywhere. When the interior of the car had been exhausted of ideas, we looked out the windows and searched the passing landscape.

Two thin girls braced themselves before crossing the busy road, hopping from foot to foot on the scalding pavement. "The Tar Heel," Lisa called out. "No, The Wait 'n' Sea. Get it? S-E-A."

A car trailing a motorboat pulled up to a gas pump. "The Shell Station!" Gretchen shouted.

Everything we saw was offered as a possible name, and the resulting list of nominees confirmed that, once you left the shoreline, Emerald Isle was sorely lacking in natural beauty. "The TV Antenna," my sister Tiffany said. "The Telephone Pole." "The Toothless Black Man Selling Shrimp from the Back of His Van."

"The Cement Mixer." "The Overturned Grocery Cart." "Gulls   45
on a Garbage Can." My mother inspired "The Cigarette Butt Thrown Out the Window" and suggested we look for ideas on the beach rather than on the highway. "I mean, my God, how depressing can you get?" She acted annoyed, but we could tell she was really enjoying it. "Give me something that suits us," she said. "Give me something that will last."

What would ultimately last were these fifteen minutes on the coastal highway, but we didn't know that then. When older, even the crankiest of us would accept them as proof that we were once a happy family: our mother young and healthy, our father the man who could snap his fingers and give us everything we wanted, the whole lot of us competing to name our good fortune.

The house was, as our parents had promised, perfect. This was an older cottage with pine-panelled walls that gave each room the thoughtful quality of a den. Light fell in strips from the louvred shutters and the furniture, which was included in the sale, reflected the tastes of a distinguished sea captain. Once we'd claimed bedrooms and laid awake all night, mentally rearranging the furniture, it would be our father who'd say, "Now hold on a minute, it's not ours yet." By the next afternoon, he had decided that the golf course wasn't so great after all. Then it rained for two straight days, and he announced that it might be wiser to buy some land, wait a few years, and think about building a place of our own. "I mean, let's be practical." Our mother put on her raincoat. She tied a plastic bag over her head and stood at the water's edge, and for the first time in our lives we knew exactly what she was thinking.

By our final day of vacation our father had decided that instead of building a place on Emerald Isle we should improve the home we already had. "Maybe add a pool," he said. "What do you kids think about that?" Nobody answered.

By the time he finished wheedling it down, the house at the beach had become a bar in the basement. It looked just like a real bar, with tall stools and nooks for wine. There was a sink for washing glasses and an assortment of cartoon napkins illustrating the lighter side of alcoholism. For a week or two my sisters and I tottered at the counter, pretending to be drunks, but then the novelty wore off and we forgot all about it.

50   On subsequent vacations, both with and without our parents, we would drive by the cottage we had once thought of as our own. Each of us referred to it by a different name, and over time qualifiers became necessary. ("You know, our house.") The summer after we didn't buy it, the new owners, or "those people," as we liked to call them, painted The Ship Shape yellow. In the late seventies, Amy noted that The Nut Hut had extended the carport and paved the driveway. Lisa was relieved when the Wait 'n' Sea returned to its original color and Tiffany was incensed when The Toothless Black Man Selling Shrimp from the Back of His Van sported a sign endorsing Jesse Helms in the 1984 senatorial campaign. Five years later my mother called to report that The Sandpiper had been badly damaged by Hurricane Hugo. "It's still there," she said, "but barely." Shortly thereafter, according to

Gretchen, The Shell Station was torn down and sold as a vacant lot.

I know that such a story does not quite work to inspire sympathy. ("My home, well, one of my homes fell through.") We had no legitimate claim to self-pity, were ineligible even to hold a grudge, but that didn't stop us from complaining.

In the coming years, our father would continue to promise what he couldn't deliver, and in time we grew to think of him as an actor auditioning for the role of a benevolent millionaire. He'd never get the part but liked the way that the words felt in his mouth. "What do you say to a new car?" he'd ask. "Who's up for a cruise to the Greek isles?" In response he expected us to play the part of an enthusiastic family, but we were unwilling to resume our old roles. As if carried by a tide, our mother drifted further and further away, first to twin beds and then down the hall to a room decorated with seascapes and baskets of sun-bleached sand dollars. It would have been nice, a place at the beach, but we already had a home. A home with a bar. Besides, had things worked out you wouldn't have been happy for us. We're not that kind of people.

Guiding Questions

1. What does it mean to live in one place and vacation in another? How might your identity change in each place?
2. How does Sedaris capture the tension between his mother and father? How does he use humor to explore certain aspects of this tension, and of his family's relationship to their vacation place?
3. What is implied when people own multiple "homes"? What emotions do owning property, to belonging to more than one place, evoke in those who do? In those who do not?

Paths for Further Exploration

1. Did your family take vacations? Were there certain places that you visited regularly? Did you have another "home" to which you journeyed? What did this place mean to you? To your family? How did it differ from your other "homes"?
2. Vacation places often create subcultures that are temporary. Describe a subculture that you have observed, documenting the ways people relate to each other and to the places they find themselves.
3. Many people live in places that are vacation destinations for others. If this is your experience, write an essay that describes the relationship between "locals" and "outsiders" created in a community where tourism plays an important role in the economy.

The Coffee Shop
ANDREA CASASSA

*Andrea Casassa, a double major in English and political science at
Boston College, is from Hopkinton, Massachusetts. She spent a year
abroad at Oxford University in England and is currently working on
an essay about the experience of traveling and being a woman abroad.
"Tips" and "Regulars" are excerpts taken from a longer nonfiction narrative written throughout the semester of a First-Year Writing Seminar. The Coffee Shop is centered on her town's coffee house, and each
chapter explores some aspect of the coffee house, from the locals who
inhabit this place to the issues plaguing the coffee industry.*

✦

I. TIPS

Good coffee is like friendship: rich, warm, and strong.

—PAN-AMERICAN COFFEE BUREAU

6:00 A.M.

Brisk New England winds tumble into the coffee shop as I open
the back door. The warm aura of cranberry scones and dark roast
beans confronts the frigid air. Mary, already hunched over a mixing bowl of poppy seed muffin mix, greets me. Quietly rattling,
the old oven readily accepts its gooey inhabitants for baking.
Newly delivered newspapers slouch patiently against the wall
waiting to reveal their stories, or to become drenched with spilled
cappuccinos. I fold a green apron around the waistband of my
jeans; after three years as an employee at the Hopkinton
Gourmet, I know too well the hazards and stains capable from
steaming coffee. With a warm cup of tea, my six A.M. lethargy
transforms into a more roused familiarity; the day begins.

Each community needs a coffee shop, not only for the obvious reasons like caffeine addictions but also for sanity. Some may
love Starbucks with their caramel coffee concoctions or the ubiq-
uitous pink and orange signs of Dunkin' Donuts, but quickly fading are the small town hubs like the Gourmet that specialize not
in fancy frappuccinos but in customers. Articles from the local
newspaper, *The Hopkinton Crier,* decorate the yellow walls of the
shop. From five-year-old Little League players to varsity field
hockey stars, town athletes frequent the store to beam at their

pictures displayed for the community to see. PTA mothers hang up flyers to promote their newest fundraisers. Fathers clad in Dockers and polo shirts discuss new business and sports.

From the road, the store appears comfortably nestled between two Victorian townhouses peering onto the main street below it. Two flower boxes wrap around the small white building; a golden pineapple separates the "Hopkinton" from the "Gourmet" on the large sign. Flapping in the wind, a sewn flag with a blue mug of steaming coffee welcomes the store's visitors. Upon entering, one immediately notices the bright yellow walls hiding behind the coffee bean jars spanning across the left of the store and the baskets of bagels in the back center. A few feet forward, the pastry counter and register leave barely enough room for the two employees to maneuver around their workspace. The coffee-grinding machine rests inches away from the sink and the shiny steel brewers crowd the neatly stacked supply of cups. One small table is positioned next to a window on the right side of the store and seven more stools squeeze into the corners, making popular window seats and practically violating fire codes. Although small, the Gourmet always seems full and, consequently, very intimate. When an actual crowd does emerge, lines spill onto the outdoor steps.

Monday through Friday, our quaint shop cranks out gallons of java and offers a plentiful array of bagels, muffins, and biscotti to the community. Groggy high school students fill their mugs and astute businessmen awaken with a shot of espresso. Cars frequently pull in and out of the three spots directly in front of the store; their drivers leave them running because their quick orders do not warrant a long stay. A small but growing town located in western Massachusetts, Hopkinton is now bursting with an abundance of kindergarten classes, Friday night football games, and eager "townies" that take pride in their community.

Once a year, these traditional New Englanders awaken to witness the start of the Boston Marathon. The town common's green transforms into a labyrinth of wide-eyed spectators, zealous newscasters, and vendors sending off almost 100,000 runners into the 26-mile stretch into the city. On typical weekend mornings, however, the town really stretches its legs and reflects on the week's disappointments and small victories. 5

7:00 A.M.

The early morning customers always seem crazy to me. Maybe I'm just jealous that I cannot muster up enough enthusiasm to match their unfailing chipper moods. Nevertheless, the "earlys" start off our day, always to get the freshest bagels, the first cup of coffee, or just to claim their rightful seats. Today Dennis, like a grand marshal leading the parade, approaches the counter first. "Fill it right to the rim," he always gently instructs, *"with just a little bit of milk. Just a little bit,* dear." About 5 foot 6, Dennis stands just a bit taller than me. Gray hair encircles his small ears, and his chin always tilts upward a little, making it seem that he is smelling the air around him. Perched with his newspaper in the corner of the shop, he overseas at least the first two hours of the day's business, taking note of all the customers, conversing with some, smiling at others, and always inquiring about my college plans. By now, I know his favorites from my list, and a thoughtful nod tells me he approves of my progress.

I relate more to another early bunch, mostly construction workers but also other Saturday morning employees, with their last minute attempts to awaken for the day with a jolt of coffee. I admit quite readily that some arrive at our store only for the pure, stimulating power of caffeine, but they still make up our Saturday morning routine and the day would seem empty without them. Paul, with a scruffy beard and mustache, slaps three dollars on the counter for his large cup, leaving an extra dollar for my tip. He tells me to wake up and grins. *Coffee, mostly black, maybe a little cream and sugar. If time allows, a lightly toasted cinnamon raison bagel smothered with butter in a bag.*

9:00 A.M.

A line wraps around the store. Pinging the floor, coffee beans from a nearby canister scatter like little Mexican jumping beans because of a clumsy patron's fumbling. Chatter buzzes, people swarm the sugar and cocoa station. I start to get dizzy from the noise. The hot toaster singes my hands, and my head begins to throb. Among the pandemonium I see Martha in the crowd and I prepare her order before she reaches the counter. Her wide frame jiggles as she chuckles at another customer's joke. A retired mother, she now religiously attends Mass and the Gourmet. Her blond bushy eyebrows rise with approval as I place a chocolate biscotti and lid-free cup of flavored coffee before her.

Many times before, Martha's countenance shrank in discontent if I forgot her order. *Small cup, one cream, one sugar, little "drop" of water, ice if you have it.* Now, I earnestly aim for perfection and she accepts me into her inner circle. Her daughter left for Israel yesterday, she relays to me with a sullen look. "If you study abroad, take your mother with you," she instructs. Traipsing towards Dennis, she engages in tête-à-tête with him about the construction of the new high school.

11:00 A.M.

Baby carriages and soccer moms disrupt the ebb and flow of a   10
more demure clientele. The end of Saturday morning cartoons brings a new tide of coffee goers. *Iced coffees, blueberry muffins warmed, chocolate milks, lots of napkins.* An occasional tantrum sends mothers fuming back out to their cars. Toys decorated with cream cheese drop to the floor by the end of the hour. The colorfully striped coffee cookies are popular commodities for this rowdy bunch, and small hands force their way into the jars lining the counter. Tottering, little Jack peers through the pastry glass at his reflection, and his fingerprints smear the surface. I cut up sesame seed bagels into bite-sized pieces as Sharon, Jack's mother, tells me about her baby shower and lets him place a handful of quarters in my tip jar. Someone grabs a handful of napkins to clean the puddle of cappuccinos just spilled on to the floor.

Managing to find stools among the makeshift playgroups, Charlie and Morgan, two "regular" patriarchs of Hopkinton, sit among the children examining the activity outside the store. The former town moderator, Charlie, sits with an aura of authority. Morgan's silver hair seems to glisten as the outside sun shines on the two. Young contrasts with old, wisdom competes with naiveté, the past converges with the future.

12:00 NOON

Cell phones ring, "Yeah, I'm at the Gourm'. What's going on tonight?" A group of my friends gather in the corner. Escaping the teenage gossip, parents usually leave the shop as students brag about their accomplishments or mishaps the night before. I drop a container of cream cheese while trying to hear the nearby conversations; I start cleaning all over again. *Three iced coffees, five croissants, lots of honey mustard with turkey and sprouts.*

1:30 P.M.

The lines stop, coffee lays stagnant, and my back aches with exhaustion. I hear the faint lull of the radio, Magic 106.7, over the sink's sputtering as I wash dishes. I sigh at the dirt smudged into the black and white tile floor and grab a mop. Predictable but distinct, another day passes. *One last bagel, a few sandwiches, a latte with skim milk, make it large.* I wipe off the green bubbled letters decorating the community bulletin board, "Fishing derby today at noon," "Soccer car wash, $5," "Polyarts festival next weekend."

I empty the jar and fold forty-six dollars in my back pocket. I wonder if Starbucks employees receive tips like I do.

15   *Hectic, exhausting, comfortable, familiar . . . just right.*

II. REGULARS

> *Coffee is one of the special things I have, instead of a social life.*
>
> —Joel Achenbach

I've been away at college for a few months now. Today, I come back to the Hopkinton Gourmet to visit some of its regulars. A few photographs of customers have been added to the growing collection on the wall since the last time I was here. Ted, the owner, insists on sneaking pictures of customers as they sip their java. Still, newspapers are stacked neatly, the small tub of Equal packets rests perfectly against the sugar, and the bagels are toasted, leaving traces of blueberry, garlic, and cinnamon in the air. In the wake of September 11th, a flag flaps in the wind and the town newspaper articles of the tragedy are neatly taped to the door.

Since the Hopkinton Gourmet opened its doors in 1992, certain customers appear at the shop day after day, week after week. These "regulars" define this small coffee shop and create a sense of family not often found in the commercialized chains. When one expected patron fails to visit, the equilibrium of the store wavers, not dramatically but noticeably. So, to learn about such a place, one must start at the center, the customers, to appreciate the dynamics of the coffee shop.

I almost laugh as Dennis, an old Hopkinton resident, swings open the door at exactly 8:00, right after church and right on schedule. After filling his mug with dark roast, I invite him to join me at a table, in his favorite seat for an interview. I start our chat by asking him why he comes to the Gourmet. He chuckles. "Well, the camaraderie, of course." Pulling something out of the pocket of his Eddie Bauer plaid shirt, he shows me a picture of Martha, his coffee shop companion, beaming above a birthday cake. "We bought her this last weekend for her birthday," he says proudly, slightly parting his thinning gray hair as he runs his hand through his scalp. The group in the photograph encircles the table where I now sit, leaning over a grinning Martha. A mother and Gourmet matron, she sits complacently and comfortably in the picture, with, of course, her cup of coffee.

When I ask him about the service at the shop, he comments on how the employees, "just know you, and they are always waiting for you with your order ready." I inquire about how this atmosphere differs from a Starbucks or Dunkin' Donuts and Dennis replies that "it's not the building, but the coffee and the people" that make him return everyday. He doesn't find that at the chain stores.

Walmarts and Starbucks replacing mom and pop stores is a   20
reality, I say. Could those sweeps ever affect the Gourmet? "Definitely not," he says without hesitation. "There exists a certain ritualism here. Everyone has their own little niche."

I take note of how true his comment really is. I turn to watch the rituals of the shop. A football coach enters the store before practice, as usual. He buys a copy of the *Herald* and the *Globe* and drinks his medium regular at a corner stool. Creatures of habit, different customers enter, drinking a specific coffee, sitting at their usual spot, living rhythmic lives.

Guiding Questions

1. According to Casassa, "Each community needs a coffee shop, not only for the obvious reasons like caffeine addictions but also for sanity." What does this place do for Casassa? What does it do for the community?
2. What do locally owned coffee shops do for communities that national chains cannot do? Conversely, what advantages do the national chains have over locally owned shops? What evidence does Casassa give to support her claim that locally owned shops "keep us connected to each other"?
3. Hopkinton assumes a personality through Casassa's use of metaphors. List some of the metaphors she chooses to describe the town and the coffee shop. What other rhetorical methods does she employ to convey the character of this place?
4. How does she use the coffee shop to tell us about herself? What does her choice of details reveal about her personality?

Paths for Further Exploration

1. Is there a place in your hometown where the community gathers? Describe its physical appearance and discuss how it functions within the community.

2. Are there places in your community that are being threatened? What argument can you make for why such places should be preserved?
3. Conduct an interview with a "regular" at a place you frequent. Make a list of what you hope to learn about the place through this interview and design questions accordingly.

Get Off at 161st and Transfer to the Truth
GIAN-KARLO CASIMIRO

Gian-Karlo Casimiro answers the question of where he is from in this essay, which describes his attempts to dispel outsiders' notions of the Bronx while questioning his own insider status. Casimiro attends Boston College, where he serves as the current external representative for the Philippine Society and is a communications major with a concentration in broadcasting. His future plans include attending Full Sail, a school for arts and music production in Orlando, Florida, after graduation. He hopes to pursue a degree in sound engineering and to produce popular music one day.

◆

I have always had mixed feelings about the Bronx, the place where I have lived for fourteen years. I'm definitely not in love with the borough and I'm not exactly thrilled to live there. I realized that it was not the right place for me early during my junior year of high school, and when researching colleges, I never bothered to spend time on New York schools. With that said, however, I do value the knowledge I gained through my experiences in this city, and there are aspects that I love about it. I find that I am both critical and defensive of the city. What annoys me is the stereotypes that have been created about the Bronx. I understand that some perceptions are justified because they have some truth to them, but like all stereotypes, they are simply too extreme and over-generalized. I have encountered many people who ask ignorant questions about the area. "Isn't that where drive-bys happen?" "Oh so are you one of those gangsters?" "Isn't that like where all the bad stuff happens?" These negative aspects do exist to an extent, but those who live here wish that others would stop talking about our home in a way that makes it seem inferior to theirs. Everything negative and positive about the Bronx is part of our culture. We accept the type of society we have created for ourselves and many people are content living here. Even I, who at times have rejected the culture, grew content with the Bronx.

Before I began to appreciate the borough, I had a desire to be different from the people in the area. My peers all seemed to act, dress, and talk alike, as if they could not think for themselves. I took pride in being studious and serious about my responsibilities, whereas work seemed to be the last thing on their minds. I didn't buy any of the clothes they wore. Before my friends at Cardinal Hayes High School opened me up to different things, I was different—an individual.

Perhaps I was trying too hard to set myself apart. I entered high school and felt like I couldn't relate to anyone. Many things—from my style of dress to my taste in music—were different from my friends'. At the time, I hated the rap that they limited themselves to, so I had to endure countless jokes about my love for rock. I felt sorry that they were not open to listening to an Incubus album. What bothered me most is the way they generalized genres. Apparently people who listen to rock are depressed and those who listen to rap are normal. Ironically, I made some generalizations of my own. Rap was the fake, gangster, sellout music that I refused to listen to. "They're not musicians. They don't even play any instruments," I argued. But when my best friend Luis forced me to have a serious listen to the genre during sophomore year, I grew to love it. Not all of it was about money and fame, and I overlooked that. I generalized the music and the people who made it. Slowly, I began to embrace this music that was so much a part of the Bronx.

My friend Drew was the one who got me interested in the urban fashion. Before that I thought it was hilarious how everyone dressed so similarly. All my peers in every part of the Bronx walk around looking like extras in a rap video. They make it a priority to dress well, which in their eyes means wearing clothes that celebrities promote; rap artists such as Jay-Z and P. Diddy have the biggest influence on their attire. Whether it is a Rocawear shirt with Sean Jean jeans or an Enyce velour suit with a myriad of matching sneakers, teens from the Bronx dress to impress every day for any occasion. They can't even go to the Laundromat without wearing the latest gear. They even use the word "exclusive" to describe their clothes whenever they wear something rare or too expensive for others, which in turn makes them feel like they are ahead of the fashion curve and gives them sense of individuality. What they fail to realize is that these clothes are specifically marketed to teenagers everywhere. Most malls have stores that carry street wear, making these "exclusive" brands just as easily accessible to suburban teens who want that look. Regardless, teens from the Bronx will spend a paycheck on an outfit (that they already own in a different color) without hesitation. Even in a private Catholic high school like Cardinal Hayes, where these clothes do not meet the dress code, students are still able to find loopholes. Instead of dress shoes, the boys wear Timberland boots or "Timbs" for short. Everyone owns over five pairs of the same design. From all black to black with blue trim and from all tan to tan with white trim, the slightest variation in color makes them willing to spend another hundred dollars. This is how they integrate their personalities into their uniforms, though. I decided to stick with my dress shoes because I wanted to be different than everyone else. However, on days where we were allowed to dress down, I wore the same clothes they did and my friends joked around and said I actually had a normal side.

5   The issue I had the toughest time adjusting to was the sense of humor that people in my school had. Racist jokes were made that would offend just about everyone if they didn't understand that my friends never meant a word of what they said. In fact, before I became comfortable with their humor, I did not know how to react. The jokes were funny and similar to some comedians' material but I felt uneasy about laughing at them because I didn't want people to be offended. Over time, however, I realized that racism was not offensive or vile to most of the people in the area. It had been reduced to mere comedy. Soon enough I began making racist comments as well. It was a form of self-defense at first. Because Asians are a minority in the area, my race was an easy target. I heard every karate and Chinese food joke imaginable. Some jokes were more tolerable than others. Jokes about me being uncomfortable eating food without chop sticks were unoriginal. Others were more offensive, but I was still able to laugh about them. They asked, "How you gonna pay for college when your mom only makes $20 a year workin' at a sweatshop?" My friends even covered their mouths around me during the SARs scare. I was forced to fire back at those types. I still cannot believe the things I said about slavery and illegal aliens. During senior year a friend said that he would get accepted to Cornell University because he had a friend on the admissions committee. I said, "What's this friend's name? Affirmative action?" It left my mouth naturally and I only realized how offensive it was after I said it.

Yet everyone still laughed because they knew I wasn't serious. And I began noticing it everywhere: groups of friends always making fun of each other's race in the parks and on public transportation. They didn't care who was listening.

I suppose the thing that made it so easy to laugh at these jokes is that teens from the Bronx embrace their social status. People realize that their standards are lower and they are guaranteed acceptance into certain schools. This realization affects their work ethic and education, and they use their backgrounds to compensate for their laziness. Students are not concerned about doing well in school; the bare minimum is sufficient for them and, to some extent, expected by teachers. The most common phrase after test results was "Oh well. At least I passed." Even the brightest students refuse to put forth an effort. Why work when plagiarized papers and copied answers are readily available? That mindset is the reason why the average SAT score was barely above 1000 when I was there. What hurt most was that Luis was adopting this attitude as well. He was barely passing some of his classes senior year and he was too unmotivated to apply to colleges, missing most of the deadlines. When I told him to stop throwing away his chances, he said, "It's all right. I'm poor and Honduran so colleges expect me to have lower grades." I was disappointed that he wanted to live down to those standards, but I understood why he responded the way he did. We were constantly being told of the advantages we had just because we lived in the Bronx. College representatives came daily, telling us that there was a need for minorities like us. My friends in other high schools said the same people were pitching the same line to them. Thus people in the Bronx naturally took advantage of that opportunity. I admit to applying to well-known universities that had a small population of minorities, especially those that had a shortage of Asians, and I was accepted to a couple. If they were giving it away, why not take it, I thought to myself; and I didn't feel like I was guilty of anything or like I was cheating whatsoever. I simply realized my situation and where I came from and accepted it.

When I finally chose a college, it was an out-of-state school. Now, having lived away from the Bronx for a year in a place that is extremely different has made it a bit easier for me to reflect on what the borough truly means to me. I still do not love it, I don't necessarily miss it, and I know in my heart that I will be spending my life in a different city after I graduate. Living there, however, has given me knowledge of what it is like to live a certain lifestyle that is viewed as underprivileged. Who made suburban middle-class homes the standard anyway? Living on a wealthy suburban campus has given me the opportunity to meet people from various places, and many of these people have stereotypical views of the Bronx. It's frustrating to see how many assumptions can be made right after I say, "I'm from the Bronx." The place that took me years to adapt to and understand should not automatically be linked to words like dangerous, violent, or less fortunate. It's true that such things do exist there, but we are content with what we have and how we choose to live and we don't want the Bronx to change much at all.

Guiding Questions

1. "The Bronx that I called home for so long is different from the public's view," Casimiro claims. How does his view of the Bronx differ from that of the public, or what he believes to be the public's view?
2. How does Casimiro's description of "the true culture of the Bronx" support or even perpetuate an outsider's understanding of the area?
3. Casimiro seems to be resisting both insiders and outsiders. Are there other moments in the essay where he seems to contradict or complicate his relationship with the Bronx? Does he see himself as an insider or outsider?
4. Compare this essay with "On Being from *Fargo*" by Tim Lindgren. How are these essays similar? How are they different?

Paths for Further Exploration

1. How might an outsider's understanding of your hometown differ from that of an insider? Are there assumptions outsiders make about your town or stereotypes they maintain about other aspects of your identity, perhaps about your culture or religion?
2. Write about a place you know only through the media or other cultural representations. Write down your assumptions about the place, then research two or three of them to see how accurate they may be.

Where I'm From
Felicia Madlock

Felicia Madlock received her master's degree in social work from Loyola University–Chicago and is a medical social worker for a trauma hospital in Chicago. Her work has appeared in several publications, and her novel, Sins of the Father, *like much of her work, centers on the issues confronting urban families living in Chicago. The following poem originally appeared in the* Journal of Ordinary Thought, *a publication that sponsors free writing workshops open to all Chicago residents. The publication's motto is "Every person is a philosopher." For more writing from this journal, see www.jot.org.*

---- ✦ ----

I am from
Malcolm X memories and Martin Luther King's dreams
I am from hands that toiled cotton, steel, and paper
And red bone women with neck snapping charisma

I am from family that stretches along the mud paths of
   The Mississippi   5
Grazing the greenery of Georgia
And reciting folktales in Tennessee

I am from hope that crept north in the darkness
Dodging demons on their quest for freedom
I am from dreams deferred   10

For I, too, am America
And life for me hasn't been no crystal stairs
I am from Langston Hughes' lyrical poetry
Frost's indecisiveness in his cross roads
Emily's sheltered world   15
And Zora's silent voice

I am from Double Dutch days
When Mary Mack was dressed in Black
And Jack be Nimble changed to Jack be Quick
I am from the dying days of Disco   20
When Funk was the fever
And House was planted in the streets of Chicago

I am from Saturday morning shopping
And Sunday School sermons
I am from corporal punishment capitalists   25
Who never believed that "Whipping" was abuse

I am from Michael Jackson mania
Prince's Purple Passion
And Boy George girly gears "garments"
30   I am from pigtails to perms
From cornrows to French-rows
From straight to kinky and somewhere in between

I am from the façade of Jane Byrne's reign
To Harold Washington's historical victory
35   I am from heroes being reduced to humans
Presidents lying to stay in the White House
And unfit leaders lying to get in the White House

I am from the Engle of the Woods
The center of Chatham
40   And the migration to the Rose of the Land

I am from BB King's Blues
Motown's memories
Al Green's Transformation
And Marvin Gaye's moments

45   I am from lust that disguised itself as love
From hearts ripped open from lies and deception
I am from dreams forgotten
In blue puddles of passion
Poison with procrastination

50   I am from hope that has been revived
Passion found
And dreams that fight to live
I am from life lessons
Moments that transfix into memories at the blink of
an eye

55   I am from poetry
My most pleasing passion
I am from Joy's jovial sound on a July's afternoon
I am from eyes that seek truth
And decipher wisdom

I am from lover's goodbyes   60
And acquaintances fleeing passing
I am from friends who have written their initials in my
Heart forever
I am from heaven and hell
And Earth's ecstasy
I am from. . . .   65

Guiding Questions

1. How does Madlock use culture in this poem? How does she invoke mass cultural experiences to define her individual sense of where she is from?
2. What role does repetition play in providing structure to this poem? What role does sensory detail play? What does the absence of concrete place descriptions do to Madlock's ability to convey a sense of place?

Paths for Further Exploration

1. What parts of mass culture create specific places in *your* life? Do you "come from" the culture of hip-hop, sports, religion, the Internet, movies, academics, or some other cultural heritage? Describe your relationship to this group and how it functions as a kind of place.

Circles

MATTHEW O'CONNOR

Matthew O'Connor, a history major at Boston College, is from Newton, Massachusetts. He spent the summer of 2004 studying German at the Goethe Institute in Baden-Wurttemburg, Germany, and hopes to continue his studies in European history via a Fulbright grant after graduation. O'Connor is an avid basketball player and reader, but tries to avoid doing both at the same time.

———————— ✦ ————————

When my parents told me that our family would be moving to Newton, I ran outside and climbed the old tree occupying our front yard. I didn't come down for lunch; hours later my father, getting the ladder, pulled me down for dinner. It wasn't that I was specifically upset that my family was moving, or that I was sulking, but merely that I needed time for my eight-year-old mind to process the notion that life existed beyond Irving Street, Watertown. I remember the idea wasn't frightening, just undefined. The thought slowly occurred to me that when my family left this place there would be people, objects, and fixtures of my everyday life that weren't coming with me.

Watertown, a small suburb bordering Boston to the west, was and remains a tight knit community due in part to the layout of the houses and streets within its borders. The homes of the working- and middle-class inhabitants sit in very close in proximity to one another, with the many little side streets connected to larger secondary roads at one of their ends, thus joining tight strings of houses together in chain link fashion and putting neighbors constantly in view. Moving to the nearby town of Newton signified a rise in class, and though Newton also borders Boston, it is much larger geographically than Watertown, and is far less dense. Houses in many areas of Newton maintain large yards with lots of foliage, making it naturally harder for neighbors to be as involved in each other's daily lives as in Watertown. A sense of losing this community was visible in my parents' faces when they talked about the move. I could sense their unease, but at that age I couldn't define it.

Suddenly my comfortable suburban home meant more than it ever had to me. My parents told us our family was too large for the house in Watertown. I thought this was a shameless lie. The house, with its ordinary white paint and no trim, wrap-around front porch and attractive lawn was more than big enough for anyone, as far as I could tell. The house had three bedrooms: one for my parents, one for my two brothers and me, and a tiny room for guests. The only full bathroom was located upstairs. The house had a big attic, which was perfect for playing hide and go seek. The basement was also large, but I never ventured there alone for fear of the furnace. A rusty black cylinder covered in soot, the furnace frightened me because of the random bursts of the loud humming noises it emitted. But other than that, the house seemed to me to have everything we could need or want, inside and out, and my brothers and I made full use of its space and opportunities for simple fun—and trouble.

At the top of the basement stairs, for example, was the most irresistible light switch in the world. It was a fire-engine red-plated, red switch for the very furnace that made going down those stairs so scary, and it was forbidden fruit. Both of my parents warned consistently about the evils that would befall me if

I ever pulled it down. But, just like the huge buttons in Looney
Tunes cartoons labeled "Self-Destruct, Do Not Push" demanded
to be pushed, The Switch had to be flipped—just once. The stunt
cost me my dinner, and since nothing else interesting immediately happened, I determined it wasn't worth it.

Being an active child, and one a bit afraid of the basement   5
(and the loss of dinner that seemed likely to accompany just
standing on the threshold of it), it was natural for me to explore
outside the house. Our front and back yards held a number of
attractions. To me, the lawns around our house created a world
unto itself, a separate magical realm. We had two good climbing
trees and a peach tree for peach fights, and scattered through the
front yard were several cherry trees. On the side of the house a
large bush that was thick on the outside but almost entirely hollow on the inside served as a base of operations for my brothers
and me as we roamed the neighborhood.

Ants always fascinated me, and in our yard there was an expansive system of anthills. The mindless scurry of tiny ants, sometimes meeting up with a spider or an ant of a different color, was
always entertaining. Sometimes I would be cruel and drown a
few unlucky ants with the hose or just cups of water, watching
what must have been floods to them swoop up and swirl the
hapless little insects to doom. Two types of ants, black and red,
remained close to their respective anthills on either side of the
lawn. They would circle around their home looking for food, always careful never to go to far, lest they meet up with their rivals;
warfare ensued any time red and black ants crossed paths. The
ants seem to know this, that wandering too far meant facing life-
threatening dangers. Sticking with their own kind in groups
around the mother anthill was their top priority, and they somehow always managed to find food close by.

Whenever the ants briefly ceased to entertain, or when rain
pushed us indoors, creative games brought my two older brothers
and I together and helped make the house feel warm. My brothers
and I slept in bunk beds, and being stuck together in one room
made us a bit nutty at times. Our favorite game was to put sleeping bags over our heads and then pull them down to the ground.
With our entire bodies mummified in the sleeping bags, we then
commenced to pound away at each other. It was hilarious
because we would be swinging blind through the sleeping bags
until one of us made contact. My oldest brother, Jon, would cheat
and take the sleeping bag off after we had already wrapped ourselves down. One day after Jon and I pushed my brother Tim out

of the room and heaved him down the stairs, my father inexplicably outlawed the game. My father's old school strictness and his habit of putting us to work on random chores made getting out of the house to play whenever we could our number one priority.

Since our parents seemed happy to have us play outside as much as possible, we were lucky that playing around the neighborhood was the best part of Watertown as far as we were concerned. Except for one kid who had "Duck Hunt," no one in the neighborhood had video games, and my brothers and our various friends spent most of our free time together exploring the neighborhood. Near our house was a three-acre, oval-shaped area of dirt and grass. There was no park there, and no houses. It was just open field with a few bushes, so the neighborhood kids used it for everything. My friends and I creatively dubbed this area The Green.

We lived on the bottom of a hill, and The Green sloped up and basically acted as a large rotary. The group had several games that we always congregated for, and when I say group I mean the same ten kids every time, ranging in age from seven to fifteen. We were connected by our ages, The Green, and the layout of our neighborhood; all of us in our homes could see each other's houses. Everyone lived around The Green. We would sometimes stray onto other streets together, but feeling neither comfortable nor welcome in these other neighborhoods, we always circled back to The Green for safety. Anybody from farther out was not part of the group and could not be trusted.

10   The neighborhood games we gathered for were creative and often dangerous. In one game, two kids would ride down from the top of the hill on cheap plastic Fisher-Price tricycles, and another kid would go down on a skateboard. The object of the game was for the riders on the tricycles to smash the skateboarder on the way down. Less violent, more traditional games like baseball, soccer, and run the bases were always in motion. One summer, one of the guys brought out a street hockey stick that he received for Christmas and, sure enough, a month later everybody on the block had a stick and the block had games going all the time.

I had some great friends in the neighborhood because of these games, and my best buddy was Teddy, who was two years older. Teddy and I succeeded in causing a lot of mischief, and in the process we spent a lot of time together. When we moved, Teddy was the hardest thing to leave behind. I had other close friends in the gang, but at the core of it for me were my brothers. They always looked out for me in the neighborhood adventures, and I'll never forget how long they spent teaching me to ride a bike at the nearby Perkins School.

Perkins was a special school for severely mentally and physically challenged children. The school was a block up the street, and we used to hop the fence to go sledding on a great hill in the winter, or to ride our bikes around the property in the summer. Perkins was understandably strict about visitors. Anyone who had not checked in was to be kicked out, and of course we had no business being there. So when guards came around during our sledding forays, we had to run, hide our snow tubes in the bushes, and mix in with the Perkins children on the playground so we wouldn't get in trouble.

Founded in 1832 in South Boston, Perkins was America's first school for blind and deaf/blind persons. Having great success in helping these people through its first decades, it needed to expand due to the rising number of families who sought it out. Perkins moved to Watertown in 1912, purchasing 38 acres by the Charles River. Much of my neighborhood was built around it and thus Perkins was and is a large part of the neighborhood's character. In 1982, Perkins began to accept students with other disabilities.[1] And so the neighborhood came to expect to occasionally see a mentor and a child walking down the street toward the river. These children were usually very quiet, much like the neighborhood itself in many ways. Most of the adults on Irving Street kept to their own lives and families, but they were always kind if you did happen to talk with them, even with all the noise we younger residents made playing on The Green and circling through our little world.

After the move, many years and a driver's license later, I circled back to the house. I did not drive around for long. The neighborhood was still intact, and since I never explored far as a child, I did not have a great distance to cover to revisit all my old haunts. As a wave of nostalgia swept through me, I remembered my mindless scurry over The Green with my brothers, the countless hours spent trying to find out all that life offered within the arms of two streets, and the contentment as we strolled back only a short distance to the home that was our base. The house was smaller than I remembered, but the warmth still lingered.

The house on Irving Street had been good to me, and the fun times I had with my brothers and neighborhood buddies cemented a strong connection to the little area. I had a happy childhood, one that a community like Watertown helps to foster. I'd like to try someday to start my own family near this place. Living in an   15 uncertain world, I would have the insurance of knowing my children would be safe in this neighborhood. My kids might scurry around but they would find, as I did, that everything they need is within a few streets. They would always feel safe circling back home.

Endnotes

1. "Perkins School for the Blind" May 30, 2002, 1 December 2003 http://www.perkins.pvtkI2.ma.us/section.php?id=53.

Guiding Questions

1. How does the image of circles function throughout the narrative?
2. How does O'Connor make thematic and structural use of the anthills he describes in his backyard?
3. How might O'Connor's sense of this house and neighborhood have been significantly different from his parents?
4. Why do you think that The Green was never organized as an official park space? How might its role in the Irving Street neighborhood have changed if it were an organized, official space?

Paths for Further Discussion

1. Describe your childhood home. How did it look through your eyes as a young child? Now broaden your description to include your neighborhood as it appeared to you then. Who were your friends? Did you have siblings? What games did you play?
2. If you can, return to your childhood home. Does your family still live there? Describe how it has changed—if it has changed at all. Has its physical appearance changed? Describe how the neighborhood looks through your adult eyes.
3. Interview parents or grandparents about their reasons for a move in their lives. If you lived through that move, compare your sense of it with theirs.
4. Do you want to live in a place similar to the one you were raised in? Explain why.

CHAPTER 2

Where Are We?

Where are you? Really—take a look around. What do you see? What do you hear? What do you smell? What do you feel? What's the first thing you notice, and why? Are you alone or with other people? Are you inside or outside? Are you in a private or a public place, or a place that's a bit of each? What do you know about the materials and substances around you? What do you know about the history—including the natural history—of the place where you are reading these words? Is it a place designed for reading and studying, or for something else? Do you know who designed it? Who built it? When and why? If it is a place that you "control," what would someone who does not know you assume about you based on what they can see there?

These questions might seem simple at first, or even silly. If you are reading this book while in a library on campus, at your desk in a classroom, on your bed in a residence hall, or in a chair in your home, you probably think you have a good sense of where you are. In many ways, you do. But if you are in such a place—a place that is familiar or quickly becoming familiar to you—you have also probably learned to take a number of things for granted, to fail to notice that place consciously.

Of course, we have to take some things for granted; if we stopped to notice every small and changing detail of the places we frequent, we would never have time for anything else. We generally reserve careful attention for extraordinary places: those that are new to us (such as a new workplace, school, or vacation spot), places that we know and will miss (a former home, a favorite hangout far away, a childhood playground or playing field), or places that are under threat of some kind (a changing neighborhood, a beach that is eroding, a patch of woods slated for development).

57

But the ordinary places we move through in the everyday "now" tend to become invisible to us unless we have some reason to look at them with fresh eyes.

Learning not to take *anything* for granted is a crucial part of good writing and of critical thinking. Thinking, researching, and writing about the everyday places we encounter can be surprisingly entertaining once we get started, and what we learn about the places we are in now can lead to provocative questions about how these places affect us—and how we shape them in turn. Knowing where we are goes a long way toward knowing why we are there, where we are going, and even who we might be.

So, think this question through again: where are you? You might answer the following questions if you are inside "your room" in a residence hall or in some kind of off-campus housing:

- What size is your room?
- What are the walls made of?
- Do you live there alone?
- Who are your neighbors? Do you get along with your roommate(s), floormate(s), or housemate(s) in this space? Can you describe the connections between those relationships and the place itself?
- How does your room affect your education, social life, love life, and sense of a private self?
- Can you think of where or to whom you might go to start finding out more about your room, or about the residence hall, apartment, or house as a whole?
- What kinds of ideas might govern the ways residence halls are made, how they are run and organized, what they look, smell, and sound like? What specific university decisions lie behind your walls, the size of your room, and the number of your roommates?

If you are at your home or your family's home, answer these questions:

- What's going on in the rest of the house or apartment building?
- Do you live with anyone else?
- What's happening right now on your street or in your neighborhood?
- How hot or cold does it tend to get in your house or building?
- Do you feel safe inside your home?
- Is your home structurally sound?

- Is it safe or unsafe to walk in certain nearby areas?
- Who makes the decisions about your home and neighborhood?
- Can you think of specific ways in which some aspects of your neighborhood affect your daily life?
- How far is your home from the other places in your life—your school, job, friends' homes, downtown areas, and so forth?
- Can you guess what people would think of you if they saw your neighborhood before they met you?
- How does what goes on in and around your home reflect larger social or cultural values?

If you are in a library, cafeteria, coffee shop, park, or some other public space, answer these questions:

- Is it quiet or noisy? Are the noises calming to you or distracting?
- What kind of light comes to where you are sitting?
- If you are at a desk or table, is it good for reading and writing?
- Does the place get used a lot for studying, or do people use it primarily for other purposes?
- If there are any students around you, what are they doing? Do certain kinds of students use different spots in the building for different tasks?
- Are there things of historical or artistic value in the building or space?
- Where are you in relation to the rest of your college campus?
- What might you learn about where you are by investigating these questions?

Thinking about place in these more thorough terms may seem difficult and artificial to you at first, but you will get the hang of things quickly. If you are new to school and to the area in which your campus is located, you will find thinking and writing about places near and new to you are great ways to orient yourself, to get a fuller, more informed sense of where you are—and of what sorts of things are "at work" in those places.

For example, writing about a particular campus green or quad could lead you to discover the history of some dispute between your school's administration and the surrounding community, or to encounter a particular tradition of the student body connected to that space, or even to a realization of how such open spaces affect education and campus life. If you begin exploring your neighborhood, you might be drawn into a discussion of local politics and zoning decisions, or into an analysis of the cultural heritages found there, or into a discussion of broader issues like technology or transportation. Even writing about something as close at hand as your dorm or bedroom could lead to an exploration of the use of energy-efficient windows to conserve fossil fuels, or to a discussion of the perils of bunk beds combined with alcohol, or to a study of how and why different kinds of students decorate their rooms. Recall some of your answers to the questions asked above: Can you imagine any of them leading to a research paper or persuasive essay?

In various ways, the essays presented in this chapter turn careful attention to ordinary places that the authors make new by looking at them with fresh and deliberate eyes. As they try to describe where they are "now," they find their investigations leading into larger issues and questions, all the while taking care to stay grounded in a specific place, to bring it alive to the reader. In "Hazardous Cargo," for example, Ray Gonzalez starts with the simple act of looking in a new way at signs on the roads throughout the El Paso, Texas, area and ends up in an unsettling discussion of local, national, and international issues. Julia Corbett's "Robotic Iguanas" begins as a simple trip out for a meal with a friend and develops into a detailed description of the restaurant with a side order of philosophical consideration of our culture's relationship to the natural world. Derek Owens ("Where I'm Writing From"), Ron Fletcher ("By Dawn's Early Light"), and Ian Frazier ("Someplace in Queens") craft their pieces in large part by just deciding to begin walking through and observing particular areas, thus combining the personal experience of and reaction to place with researched facts about local history, culture, and even geology. Finally, Jeffrey Lockwood's "Becoming Native" offers broad and even abstract considerations of how and why people come to belong to places in large part through a strong sensory description of what it means to relate to place.

Description then is one of the key skills you will develop when you write about place—indeed, you will build upon the descriptive skills you began to develop in the last chapter when you were writing largely from memory. As you'll see in these essays, good place-based writing depends a great deal upon the writer's ability to convey a sense of the physical reality of the space, and upon the ability to know what to leave out. Although a single physical detail may be too small to be effective, a whole list of them would quickly bore the reader. The careful writer must thus learn how to recognize "choice details," those observations that will be both particular to a place and evocative of some larger sense of it. As you develop your own writing on place, you will learn to pay attention to physical details without becoming hostage to them. (Keeping a place journal is a great idea—that way you can record any and every minute physical detail that strikes you as you explore a place and can later choose the best or most effective of them.) When you write about the places in your past, you call up memories and use your imagination to enhance the details; when you write about the places of your present, you will find ways to generate details grounded in the moment.

As you explore the places around you, you will also learn how to use specialized research sources to help you understand them—from online databases, to dedicated library holdings, to personal interviews with experts, to local newspapers and historical societies. You may learn a bit about art and architecture, infrastructure planning, and even basic sociology as you explore the places around you. Writing about place can also lead you to a more informed knowledge of the natural world, as you may discover that recognizing things like watersheds, tree canopy corridors, micro climates, and other natural aspects of places are crucial to a full understanding of the many forces that create and shape them. Finally, as you learn to spot the human values and choices that lay behind the reality of the places you encounter, you will learn to analyze places as you would a text or a painting, to think and write about the larger ideas that shape places and the ways that places shape ideas.

So, where are you? Enjoy—your explorations are just getting started.

Where I'm Writing From
DEREK OWENS

Derek Owens teaches at St. John's University in Queens, New York, where he is the director of the Writing Center. In his book Composition and Sustainability: Teaching for a Threatened Generation, *where this essay appears, he asks college writing teachers and their students to discover the links between writing and the environments where they live, work, and study. Owens demonstrates how he has explored where he lives, a suburban neighborhood in Ronkonkoma, Long Island, New York. By combining human history with natural history, Owens attempts to explain what home means for him as a*

*teacher, husband, father, and citizen, and he invites his readers to
consider how teenagers in particular might respond to such suburban spaces.*

✦

Where the hell is Ronkonkomano?
— A character in the film *200 Cigarettes*

I am writing this book at the corner of Lake Promenade and
Second Street in the hamlet of Lake Ronkonkoma, in the town-
ship of Brookhaven (the largest in New York state), which is located in Suffolk County, a chunk of land that forms the eastern
half of Long Island. My house is in the exact center of this island.
In 1994 I got a job at St. John's University, which is located in
Queens, on the western half of the island, but we moved farther
out east because my wife's family is here—her parents, her sisters'
families, her aunt and uncle, her cousins—most of them less than
five minutes away. Close extended families are always something
to celebrate, but such tribal islands are crucial when you live in
the middle of a sea of suburban sprawl.[1]

Sixty thousand years ago a mile-high glacier called the
Wisconsinan bulldozed its way in slow motion down through
Canada and New England and didn't stop until it reached just
about where I'm sitting right now. Warmer temperatures caused
it to melt and retreat, leaving behind the detritus (mud, sand,
gravel, boulders) that geologists now call the Ronkonkoma Termi-
nal Moraine, a line of glacier droppings (including rocks, called
"erratics" or "messengers," sheared off of the tops of northern
mountains) that extends all the way to Montauk Point, the east-
ernmost tip of New York State. A few thousand years later the
very same glacier came back and did it all over again, dumping
another string of debris stretching the entire length of the island,
this one running from Brooklyn to Orient Point, the northern
fork of the island. When the ice began to melt, the land "began to
rebound the way a small boat bobs back up when people step out
of it" (Isachsen et al. 177). As the ice retreated, mammoth chunks
broke loose, got buried, and eventually melted within the ground,
forming kettle holes. One of the largest is Lake Ronkonkoma, the
freshwater lake that is a fifteen-minute walk from where I sit.
Eventually—perhaps as recently as six thousand years ago—Long

Island evolved into its present-day shape, making it, geologically speaking, a baby compared with the rest of the state. The variety of ecosystems caused by the proximity of outwash and moraines led to hardwood forests, salt marshes, and even prairies (a geological anomaly now thought to be the result of periodic burning by American Indians), which, combined, supported an unusual diversity of flora and fauna. Five thousand years ago, the first humans settled in the area—Archaic American Indians of the Orient phase, followed by American Indians of the Woodland phase. These were the first people to clear forests for agricultural purposes. Contact with Europeans occurred five hundred years ago, and, just two centuries later, most of the American Indian population had disappeared or blended with European ethnicities as a result of factors including genocide, slavery, alcoholism, smallpox, and intermarriage. In the seventeenth century, the four American Indian communities around Lake Ronkonkoma were conned into relinquishing water rights (Curtis 5) to settlers who, from the beginning, had a hard time pronouncing, let alone spelling, the name of the area (local historical documents include, for example, references to "Ronconkomy Plains" and "Rocconkkemy Pond").[2] Three separate townships now abut the lake, and the lack of coordination between the localities has contributed to the lake's steady decline since the 1950s.

By 1850 the Long Island Rail Road (LIRR) had already spanned the length of Long Island, making wealthy New Yorkers aware of the lake and turning the area into a "millionaire's playground" around the turn of the nineteenth century. Mansions sprouted around the perimeter of the lake, along with dozens of hotels, lodges, and beach pavilions. Postcards from this period show men lounging in flannel bathing suits and children climbing two-story-tall water slides or scampering like mice in giant water wheels. Summer dances were held on Saturday nights in the halls bordering the lake; in winter, scooters and iceboats raced across the ice. During prohibition, houses of prostitution and speakeasies popped up in the surrounding woods, and one could buy "needle beer" that made one's fingers tingle (Curtis 100). During the 1920s, anti-Catholic sentiment helped create an active Ku Klux Klan presence: one conductor on the Long Island Rail Road actually sold KKK outfits on the Greenport line (Curtis 134).[3]

In the 1940s, MacArthur Airport opened two miles away from the Lake. (Our house is situated along one of the flight paths; you can almost make out the passengers in the windows of the Southwest jets that pass overhead.) An auction sale catalog from 1937 advertised the selling of two hundred lots near the lake, emphasizing the easy commute from this "gem of Long Island" to Penn Station via twenty-four daily trains. The population surged as summer cottages were converted for year-round living. (My own single-story, two-bedroom home, while not large by middle-class Long Island standards, started out as a bungalow, and has been added onto three or four times in the last four decades.) A local historian writes that "many new developments appeared, and unfortunately some of the promoters emphasized cheapness rather than quality which attracted some buyers who were less desirable," and that "the crowning blow to the town" came when a significant woodland stretch was sold to developers (Curtis 148). Development continued. Lakeside pavilions were sold, and those left abandoned were burned. In the 1960s and 1970s "unrestricted dumping of fill over the banks of the lake destroyed many trees and left unsightly yellow gashes here and there on the east side of the lake": "Large sections of the Great Swamp were filled in and the once beautiful lake was becoming an eye sore." In 1975 the entire lake was closed for three days due to pollution from storm drains carrying runoff into the water (Curtis 161).

Today Lake Ronkonkoma is a working- and middle-class suburb, indistinguishable from a hundred other suburbs on the island, most of them spilling into each other so that one's sense of boundaries comes not from any visual sense of "village limits" but from proximity to highways and strip malls. (In his stand-up days, the comedian Jerry Seinfeld, who grew up half an hour away in Massapequa, joked that the town's name was Indian for "near the mall.")

If you walk out my front door and view the neighborhood, you will see streets that are safe and quiet, except on occasional summer days when neighborhood kids and sometimes their fathers race motorcycles, looking furtively at intersections for signs of cops. Up to 25 percent of the homes in the area are rentals converted into two or more illegal apartments. Despite the fact that when the house next door was rented out the new tenants found the basement littered with vials and syringes, obvious drug activity in the neighborhood is virtually nonexistent, save for an occasional teenager shuffling down the street smoking a joint, or a pipe tossed into the bushes. An abandoned shopping cart across the street is evidence of the "sober house" up the street, a home containing eight apartments (all legal, surprisingly) rented out to men trying to get back on their feet. These men are some of the more visible members of the community, walking (their drivers'

licenses have been revoked) six blocks to a minimarket for gro-
ceries. Because these men are not permitted to have overnight
guests, on a few occasions women have spent the night sleeping
in cars outside our house.

Like much of suburbia in Suffolk County, the streets here
have no sidewalks, just sandy shoulders. The side streets are often
very wide—so wide in fact that five, possibly even six, cars could
park side by side across the width of the street and still not touch
the lawns on either side.

> It has been established . . . that suburban streets all over America
> ought to be as wide as two-lane country highways, regardless of
> whether this promotes driving at excessive speeds where chil-
> dren play, or destroys the spatial relationship between the houses
> on the street. Back in the 1950s, when these formulas were de-
> vised, the width of residential streets was tied closely to the idea
> of a probable nuclear war with the Russians. And in the after-
> math of a war, it was believed, wide streets would make it easier
> to clean up the mess with heavy equipment. (Kunstler 113–14)[4]

If you walk five blocks north from our house you will come to
a service road that runs parallel to the Long Island Expressway
(LIE), with its (increasingly slow-moving) current of 24/7 traffic.
At night the hiss of cars in the distance spills in through our
bedroom skylight.

In 1998 they started widening the highway, extending the
HOV lanes. Although HOV stands for "high occupancy vehicle,"
in this case two people—even if that second person is a baby—are
considered "high occupancy." The HOV lanes have been added to
decrease congestion by encouraging carpooling. Traffic, even out
here, ninety minutes from Manhattan—off peak—is thick: on
weekdays as early as 6:30 A.M. the westbound lane of the LIE can
crawl at 15 m.p.h. But studies show the HOV lanes to be ineffec-
tive. In a car culture like Long Island's, people are reluctant to
carpool (the newspapers occasionally report stories of drivers getting caught in HOV lanes with mannequins sitting next to them
or cabbage patch dolls in baby seats), and, even when they do, the
time it takes to navigate the crowded secondary highways to pick
up one's passengers requires people to get up that much earlier.

> So you think traffic on Long Island is bad now? Stick around.
> In a mere 22 years, it will be unbearable unless something
> is done.

That's the prediction of a team of consultants hired by the state Department of Transportation.

Their study, released by the department last week, makes it clear that existing and planned HOV lanes on the Long Island Expressway aren't going to solve anything. . . . The forecasters say that by 2020, the amount of time Long Islanders are delayed in traffic will nearly double. The 1,091 miles of congested lanes during the morning rush will increase by a whopping 75 percent. And it will take longer to get where we're going; the average travel speed during morning and evening rush hours will decrease by 17 percent.

. . . The big problem is that Long Island's highway system is close to overflowing already, according to the experts. Even a small increase in the number of cars on the road can cause big problems. (Adcock)

Yet construction of the new lanes continues. By the time they are finished, the LIE will be twelve lanes wide in places: the outside shoulder, three lanes of traffic, an on-off lane for entering and leaving the HOV lane, and the HOV lane itself—times two. (See Figure 1 for a construction photo.)

10   If you want to walk more than five blocks north from my house you will have to walk under the LIE, which means crossing a busy service road. Continue for another five blocks and you will find yourself looking at Lake Ronkonkoma. Although the lake is described as "the jewel" of the community, there is no boardwalk, sidewalk, or even pathway encircling the lake—just a perimeter road (dangerous to walk on due to lack of shoulders), scattered homes in some areas, a restaurant, low-income apartments, and a trailer park. There are three beaches, but each resides in one of the three localities bordering the lake, so residents are permitted to use only one of them. (See Figure 2.)

If you walk several blocks east or west from my house you will arrive at busy four-lane streets (seven-lane, if you count the wide shoulders and the center turning lanes), which serve as effective pedestrian barriers, boxing in and thereby defining the parameters of our little "neighborhood." Both roads were widened in the last decade. One street has a light that sometimes changes color before you can reach the other side; the other is an artery connecting the expressway to the Long Island Rail Road and, beyond that, Veteran's Highway. I am reluctant to take walks with my son in this direction because the traffic on Ronkonkoma Avenue is constant and fast-moving (I was nearly run over early

FIGURE 1. *May 14, 1998, 3:55 P.M. Looking down at HOV lane construction on the Long Island Expressway from the Ronkonkoma Avenue overpass between exits 59 and 60, about forty-five miles from Manhattan. "The Long Island Expressway was built without rapid transit—and without provision for rapid transit in the future. And as each section of the superhighway opened [beginning in 1955], it was jammed—with traffic jams of immense dimensions. [Robert Moses'] dream became a nightmare—an enduring, year-after-year nightmare—for tens of thousands of other men. Year by year, the huge road bulled its way eastward, through Queens, across Nassau County, deeper and deeper into Suffolk; it would take fifteen years to build it out to Riverhead. And as each section opened, as each piece of Moses' largest road-building achievement fell into place, the congestion grew worse. The Long Island Expressway's designed daily capacity was 80,000 vehicles. By 1963, it was carrying 132,000 vehicles per day, a load that jammed the expressway even at 'off' hours— during the rush hours, the expressway was solid with cars, congealed with them, chaos solidified. The drivers trapped on it nicknamed Moses' longest road 'the world's longest parking lot.'"* (Caro, Power Broker 949) *Photo by Derek Owens.*

FIGURE 2.   *A view of Lake Ronkonkoma (obstructed by low-income housing). Photo by Derek Owens.*

one morning while walking to the train station). On the other hand, living so close to the Ronkonkoma LIRR station (see Figures 3 and 4) is helpful since I take the train to work. (My daily commute is almost two hours, each way: a fifteen-minute walk to the train station, a one-hour train ride to Jamaica, Queens, a fifteen-minute wait for the Q30 or Q31 bus, and another twenty- to twenty-five-minute ride to campus.)

If you choose to walk south from my house you can go only two blocks before coming to a wooded acre of (for the moment)[5] undeveloped land, which ends at the railroad tracks. A tall fence prevents one from crossing the tracks, which are electrified and will cause third-degree burns and possibly death if one touches the third rail. It is in this wooded plot of land that in the late summer of 1997 I found, hidden amid the black oaks and scrub pines, the remains of a campsite.

They had been living in two ripped tents, the smaller one erected inside the larger one, apparently in an attempt to keep out rain and mosquitoes. Filthy clothes and broken furniture were strewn everywhere. From the smell of the cheese and chopped

FIGURES 3 and 4. Abandoned stores and empty lots at the Ronkonkoma train station. In 1995 a new multimillion-dollar train station was built here, this being the busiest LIRR hub east of Queens. But the new station has not led to the revitalization of local businesses. A billboard in the center of an empty lot next to the train station promises future stores as early as 1997, but as of 2001 the lot remains empty. Photos by Derek Owens.

meat left in a plastic foam cooler, and the remains of a cat coated with maggots and wrapped in a blanket, the site had been abandoned for several weeks. (See Figure 5.) The next day I made an attempt to clean it up but only got so far as to fill a half a dozen garbage bags before I grew too disgusted and gave up. In the process, I found a shoebox of old photographs and a diary. The two squatters had been teenage girls who had taken to living back here in this tiny patch of woods, subsisting for a time by cashing in on a stepfather's social security checks. I wondered what had caused them to leave so suddenly.

Despite the filth they left behind, part of me admired them. In Ronkonkoma, like most suburbs, teenagers, along with elderly persons, are the ones most victimized by the absence of a public commons, of meeting places, of coffee shops or bookstores or independent movie theaters or parks. As a result, many teenagers skulk around in small bands, knocking over fences, stealing the occasional mailbox, and parking at night in the dark beneath shot-out streetlights to hang out, get stoned, or have sex (twice I've found used condoms on the shoulder outside our

FIGURE 5.   Squatters in suburbia. Photo by Derek Owens.

house, and, once, a discarded early pregnancy test kit in the bushes).

> As a teenager I visited my old suburban chums back on Long Island from time to time and I did not envy their lot in life. By puberty, they had entered a kind of coma. There was so little for them to do in Northwood, and hardly any worthwhile destination reachable by bike or foot, for now all the surrounding territory was composed of similar one-dimensional housing developments punctuated at intervals by equally boring shopping plazas. Since they had no public gathering places, teens congregated in furtive little holes—bedrooms and basements—to smoke pot and imitate the rock and roll bands who played on the radio. Otherwise, teen life there was reduced to waiting for that transforming moment of becoming a licensed driver. (Kunstler 14)

One writer has suggested, not completely tongue in cheek, 15 that it is the sameness of the Long Island landscape, perfected early on in that famous suburb of Levittown, that makes Nassau and Suffolk county produce more than their share of kidnappers, serial killers, snipers, teenage killers, spouse murderers, and other dangerous individuals. In "Long Island, Babylon," Ron Rosenbaum implies that the inability to situate oneself psychologically or physically within a specific space distinguishable from other spaces leads to psychosis. Moreover, Rosenbaum sees the percolation of antisocial behavior on Long Island as a harbinger for the rest of the country:

> Long Island, after all, was supposed to be the future *before* the future. We always had a head start on the life cycle of suburban baby-boom culture because we were the first-born burbs of the baby boom; a burbland created almost all at once, very fast and virtually ex nihilo, right after the war, a self-contained social organism. An organism whose sociobiological clock started ticking a little earlier than subsequent burbs, and whose shrill alarms now seem to signal that it has raced through its mature stage and is now rocketing headlong into the social-organism equivalent of senile dementia. (628)

Others have called attention to what some see as a disproportionate number of famous crimes associated with Nassau and Suffolk county (Demoretcky; Jensen; Wacker). Two weeks after the April 1999 high school massacre in Colorado, an article appeared

in the *New York Times* speculating about the role of suburban
sprawl in fostering the kind of environment where such tragedies
occur: "At a time when the renegade sprawl of suburbs themselves
is being intensely scrutinized, the troubling vision of a nation re-
pioneered in vast tracts of disconnected communities has produced uneasy discussion about the psychological disorientation
they might house" (Hamilton, "Suburban Design" F1).

At least the two squatters near my house had made, for a
piece of their summer, a hovel of their own away from others'
eyes, tucked away by the tracks in a copse of trees sandwiched between the Quality Muffler Shop and a dirt parking lot owned by
the LIRR. As disgusted with them as I was for having defiled that
place, I am more ashamed of the planners and architects and developers, and their backers, who have bequeathed to other people's children what James Kunstler calls "a landscape of scary
places, the geography of nowhere, that has simply ceased to be a
credible human habitat" (15). If their community leaders had exhibited no imagination in designing neighborhoods and had polluted the environs with industrial parks and strip malls, one
could hardly criticize these girls for desecrating their own hidden
home, which was, after all, distinctly *their* mess, and not a copy of
a copy of someone else's idea of what a home or neighborhood
should look like. Embarrassing as it was, this pathetic campsite
had become, for a few weeks, their space, an island constructed
in the center of an island marked by unchecked sprawl.

Endnotes

1. Because of the confusing mélange of towns and villages overlapping
   one another across the island, coupled with the absence of village
   centers, Long Islanders often identify themselves according to the
   exit on the Long Island Expressway nearest their home. When people ask me where I live, all I need to say is "near exit 60." For many
   Long Islanders, our sense of place is often determined by commut-
   ing distance—to Manhattan, to work, or to family in the area.
2. In the 1999 film *200 Cigarettes* two teenagers from Ronkonkoma
   (Christina Ricci and Gaby Hoffman) spend New Year's Eve on the
   Lower East Side. One of the film's recurring jokes is that no one can
   understand where exactly the two young women come from or what
   they say, given the odd name of their town and their impenetrable
   "Lawn Guyland" accents.
3. This active KKK presence is, sadly, less surprising when one
   considers that during the 1700s roughly 20 percent of Long Island's

population consisted of slaves, mostly Black but also American Indian. One historian (amazingly) equates ownership of slaves with Long Island's contemporary car culture: "Slaveholding was to colonial status on Long Island what car-owning is to contemporary status: prosperous families owned fourteen or more slaves, while poorer residents could afford only one or two" (Bookbinder 39). An insensitive comparison for obvious reasons—car owners around here spend considerable money "detailing" their machines, not torturing, raping, and murdering them—the analogy is also backwards: to live in suburban sprawl means to be a slave to one's car, or, rather, to the planners who built these communities designed around automobile transportation.

4. "The influence of the Cold War was profound. In the 1950s, the civil Defense Committee of AASHTO, the American Association of State Highway Transportation Officials, was a dominant force in the determination of street design criteria. Its prescription was straightforward: street design must facilitate evacuation before, and cleanup after, a major 'nuclear event'" (Duany et al. 65). Ironically, fear of the bomb is what drew so many "come-outers" to the suburbs in the first place, away from urban centers that had become atomic bomb targets (Stilgoe 301).

5. Portions of this wooded lot have since been bulldozed to make way for a road widening project; the rest is up for sale.

Works Cited

Adcock, Sylvia. "A Look at Delays to Come." *Newsday* 3 May 1998: A3.

Bookbinder, Bernie. *Long Island: People and Places, Past and Present.* New York: Abrams, 1983.

Caro, Robert A. "The City-Shaper." *The New Yorker* 5 Jan. 1998: 38–50, 52–55.

———. *The Power Broker: Robert Moses and the Fall of New York.* New York: Vintage, 1974.

Curtis, Ann Farnum. *Three Waves: The Story of Lake Ronkonkoma.* Ronkonkoma, New York: Review Publishing. 1993.

Demoretcky, Tom. "Crime in the Suburbs: A Deadly Parade of Violence Brings Pain to Peaceful Neighborhoods." *Newsday* 21 June 1998: H16.

Hamilton, William L. "How Suburban Design Is Failing Teen-Agers." *New York Times* 6 May 1999: F1+.

Isachsen, Y. W., et al., eds. *Geology of New York: A Simplified Account.* Albany: New York State Museum/Geological Survey, State Education Department, State U of New York, 1991.

Jensen, Bill. "A True-Crime Tour." *Long Island Voice* 15–21 October 1998: 16–18.

Kunstler, James Howard. *The Geography of Nowhere: The Rise and Decline of America's Man-Made Landscape*. New York: Simon, 1993.

Rosenbaum, Ron. "Long Island, Babylon." *The Secret Parts of Fortune: Three Decades of Intense Investigations and Edgy Enthusiasms*. New York: Random, 2000: 612–628.

Wacker, Bob. "Why Living Here Can Be Murder." *Long Island Voice* 15–21 October 1998: 154.

Guiding Questions

1. How does it make you feel when Owens uses the second person, and tells you what you would see if you walked north, south, east, or west from his house?

2. Why do you think Owens spends as much time as he does early in the essay on the geological and other natural histories of Long Island and Lake Ronkonkoma?

3. Owens mentions a theory that central Long Island's historic prairies—a natural anomaly—might actually have been caused by the actions of Native American inhabitants. Why do you think he makes sure to include this point? Are there implications here for the rest of his essay?

4. Both Lake Ronkonkoma and the Long Island Expressway figure prominently in Owens's neighborhood and in the essay. How does he describe each of them? What kinds of contrasts or similarities does he draw?

5. Are you surprised by how long it takes Owens to get to work in Queens (which is also on Long Island, less than 90 miles away from Ronkonkoma)? Do you think he expects or wants you to be surprised?

6. How would you describe the kinds of research Owens does for this piece? What kinds of sources does he read in order to make sense of his place? How does he integrate these secondary sources with his own observations?

Paths for Further Exploration

1. Write a neighborhood narrative, following the pattern that Owens uses. Leave your home or residence hall (and get off campus, too, if you can) and walk in all four directions, explaining to your readers what they would encounter if they were to do the same. Take pictures and make lists of what you see, and do some research on one or two things that particularly capture your interest (an old building, a brook, a busy intersection, an abandoned field, etc.). (See Chapter 4 for tips on how to research local histories.)

2. Find out something about the natural history of your hometown neighborhood or campus neighborhood and write about how those environmental

factors may have affected what humans have done with the place, or may even be affecting how you experience it today. (See Chapter 4 for tips on how to get started on this kind of research.)

3. Write about your own commute—whether to classes or to a job you hold now or have held in the past. How long does it take you? How many different modes of transportation do you have to use, including your own walking? Do you experience the places you commute through in any special way? If you do not think you have enough to write about, consider writing about someone else's commute. Interview that person to find out as much as you can about how he or she gets to work or school.

4. Owens talks about the boredom that many teens experience in suburban communities that were not designed with them in mind, and he cites various authorities who argue boredom and sameness can lead to psychosis. If you have been bored in a place where you lived, write about why the place was boring, how you tried to make it interesting, and how boredom affected you. Do you understand Owens's depiction of the sameness and nowhereness of suburban teenage life?

En Mi Cucina/In My Kitchen
GABRIELA DE LA HUERTA

Gabriela de la Huerta was born in Tlaxcala, Mexico. She arrived in the United States in September 1997. Gabriela loves to write and to knit. She has two children, Diana and Gerardo, and her principal goal is to keep her family together. This poem first appeared in the Journal of Ordinary Thought, *a publication that sponsors free writing workshops open to all Chicago residents. The publication's motto is "Every person is a philosopher." For more writing from this journal, see www.jot.org.*

———————— ✦ ————————

*La cocina para mí es un lugar muy
especial porque paso un buen tiempo,
porque allí se prepara los alimentos
diaramente. Me encuentro sola, es
un día normal. Mis hijos están en
la escuela. Mi esposo fue al trabajo*

5

Estoy escuchando el ruido del
refrigerador, es un ruido continuo
que hay en la cocina
Disfruto del olor a mole que estoy   10
cocinando para la comida del dia de
hoy, para disfrutar en familia. ¡UM
UM qué rico! Pero, siento un frio
inmenso que me duele el cuerpo, un
frio por el cambio del tiempo y por   15
la soledad que hay en mi casa. Me
gusta disfrutar un chocolate caliente
con canela, y un pan que trajo una
amiga. Disfruto de mi cocina. Me
levanto y veo por la ventana caer   20
las hojas de los árboles y algunas
personas caminando con prisa y yo
me encuentro en mi cocina.

                                  * * *

My kitchen is a very special place
because I spend a good part of my
day there, because every day I prepare
the meals there. I am alone—it's a
normal day. My children are in   5
school. My husband has gone to
work. I am listening to the sound of
the refrigerator; it is a continuous
noise in the kitchen.
I enjoy the smell of the mole I am   10
cooking for today's meal, which we
will enjoy as a family. Yum, yum,
how delicious! But I feel an immense
chill that hurts my body, a cold that
comes with the change of the weather   15
and the solitude in my house. I
like to enjoy a hot chocolate with
cinnamon, with a piece of bread my
friend brought me. I enjoy my
kitchen. I get up and look through   20
the window. I see leaves falling from

the trees and people hurrying, and I
find myself in my kitchen.

Guiding Questions

1. De la Huerta's description of her kitchen seems like it could just as easily
   have been written in prose as in poetry. What is gained by her decision to
   use poetic line breaks? How do the conventions of poetry affect the descriptive power of the piece and its presentation of images?
2. If you speak or read Spanish as well as English, think about what it means for
   the Spanish version of the poem to appear first. What would have changed
   about your response if the English version had been first? Are there some
   places you feel you can best describe in a language other than English?
3. Why does the kitchen seem to be a particularly important place in de la
   Huerta's life? What goes on in kitchens that tends to make them central
   places? What does it mean in *your* family to invite someone into the kitchen?
4. Reread Kimberly Wheaton's "Mom and the Kitchen" and describe how this
   kitchen functions differently from de la Huerta's.

Paths for Further Exploration

1. Try writing a brief poem about a single room. Pay the kind of close attention
   to sensory detail and mood that de la Huerta does. Now change the poem
   into a prose piece. What happens to the description?
2. Write a short essay about a contradictory place like de la Huerta's kitchen—
   a place where you can be alone but feel the presence of others in the room
   or where you can be inside but have a good sense of the outside world.

Structured Chaos
EMILY KEANE

*This essay focuses on a place familiar to almost any college student:
a campus dining hall. A confusing and busy zone of bad, overpriced
food, last-minute studying, fundraisers, and hundreds of flyers announcing an endless stream of events, the dining area nevertheless
maintains a ruthless utility: students flow in, grab food, gulp it
down, and flow out. Emily Keane's sense of that basic organizing
principle underneath all the scattered energy of the place may just*

make "Pizza Surprise" a bit more understandable. Keane is an international studies major and theology minor at Boston College. She plans to go Africa with the Peace Corps after graduation and would eventually like to work for a nonprofit organization involved with African refugee issues.

✦

Walking into the room is slightly disorienting—to say the least. From opposite corners of the room mounted televisions play music videos. With booming bass lines and outrageous lead singers, the trendy bands do their best to capture your attention and immerse you in their worlds. Yet while they enjoy their ephemeral fame, which the clock ticks closer to fifteen minutes, the hundreds of students talking, yelling, laughing, and chewing loudly give new meaning to the phrase "background music." An onslaught of hot pink, sunflower yellow, and sky blue paper is strategically placed around the room to seize your attention via key phrases such as "Wanna Volunteer?", "Spring Break!", and "Guest Speaker on Wednesday!" The bold lettering saturated with exclamation points exudes anxiety, hoping someone will take interest and look at its excited message more closely.

Artificial light from above settles on the gray tables made for four. More often than not the tables are pushed together to accommodate large clusters of students from the same dorm having lunch together, as is their ritual when their schedules allow. Backpacks, notebooks, and jackets fight for space among trays, cups, and elbows. Information on upcoming assignments and tests struggles to be heard as upcoming weekend plans are gushed to the group. These frenzied conversations surge with energy as students analyze their best options for Friday and Saturday night adventures.

In contrast, rays from the sun cascade onto other, quiet tables by the windows, highlighting their single occupants. Engrossed by notes for the next class, some tune out all of the surrounding distractions and use this room as an unconventional library. Others sit alone simply to ponder something on their minds and unearth some inner clarity. Whatever their reasons, these people seem to have a certain independent streak in their sense of self. They don't seem to hate solidarity; they simply have an affinity for solitude even within the crowd.

For some students, the large room serves merely as a shortcut from point A to point B. Some pass through leisurely in the company of friends, sauntering and enjoying light conversation. Others are on a mission to get from one end of the room to the other in as little time as possible, dashing off to their next class or meeting. Girls' heeled shoes strike the floor, providing a staccato, syncopated rhythm for the room as they pass through announcing their busy purpose.

Walking into the food service area itself is like walking into   5 structured chaos. Dodging trays, food stands, and lines of people, it is wise to know where you are headed before you enter. If you don't, you become a wanderer, aimlessly drifting from station to station while trying to decide exactly what you want for lunch. In this fast-paced environment, such wanderers become unwanted speed bumps for the rest of the traffic.

In contrast to the boring beige walls of the eating area, the serving area's walls are bright, white ceramic tiles. They provide a unique canvas for the vivid color palette splashed within their bounds, flaunting the multitude of food choices. Each station and food stand draws you in, wanting to show you what it has to offer with its own colors, smells, and flavors. Each bag of chips and cookies glints in the light, enticing you to take them—just this once.

Most that enter become part of the vast lines that wind within the small enclosure. Waiting for a coveted wrap sandwich leaves you a large amount of time to think. Your main focus starts to become the constant sounds: the drone of the refrigerator units, the beeping of the register as people check out, and the cubes of ice tumbling on top of each other into a plastic cup, followed by soda swooshing from the fountain. The sticky refrigerator doors "pop" as they open and quietly bump when they are sealed again, and the radio is just audible as it plays in the kitchen giving the workers something to hum along to—adding to the steady cacophony of the background symphony.

Your eyes are drawn to the neon blue signs on each side of the room announcing that below them are BEVERAGES. The transparent glass and bright white lights down the insides of the refrigerators illuminate the diverse group of beverages within. As though not wanting to be forgotten, a cherry red neon sign proclaims the existence of SALAD in the back. Even the soup station, with its three different types each day, lights up a bowl of steamy soup and projects the colors onto the white tiles and faces gathered around this modern hearth.

The numerous options available for a wrap sandwich are presented behind a shiny protective glass covering. The khaki, sallow green, and intense golden yellow tortillas ("Plain," "Spinach," and "Garden Vegetable") rest in clear plastic bags on top of the counter. The dim light settles on bright green romaine lettuce chopped into sections, a far more appealing choice than the sickly white shredded iceberg. The thinly sliced red tomatoes and chunks of shiny chopped onions actually look good to eat. They sit next to a variety of creamy colored cheeses which all look exactly the same. (Luckily for the Swiss, it can be distinguished by its holes.) There are the traditional luncheon meats—the sliced pale pink turkey and the watermelon-colored ham—but also unconventional choices. Disturbingly orange chunks of barbeque chicken look they've been there since last week, and the chunky white tuna fish is complete with an immersed ice cream scooper to add to its dubious appeal.

10   The workers, in short-sleeved polo shirts with a cursive BCDS insignia, use their rubber-gloved hands to make the sandwiches efficiently, tailoring whatever combination is requested. The wrap sandwiches are a highly craved item in the dining hall. A large line assembles outside the gates waiting for them to open at eleven in order to beat the rush later in the day. It is a scene similar to a store opening the day after Christmas, the customers eager to find a decent sale. Once the gates are open, the lines only grow longer. It can take up to twenty minutes to get a freshly made sandwich, but people don't seem to mind. At the peak of the day, eating in this dining hall is a privilege. Students carry their wraps in their hands like trophies. Stopping right outside the exit, their eyes scan the room to find an open table. When that fails, they look around for friends, or even acquaintances, to squeeze in just one more.

Even when the serving area closes for the day, the room still thrives. Looking into the garbage cans at the end of the afternoon is a good way to judge how busy the day has been; usually they are overflowing. Despite the lack of food service, some students study until only the harsh ceiling light remains while others catch up on the day's events as they walk through the room. In the early evening, large clubs hold meetings and line up the chairs in the main flow of traffic to assemble a makeshift auditorium. Even when the doors are locked for the night, the hum of the refrigerators can still be heard. The lights within them are the only ones left on, serving as the night light for the now mysteriously quiet arena.

The televisions display gray lifeless screens and the chairs scattered throughout the room are now unoccupied. Yet the empty tables still pulse with life. Some bear the remnants of past lunch, a salt or pepper shaker, or a small flyer *still* trying to announce the arrival of the guest speaker on Wednesday.

Guiding Questions

1. How does Keane use various sense-based descriptions to put you in the place? What does the abundance of color, noise, and smells suggest about the design principles behind student dining halls?
2. How many different functions does this place seem to serve? Does it serve all of them equally well?
3. What does Keane suggest that you can determine about a student by watching how he or she behaves in the dining hall?

Paths for Further Exploration

1. Write about a student dining hall on your campus. If you can, contrast it with a faculty dining area, or even with a nearby restaurant. In the student area, pay particular attention to how students seem to use space to interact with each other.
2. Examine any busy place to see how it might be designed to promote certain kinds of traffic flows through its boundaries and to discourage others.
3. Explain what your ideal student dining hall would look like, how it would work, and what it would feel like to eat there. Include a diagram or two if you are artistically inclined.

By Dawn's Early Light
RON FLETCHER

Ron Fletcher teaches English at Boston College High School and his reporting regularly appears in the Boston Globe *and the* Boston Phoenix; *he is also at work on his first novel. This "slice of life" article from the* Boston Globe *shows us that familiar places—such as urban neighborhoods—can become essentially different places when we change our perspective on them in even one significant way. Here, Fletcher changes our perspective by taking us through the city at a time most of us never see it. In doing so, he not only makes the everyday urban landscape seem strange but also encounters a secret second society of neighbors, those up with (or before) the sun.*

――――――――――――― ✦ ―――――――――――

In a city that does sleep, the pulse of the Charles River slows, its pre-dawn repose a black mirror for solitary headlights that wind down Storrow Drive. Delivery trucks sail through downtown traffic lights that flash yellow above near-empty intersections. The occasional jogger, dog walker, or roller-blader commands an open sidewalk. An empties-laden shopping cart rattles down the alleyways behind Comm. Ave. condos with curtains drawn. And stiletto heels click and clack along the streets of Bay Village, where turning the clocks back means gaining an hour to ply the oldest trade.

"Four a.m. in Boston is another world," says Steve Hobbs, whose work as a floral designer has him up before the sun. "You see everything. Well, everything that those who get to work at 9 a.m. miss."

For those who set their alarms for the small hours, Boston offers ample free parking, a lack of coffee shops, and an expansive calm. Early risers talk often about the ways space and pace shift throughout hours four, five, and six. They turn to recurring sounds and sights rather than clocks or watches for a sense of time.

Last week's return to standard time matters little to them. "When the sun comes up, it wakes a tree full of birds right in front of the shop," says Dave House, co-owner of Flat Black, the coffee shop in Lower Mills. "They chirp away for about 15 minutes. When they stop, the day begins."

5   For Marlon George at the Franklin Park Golf Course, there is the morning ritual of placing 18 blue flags on the dew-dappled or, now, sometimes frosted greens. He drives his cart from hole to hole in the company of other early birds to the course: geese, seagulls, and the occasional hawk. "There's always some kind of activity at the course," says George, "people walking or jogging or looking to get an early nine holes in."

A solid three-iron away from the links, Steve Sullivan pushes a broom along the curb outside the Shattuck Shelter. A resident as well as a member of the shelter's work crew, Sullivan earns minimum wage as he sweeps up damp leaves, cigarette butts, scratch tickets, and a few bottle caps. The hour of 5 a.m. appeals to him.

"I do appreciate a little solitude," says Sullivan, 45, who had worked full time as a truck driver before he lost his license and landed at the shelter last March. "To find a quiet moment when you live with a couple hundred people is pretty nice."

As the black sky lightens to dark blue, Sullivan completes his outdoor chores, walks through the gray cigarette smoke exhaled by a handful of fellow early risers, and prepares the shelter's cafeteria for a 6:40 a.m. breakfast. He moves silently past a row of occupied bunk beds toward the labyrinth of hallways that will lead him to the cafeteria, where trays of scrambled eggs and crates of single-serve OJ and milk cartons await the guests.

Sullivan sees little unique in his appreciation of the early-morning hours. "There are a lot of people staying here who get up very early and go straight off to work or to look for a job," he said, enjoying his own breakfast after having prepared and served more than 100 himself. "When the average rent [in Boston] is over $1,000, what are the chances of someone making minimum wage getting a place? If you're lucky, you find some steady work and make enough to get a room."

Working alongside Sullivan is Peter Lewis, who has spent two   10
years at the shelter. This year, he says, is about continuing to break the habits that hobbled him last year. Progress has opened his eyes to dawn's early light.

"Sunrise didn't mean too much last year," says Lewis, "but I appreciate it now, what it represents: something beneficial, something peaceful. Sometimes I catch it while I'm working." He points to the cafeteria's wall of windows. "But most of the time I'm too concerned with what's going on in here to notice it."

Rene Morales has seen his share of sunrises through a window as well. Since 1974, the native of Guatemala has been mixing dough and making breads at Quinzani's Bakery on Harrison Avenue in the South End. Describing himself as a "morning person," Morales, 59, flits around the heavy machinery that cranks out 5,000-plus dinner rolls per hour. He punctuates his 4 a.m. to noon shift with a well-timed break.

"You see that window?" asks Morales, pointing a flour-dusted finger. "When I can, I go there and watch the sun come out. The daylight makes you keep going. It energizes you."

Many who work the predawn shift speak of having two days in one. Restored by a post-work nap, they enjoy an afternoon and early evening all their own. Not Morales.

"I go home, take a shower, have lunch, then go to my second   15
job at South Shore Hospital," says Morales. No boast, no grouse. "At 8 [p.m.], I go home, get some sleep, then come here. That's my life." He smiles, then mentions he has a chance to sleep late on Sundays. "I get up at 9 a.m.," says Morales, "then go out for breakfast with my beautiful wife and my beautiful daughter."

Outside of the bakery, Javier Ayla loads paper bags of still-warm bread onto a delivery truck he will drive from 5 a.m. until 1 p.m. He says that the end of daylight savings time matters little to him. "I'm still working and it's still dark out," says the young father, who rises daily at 2:30. "I just have to make sure that I get up at the right time."

A few blocks away, the alarm clock–like beeping of a delivery truck in reverse gear snaps to attention the small staff of Back Bay Wholesale Flowers. The loading-dock door is raised like a stage curtain to reveal a choreographed ballet of retrieval, unboxing, plunging into water, refrigeration, and the displaying of flowers picked in Ecuador or Holland less than 24 hours ago. Europe or South America, to New York City, Boston, then, perhaps, your dining room table.

"It's amazing," says Wayne Robinson, who owns a flower shop in Easton. "If it wasn't for these guys here, we'd be selling carnations and mums from oh, I don't know—Woburn." He then points out one of his own creations, a fall floral arrangement in a 4-foot glass vase, filled with eight bags of candy corn.

A whit more subdued is Steve Hobbs, designer for Exotic Flowers of Boston. The 30-year veteran who learned the trade from his father sips a cup of coffee as the staff trots out buckets and boxes of fresh flowers. Color and fragrance fill the room, surfeiting the senses.

20   "This is wonderful, just wonderful," says Hobbs, who eyes a display of gerbera daisies that capture the colors of fall. "People think that autumn in a flower shop is all about gourds, pumpkins, hay, and cornstalks. As you can see, it is not.

"But you have to get here early for the best stuff," adds Hobbs. "Show up at 9 and you're looking at a few boxes of yellow and orange daisies not the glorious colors you see now."

From the flower district to the fish piers, the newsstands to the bakeries, the early-morning hours offer a commerce of daily consumption, a trafficking in the timely and ephemeral. Dawn dramatizes transition. And witnessing dark give way to light each day seems to offer something salutary.

"The light," said baker Rene Morales, "it's like life."

Guiding Questions

1. The autumnal setting of the clock back one hour seems to have inspired this article. Why do you think Fletcher found that a useful writing prompt? What kinds of things about time, place, and routine do you think it made him consider?

2. Do the people Fletcher encounters at these early hours seem to have certain traits or lifestyles in common? Do the same kinds of places seem to be occupied before dawn in the same way as during the regular day? If so, why?

3. The natural world seems particularly present in the city at these early hours. Why might that be so?

Paths for Further Exploration

1. Set your alarm for 4 A.M. some morning and write a description of what your neighborhood or campus looks and feels like at that time of day. Consider writing a twenty-four-hour description of these places, observing the place for at least a few minutes during every hour. (Break up this assignment into several days of observation, though, as doing twenty-four hours straight probably is not a healthy or safe idea.) Webcams may help you in this assignment (see Chapter 4 for the Web site of a directory of public webcams, and check your school's home page and admissions office page to see any webcams that may be on your campus).

2. Imagine other ways to alter your perspective on a familiar place. How would these change your sense of it? Give yourself an assignment and write about what you observe. For example, what if you could not see or hear in a particular place? What if you could not speak to anyone there? What if you were much shorter or taller? What if you were much older or younger than you are? Be creative.

3. Find out what specific tasks need to be done in your neighborhood or on your campus to make them "ready" for you and interview the people who perform those tasks, such as the workers in a dining hall, bakers, or delivery drivers. Examine how your sense of the place is different from and similar to theirs. Once you have met some of these people, note how, if at all, your understanding of the places you share is altered.

Hazardous Cargo
RAY GONZALEZ

In this investigative essay, Ray Gonzalez analyzes how aspects of places can remain largely unknown by most who live there, even when those aspects pose a great threat. Raising questions about environmental justice and showing that what you do not know can hurt you, Gonzalez asks us to consider just how much we might not know about where we are, and who benefits from our ignorance. Gonzalez is a professor in the English department at the University of Minnesota, where he teaches creative writing, U.S. Latino literature, poetry, and creative nonfiction. A much-published poet, essayist, editor, and novelist, Gonzalez has won numerous awards for works such as The Hawk Temple at Tierra Grande, The

Underground Heart, *and* Turtle Pictures. *He was the founding editor of* Luna: A Journal of Poetry and Translation.

———————— ✦ ————————

My car engine idles on the shoulder of the two-lane road, about one hundred yards from the entrance to Caldwell-Briseno Industries, a thriving solid waste disposal facility in Sunland Park, New Mexico, ten miles northwest of downtown El Paso. I can't see what lies behind the metal fence, its threads tightly wound together, barbed wire running along its top for hundreds of feet. I think I see mounds of dirt beyond the barrier and warehouse buildings spread throughout, but the long row of diesel trucks blocks my view. Eight of them are lined up at the gate, waiting to be checked off and allowed to enter and deposit whatever hidden cargo they are carrying. The entrance is reinforced by a guardhouse, three men in uniform standing inside the glass, watching the slow-moving parade of vehicles.

I sit in my car with the windows closed because the exhausts from the trucks spread fumes everywhere. The plant is near the Rio Grande, and Cristo Rey, the mountain with the statue of Christ at the top, looms over the area, its brown slopes two miles away. A friend in El Paso told me about this place and said they found a good location because acres of cottonwoods, salt cedar, and other river vegetation surround the perimeters of the dumpsite. Most people don't know of its existence or what is left here after empty trucks roar away. As I count the vehicles, two more pass me and get in line, and I wonder if anyone ever questions why so many loud trucks turn into this area off the main highways on the west side of the city.

I wanted to see how a waste dump so close to town operates, perhaps even talk to some residents of Sunland Park, but my plans are cut short when a white, four-wheel-drive van screeches to a stop next to my car, the blue and green Caldwell-Briseno logo painted on its doors. The uniformed driver, decked out in sunglasses and blue baseball cap with the logo on it, stares at me until I lower my window. He lowers his passenger-side window, and I see he is Mexican-American.

"I'm sorry, sir, but you can't stop your car here," he says politely.

5   "I was just driving through and wanted to see all the trucks," I tell him above the roar of the waiting line down the road.

"You can't stop here." He looks over his shoulder as a radio squawks inside his van. "Turn around right here and you can get back to Doniphan."

"Isn't this a public road?" I point toward the street that goes past the gates.

He looks at me without answering, his brown face with its thin, well-trimmed moustache glistening under his cap. "Turn around right here, sir. No unauthorized vehicles are allowed to stop here."

"Okay," and I wave goodbye. He pulls forward so I can make a U-turn before another truck arrives and blocks me on the shoulder. I spin around and head back toward town. Four more lumbering, weighed-down trucks churn toward the facility before I reach the main road out of Sunland Park. Before I get on Doniphan, it hits me. None of the trucks in the long line or the ones approaching are painted with company logos, lettering, or signs on them. Every truck is anonymous and I can't tell to whom they belong or what they carry. It can't be a coincidence that none of them are marked, though some have New Mexico and Texas license plates, while others carry Chihuahua, Mexico, plates.

These trucks remind me of the black helicopters on *The X-Files* television series. Once you realize "the truth is out there," you can't help but spot them on the highways. There is no way to keep an accurate count of how many of these highly visible, yet invisible, trucks carry millions of gallons of toxic chemicals from American plants and maquiladoras across the border in Juárez. In a way, it is a silent operation, an invisible network that basically runs unimpeded. Since these diesel trucks and rigs blend into normal business traffic, no one is going to ask them to stop and find out what time bombs are riding in the back. Despite laws regulating these border factories, hazardous waste gets dumped on the border every day.

These trucks have appeared at a waste facility by supposedly following designated routes marked by HC signs. They are everywhere I look in the southern New Mexico and El Paso area. White diamond-shaped highway signs with the big, green letters "HC" on them. Hazardous Cargo. HC signs point the way—the lawful stops, turns, and streets to get out of one area and show up with your chemical mess in another. I don't know when they first went up because they were not posted on highways and roads when I was a boy in El Paso. These warnings are a recent response to government regulations on shipping materials that have probably been sent through the area undetected and unregulated for decades. Now, I spot dozens of HC signs on main streets in El Paso, entry ramps to the freeway, and on Interstate 25 heading north toward Las Cruces. Some of the key places to find them are on the international bridges between Juárez and El Paso. If you

10

look closely among the hundreds of cars and trucks lined up to cross each way, you will spot an HC sign.

The Southwest is the most nuclear-polluted and chemically ruined area of the U.S. It is the location for top-secret military installations and radioactive waste sites. Interstate 25 is the route to White Sands Missile Range, Los Alamos Nuclear Laboratory, and Cheyenne Mountain in Colorado. Secret cargoes are shipped, transferred, and secretly shifted on huge trucks every day across Arizona, New Mexico, and west Texas, I-25 the main artery that sends government and industrial waste toward its final resting place. One of the newest dumping sites is the Waste Isolation Pilot Plant, mined 2,150 feet below an ancient salt formation thirty miles southeast of Carlsbad, New Mexico. Los Alamos National Laboratory had the honor of being the first to dump what is called "transuranic waste" at the Carlsbad site. Transuranic wastes are generated primarily during the research, development, and production of nuclear weapons. This waste includes everything from laboratory clothing, tools, glove boxes, and rubber gloves, to glassware and air filters. Trucks rumbling south on I-25, and passing through El Paso, carry the waste in Transuranic Packing Transporters—reusable shipping casks, three to a truck, and each filled with fifty-five-gallon steel drums of matter to be buried under the desert.

There are daily hazardous cargo caravans no one knows about, with most of the people living in the area not paying attention to the growing business of dumping dangerous materials and leftovers from a region undergoing tremendous economic and industrial changes. When state or city governments do find out, there is little they can do to stop the dangerous materials from passing through their area, though the Western Governors' Association, made up of several western state government offices, spent ten years preparing regulations to oversee dangerous shipments, but they have not stopped the increasing tide of waste or new companies making money by taking care of the sludge. Flooding the landscape with HC signs and keeping the trucks on these designated routes are victories from long-fought legislative and economic battles between federal and state agencies. Decorating the El Paso landscape with HC signs also means these designated routes are here to stay, bringing the risk of chemical spills and public endangerment with them.

Hazardous cargo has become big business because the passage of NAFTA a few years ago meant more trade and more factories having to get rid of their manufacturing messes. In January 1997, Mexican president Ernesto Zedillo inaugurated what he

called the "NAFTA highway" to boost further trade between the
U.S. and Mexico. He dedicated sixty-two miles of a highway running through the state of San Luis Potosi, about halfway between
Mexico City and Laredo, Texas, and promised thirty-eight million
dollars to complete it. By 1998 trucks were moving 160,000 tons
of products daily along the partially finished highway, about half
the cargo weight moved between the two countries in a twenty-
four-hour period. When it signed NAFTA, Mexico insisted
that any dangerous materials generated by the maquiladoras,
U.S.–owned factories in Mexico, must be transported back to the
country of origin even though a 1997 report, by Mexico's National
Institute of Ecology, claimed that only 12 percent of eight million
tons of hazardous wastes receives adequate treatment. Thus,
more HC signs sprang up all over the El Paso area and literally
hundreds more trucks and vans began clogging the freeways. In
public documents, Caldwell-Briseno estimates 300 vehicles pass
through its gates per day. Of those, it reports that 250 are commercial disposal trucks full of cargo directly from Juárez
maquiladoras. These carriers dump six thousand cubic yards per
day or eighteen hundred tons of waste every twenty-four hours.
Sunland Park is ten miles northwest of downtown El Paso. The
roads around El Paso, and other areas along the U.S.–Mexican
border, are packed with heavy trucks and vans, though many local citizens might say it is part of becoming a major city.

One of the few encouraging steps taken, in an attempt to con-   15
trol these hazardous materials, took place in 1996. The Mexican
city of Nogales, on the Arizona border, conducted a hazardous
waste worker training program. They gathered one hundred
Mexican workers from maquiladoras in the San Luis and Mexicali
areas. The five-day program consisted of lectures on the marking,
packaging, and filling out of shipping forms, placarding, and driver
training. As one of the few training programs on either side of the
border, it received media attention and promises by the Daewoo
Electronics maquiladora in San Luis that it would increase its programs for workers and encourage other industries to do the same.

Five years later the only media stories you hear are the ones
about the increasing number of workers with medical problems
caused by working conditions, the murdered Mexican girls who
work in the factories, and the growing level of contamination in the
Rio Grande. In the meantime, the HC signs shake in the hot wind
of a desert summer. How many truck drivers that know these
marked routes have been trained in moving industrial waste,
hydrocarbon-affected soils, and radioactive sludge? New Mexico

passed a law in 1986 requiring that all hazardous waste be exported out of the state. Chances are they are not dropping it in the El Paso area because that is too close to home, so the growing number of trucks on border highways mainly come from U.S. companies producing industrial trash right across the river in Mexico.

The white diamond signs that guide these trucks to the landfill blend into the thousands of billboards, traffic lights, and highway directional signs. They have been erected to make sure the risky fallout from thriving border commerce does not wander from the plotted path and into "safe" parts of neighborhoods. Their drivers must know the routes from memory by now but, as I count the HC markers, I realize the only freeway in El Paso is a legal route and so is every major street in town! I have never heard about any toxic spills in the El Paso area, yet the proliferation of the white signs on city streets and its lone freeway says the legal route is the only route. It should be evident to any El Pasoan who has noticed the former sleepy town now has heavy rush hours and gridlock that a good portion of the traffic causing these problems are long parades of large diesel trucks carrying their secret cargoes from a thriving border, industrial revolution.

I walked around Paisano Street and asked a few people if they knew what the HC sign down the block stood for. Not one out of eight people I stopped knew what it meant. Five said they had never noticed the sign before; one of them, a young comedian with a smirk on his face, answered, "Doesn't that mean Hispanic Culture?" The other three thought they were directional signs to Juárez.

In 1999 an environmental group working with state officials managed to keep a radioactive waste site from being constructed in Sierra Blanca, about a hundred miles southeast of El Paso, though the fight to stop the Carlsbad site failed. The underground dump in the salt flats of southeastern New Mexico is only a few years old and is being watched and regulated by a number of state and federal agencies. The volatile issues these facilities raise come and go in the media, though the inadequate highways being used to truck NAFTA waste are starting to get some attention as more stories about dangerous breakdowns by Mexican trucks keep appearing. One estimate claims that by the year 2010, traffic on 1-25 will have increased by 88 percent.

20   HC. I drive the streets of my hometown in the hundred-degree heat of June searching for more signs. They start to appear as I move across town. The white diamonds are everywhere because I am looking for them, their green letters on white rather unnoticeable, if you think about it. While I drive around town counting HC signs, the radio reports that in northern New Mexico, the Los

Alamos fire is out of control. It has destroyed dozens of houses and rolled over parts of the nuclear laboratory compound. Government officials claim there is no danger of the fire reaching concrete-covered storage sites. I drive the streets of El Paso and find what I have been looking for in the furnace of the afternoon.

I am back on Paisano, one of the streets closest to the Rio Grande channel, and a quick route to Caldwell-Briseno, a few miles away. There are two HC signs close to each other near the last exit before downtown El Paso. Both are spray painted in graffiti, the only defaced ones I have found all day. The first diamond glows in orange letters that turn the HC into AO, perhaps an attempt to abbreviate "asshole." The second is more creative. Someone has used black paint to change the green H into two black crosses—✝✝—and the O into a black peace sign from the sixties—☮. I had no idea today's taggers knew that old symbol. At the red traffic light, my car waits in the middle of a three-lane side road leading to the freeway. The lanes on either side of me are filled by several diesel rigs, their long, sleek bodies humming quietly as their drivers wait for the light to change, black smoke from their exhaust pipes swirling toward the blue sky of a busy, working day.

Guiding Questions

1. How does Gonzalez convey the secrecy that surrounds the solid waste disposal facility? What details does he focus on to give a sense of how this place within a place has managed to stay out of most people's minds?
2. What do you think prevents most people from being aware of—or even seeing—the network of "Hazardous Cargo" signs on the roads in and around El Paso?
3. Why does Gonzalez describe his efforts to spot the HC signs as "looking for white diamonds"? Is there a historical irony in his use of this phrase?

Paths for Further Exploration

1. Hazardous waste has to go *somewhere*, and it has to go through other places to get there. Do some research on the issue and present your ideas of "best practices" regarding the transportation and long-term storage or disposal of such wastes, paying particular attention to how you think decisions should be made about which places will be most affected. Be sure to articulate the *values* behind your ideas.
2. Find a "secret" network or system in a place you think you know well, something significant that is happening there (or through there) that most people do not know about. (Maybe find out if hazardous cargoes of any kind are moving through your town.)

3. Once Gonazales begins paying attention to HC signs, he begins to see them everywhere. Pick something to observe on campus, in your neighborhood, or along your daily commute, and keep track of how many times you notice it. Do you notice any patterns? Do these patterns reveal a secret network or system in the area, something going on there (or through there) that most people do not know about?
4. Trace the waste produced by your college or by your hometown. How much waste is generated? What kind is it, where does it go, and how does it get there?

A Nation Divided
ROSE ARRIETA

Rose Arrieta has worked in print and broadcast journalism as a news writer at San Francisco's KCBS and as a reporter for El Tecolote, *a bilingual, biweekly newspaper. In 2002, Arrieta won a grant from the Independent Press Association's George Washington Williams Fellowship for Journalists of Color to report on border issues. In this essay, which first appeared in* Orion *(www.oriononline.org), Arrieta describes the situation of the Tohono O'odham and other peoples who find themselves on the wrong sides of the border laws of nations and cultures around them. One of the ways we define a place is by understanding it to be separate from another distinct place. But what happens to a people whose sense of themselves is deeply connected to place when outsiders redraw the lines of those definitions? And in an increasingly small and threatened world, how do we strike the right balance between being able to be secure within borders but free enough to cross them?*

---◆---

A na Antone skillfully maneuvers the four-wheel-drive vehicle, peering over the dash, pausing every so often to negotiate the deep potholes, large rocks, and tree branches scattered on this bumpy dirt road just north of the U.S.-Mexico border. The surrounding desert is dotted with ocotillo shrubs, palo verde trees, and saguaro cacti. Full, heavy mesquite trees hang low. Greasewood bushes, about four feet high and a deep leafy green, hug the earth. Somewhere out there, families of *javelinas* (wild pigs) snort around for seeds and berries; cows poke along the landscape; and white-winged doves, woodpeckers, and hawks swoop through the Sonoran Desert skies.

Antone is headed home. Although she lives in Sells, Arizona, her birthplace and ancestral home is south of the border in the Tohono O'odham community of Ce:dagi Wahia—known in Spanish as Pozo Verde. The village is just twenty miles from the San Miguel Gate, an unofficial border crossing on a route used by the Tohono O'odham for centuries.

"That's the road my people traveled when they went back and forth to visit our relatives, the Pima at Salt River, and Gila River," says Antone softly. "But by the time I started remembering things, that wasn't happening anymore. By then, the boundary was there." Today, the Tohono O'odham Nation straddles the border, with members living on both sides.

Antone, fifty-four, with short dark hair and a pleasant smile, works as a mental health counselor for the Tohono O'odham Health Services Department in Sells. Sitting next to her is forty-five-year-old Lavern Jose, a Health Services health care worker. Jose's job is to bring elders from south of the border to their medical appointments in Sells. A woman of force and vigor, she grinds her own corn masa for the tamales that she cooks over the wood stove at her home in Tecolote, Arizona. She used to help her dad rope cattle and can get a broken vehicle up and running in short order. It is perhaps this strength that steels her against intimidation by U.S. border agents.

As tribal members, Jose's patients can receive medical care 5 provided by the Tohono O'odham Nation. But that care, like all other tribal services, is located at the nation's headquarters in Sells, on the increasingly inaccessible U.S. side of the border.

"They have lights in the front, spotlights—that's how they pull us over," Antone says, referring to the vans of border agents. "Lot of time they will just follow us for a long distance and never turn on the spotlights. Some will even drive alongside your vehicle. In November it happened almost every week. I was stopped once; other times I was followed all the way to my house in Sells."

With a reporter in the car and no patients as passengers, there is a good chance we won't get stopped on our way back into the U.S. But Jose and her patients aren't always so lucky. "I tell them things will be okay," Jose says, recalling the fear in the eyes of patients who are well into their eighties or nineties. "We've had different agencies point guns at us. Whatever they learned in training—they shouldn't be using it on the elderlies. The agents have no respect."

***

Antone and Jose are maneuvering in a militarized zone. Since 1994, when Congress passed the immigration-control measure Operation Gatekeeper, a record number of border agents have been descending on the Tohono O'odham Nation. Border officials acknowledge that the tribe's seventy-five-mile section of the border is now patrolled by seventeen hundred agents, the largest number ever—not including a battalion of customs agents.

Operation Gatekeeper, designed to crack down on illegal immigration in the San Diego area, diverted migrants to the less crowded Sonoran Desert and Tohono O'odham land. Within a year or two, hundreds of tribe members "started calling the vice chairman's office because they were being stopped and asked for documents," says tribal general counsel Margo Cowan. "Some of them were roughed up—dragged out of their cars, spoken to with profanity, told they had to get documents or they would be arrested and deported. Some were arrested. Some were deported."

10   Among other activities, tribal officials report an increase in vehicle surveillance, gunpoint questioning, and the use of helicopters, which roar overhead to spot migrants. Like migrants, Tohono O'odham tribe members are subject to arrest and detention in any one of a handful of jails along the border. Some detainees are held up to twelve hours before they are released in the border city of Nogales, Arizona. Others are transferred to detention facilities in Florence or Eloy for stays of up to six weeks, according to border patrol spokesman Frank Amarillas.

Cowan says the nation has filed at least one hundred written complaints with U.S. border authorities in the past nine years, on allegations ranging from wrongful detentions to property damage. While Mario Villareal, spokesman for the U.S. Bureau of Customs and Border Protection, says he is not familiar with the complaints, Clyde Benzenhoefer, a border patrol official who worked in the Tohono O'odham region until 2000, acknowledges having received written complaints, although "nowhere close to a hundred."

In 1997, agents arrested a seven-year-old Tohono O'odham boy traveling to a heart specialist at the Sells clinic, says Cowan. The boy and his grandparents were jailed and deported for lack of documentation, their vehicle seized. In February 2003, a woman was turned away for prenatal care for similar reasons; she later miscarried, Jose adds. Many of Jose's patients are elderly, and require regular visits to the health clinic. "A lot of our people have diabetes," she says. "My heart is there for them."

The Tohono O'odham tribe, with a Connecticut-sized reservation on the U.S. side, has twenty-eight thousand members,

fourteen hundred of whom live south of the international border
that has bisected their homeland for one hundred fifty years.
Since the 1930s, that divide has been marked by barbed-wire cattle fences; so far, tribe members have been spared the imposing
metal walls that seal the border in areas like San Diego. But the
country's recent immigration-control policies have drastically
changed every facet of Tohono O'odham life.

Because of the border and its enforcement, ancestors' graves
are unvisited; relatives go years without seeing family; and fies-
tas, wakes, and ceremonial offerings go unattended. Elders, ham-
pered from crossing for a number of reasons, fail to share
traditional stories, and to pass on knowledge about the past,
about plants and animals, and about caring for their desert
home—knowledge that is vital to the tribe. "We were brought into
this world for a purpose," says Joseph Joaquin, Tohono O'odham
cultural resources specialist, "to be the caretakers of this land."

Even the gathering of native plants, a mainstay of traditional   15
culture, is no longer without hassle. Tohono O'odham women just
north of the border still go out early in the morning to collect
saguaro to make jams and ceremonial wines. "But now the border
patrol often pulls up and starts asking for identification," says Jose.

"From time immemorial this has been our land," says tribal
vice chair Henry Ramon. "It doesn't make sense that we should be
questioned about who we are—we know who we are."

The Tohono O'odham is the only border tribe whose Mexican
members are officially recognized by the U.S. government. But
members of the Yaqui, Cocopah, Quechan, Kumeyaay, and Kick-
apoo nations have also traversed the two-thousand-mile border
that runs from California to Texas in order to maintain ties with
tribe members in Mexico.

Before 1994, members of all these nations could cross the
border both ways with little trouble. Operation Gatekeeper, which
followed on the heels of Texas's Hold the Line initiative at the El
Paso crossing, ended the informal recognition of tribal peoples'
right to travel within their traditional homelands. The 1999 federal Operation Safeguard, targeting the Nogales border south of
Tucson, intensified the clampdown. September 11 further height-
ened the tensions, sending the number of border agents to an all-
time high, from 7,300 in 1998 to 10,200. "Everyone," as one Yaqui
cultural leader puts it, "becomes a suspected terrorist now."

Last January, the Department of Homeland Security folded
an array of functions from several border-related agencies into
two bureaus: the Bureau of Customs and Border Protection

handles inspections, while the Bureau of Immigration and Customs Enforcement handles enforcement. Warren McBroom, associate general counsel of the enforcement bureau, says that some fifteen hundred undocumented non-O'odham migrants could be occupying the U.S. side of the nation's land on any given day. The O'odham generally accept that estimate. Their own police force cooperates with the border patrol and has been shot at by drug runners, according to Cowan. But this ramped-up border security, meant to curtail illegal immigration, drug trafficking, and terrorism, is causing trouble for the Tohono O'odham.

20   Ana Antone got a sense of the new Homeland Security Department's policies late one night in November of 2002, as she was returning home from a ceremony in Pozo Verde honoring the ancestors. Antone's group had just pulled through the San Miguel Gate. "A border patrol van drove right in front of us," she says. "My friend had to slam on her brakes." Agents in four separate vehicles approached their vehicle on foot and pointed guns at them. "This is our home," she says in a quiet, firm tone. "Who gave them the right to treat us the way they do?"

In 1999, following complaints about harassment at the border, the U.S. government agreed to issue visas to facilitate passage to and from the fourteen O'odham communities in Sonora, Mexico. The program has had limited success. Visas were issued during a ten-week period from November, 2000 to January, 2001. Many tribe members didn't apply during that period, and since then have reported difficulties obtaining the document, according to Cowan. To apply, members from south of the border were required to display Mexican passports, but about four hundred O'odham had never obtained passports. Some refused to apply for them because "to do so was to deny their own nation," Cowan explains. On the U.S. side, many didn't apply for the visas because they feared deportation; several hundred tribe members born south of the border now live in Arizona, where they are as vulnerable to arrest as undocumented immigrants.

The Tohono O'odham Nation also estimates that seven thousand members, a quarter of its population, were born on U.S. soil but cannot prove it. The reason: they have no birth certificate. "We were born in our own homes by a special medicine woman who does births," says Ramon. "Now we are paying the penalty." Some, like Antone, have served in the U.S. military, which is open to non-citizens, but now find they cannot even apply for a passport.

Tribe members also complain about the indignity and inconvenience the visas represent. The required documents are only accepted at official U.S. ports of entry, but the nearest ones are outside the nation's land, reached by miles of poorly maintained roads, says Silvia Parra, executive director of the nation's Health and Human Services Department. Most people are accustomed to using a number of traditional crossings, many of them cattle guards like the San Miguel Gate, which are no longer legal. And once they make the trek to an official port of entry and show proper documentation, tribe members must still obtain and carry a special immigration permit, usually good for only one day.

Warren McBroom contends that the agencies have a good relationship with the tribe. "If you cross by a port of entry using your documents," he says, "you won't have any problems."

Yet even documented members from Mexico have reported   25 trouble. According to Joaquin, border patrol agents don't always honor the U.S. visas, saying that "it's not a passport." That charge is denied by U.S. officials. Neither the U.S. border patrol nor the tribe has counted how many tribe members have been turned away from crossing the nation's border points, or determined the reasons.

To tribe members, the situation is increasingly unacceptable. "These gatekeepers are telling them they can't come on their own land," says Cowan. "That is very offensive. They are not Mexican. They are Tohono O'odham."

For their part, border guards have little patience for nuanced explanations about tribal identity, missing documents, or historical passageways, says Cowan. Many agents have no experience with the desert, indigenous culture, or the border area, she says. "The agents are typically sent in for six-week tours of duty from all over the United States," Cowan explains. "You [often] have rookies, and people itching for a fight." Not surprisingly, O'odham elders respond with dismay. "These people are very private. They believe that they were created from the sand of this sacred desert," says Cowan. "For them, harsh words and harsh actions and people who don't belong disrupt the harmony."

Before the border was established, Tohono O'odham villagers in places like Quitovaca, Bacoachi, Caborca, Pitiquito, or Pozo Verde freely moved south and north to visit their relatives, to barter, to share stories. According to tribal cultural affairs manager and archaeologist Peter Steere, some modern border-crossing roads follow prehistoric trade routes along the river valleys. They connected the Tohono O'odham, who lived in the western desert, with the Akimel O'odham (Pima), who lived along the Santa Cruz and nearby rivers. The tribes spoke a mutually understandable dialect. The Tohono might trade baskets, beans, foodstuffs, or labor for

"pottery, basketry, meat, deer hides, or mesquite or ironwood carvings," Steere says.

The network of ancient trade routes covered a large swath of
territory. "One of the great traditions was going to bring salt from
the Sea of Cortez," says Raquel Rubio-Goldsmith, adjunct professor of Mexican-American studies at the University of Arizona. "It
was a rite of passage [for] young men. And it indicates the range
of land they moved in."

30   That range of land was bisected following the 1853 Gadsden
Purchase, which imposed a string of six-foot-tall metal pillars
across Tohono O'odham territory, and opened the way for the
U.S. to build a southern transcontinental railroad. The Gadsden
Purchase added thirty thousand square miles south of the Gila
River to the vast stretch of the Southwest that Mexico had ceded
six years earlier, through the Guadalupe Hidalgo Treaty that
ended the Mexican War.

"No one showed the Tohono O'odham the respect to invite
them to the table," says Cowan. "It was bought and sold out from
under them."

By the 1930s, according to Steere, the U.S. had built cattle
fences and border inspection stations to prevent the entry of hoof-
and-mouth disease from Mexican cattle. Following World War II,
the U.S. began establishing border checkpoints. And around that
time, the pilgrimage to the Sea of Cortez was halted when U.S.
border agents refused to let the salt into the country, says Joaquin.

But for the most part, people still traversed the border freely,
even when Lavern Jose was a young girl going to visit relatives in
Mexico. "My grandparents never said 'We're in Sonora,'" she recalls, "just that they were going back to the ranch."

Today, because of the threat of detention, deportation, harassment, or just inconvenience, Tohono O'odham travel less
freely. Many are blocked or discouraged from making the trek to
honor what is perhaps the O'odham's most revered mountain—
seventy-seven-hundred-foot Baboquivari Peak. It rises high above
the lands overlooking the Tohono O'odham Nation on the U.S.
side. Each March, Felix Antone, Ana's brother, leads a pilgrimage
there to make offerings before the start of the Unity Run from
Pozo Verde to Salt River, a ritual he initiated five years ago to
connect O'odham youth with their elders.

35   Antone, sixty-seven, is considered a healer. Wearing a white
cowboy hat, dark blue plaid shirt, Levis, and boots, his skin the
color of polished mahogany, Antone speaks thoughtfully about
Baboquivari Peak. "There is a cave there where the creator we call

I'itol lives. That's where we take the young children and where we talk to them about our old way of life," he says. "We go out there and camp all night, and sing and tell stories. Every morning, we go to the cave, and make offerings to the creator." Such offerings preserve a ritual the tribe has practiced "forever."

Now a shadow hangs over ceremonies that require cross-border travel. Antone says that when he was a young boy, "that border line didn't mean anything to me. Or maybe for those of us who live on both sides of the border it really didn't exist. But now, as the years go by, things are getting harder."

For Antone and the Tohono O'odham Nation, the solution may rest with a bill reintroduced by Arizona Congressman Raul Grijalva in February. It would amend the Immigration and Nationality Act of 1952 to grant U.S. citizenship to all enrolled tribal members who carry a tribal card. That card—not a U.S. or Mexican passport—would then authorize all crossings, reinforcing the tribe's identity as a nation. Since 9/11, the bill, H.R. 731, has been held up in the House Immigrations and Claims subcommittee. But the tribe has 112 co-sponsors from forty states including California, Arizona, New Mexico, and Texas. Border patrol spokesman Russell Ahr points out that the U.S. grants residency status, and permanent rights of passage, to all officially recognized North American Indians born in Canada. "If there is already a norm for Canada," he asks, "why is there no discussion of applying that to Mexico and that country's Indians?"

The indigenous nations along the U.S.-Mexico border are asking that same question. Leaving the quest for a citizenship bill to the O'odham, other border tribes are pursuing their own methods for maintaining cross-border links.

Yaqui ceremonial leader Jose Matus helps coordinate cultural exchanges as co-founder of the Tucson-based Alianza Indigena Sin Fronteras (Indigenous Alliance Without Borders), which defends the right-of-way of indigenous peoples on their lands. About ten thousand Yaquis live in southern Arizona, but about forty thousand live in Mexico, where they practice a traditional subsistence lifestyle. They have no running water, electricity, or paved roads, and little experience with U.S. bureaucracy. An agreement hammered out by the Alianza, the Pasqua Yaqui tribal government, and the Yoemem Tekia Foundation waives strict visa requirements for Yaqui cultural events.

In December 2002, Matus followed the protocol of the agreement, informing border agents that he would be crossing with a   40 contingent of his tribe's dancers and singers from Rio Yaqui, Sonora—about four hundred miles south of the border. Matus and his group got through. Still, "three or four of them were heavily questioned about what they were doing and why," says Matus. "We realize that passports could be confiscated at any given moment on the whim of a border agent, especially from a person who can't answer the questions or understand them. They get very intimidated."

Cultural relations were severely strained in 1994, when a group of Yaqui deer dancers was coming across the Nogales port of entry. They were on their way to perform a traditional ceremony involving a sacred deer head, which can only be touched by the dancer using it. A border agent broke open the deer head to make sure there were no drugs inside. "We believe it is an omen when something happens like that," says Matus. "The dancer did not participate in the ceremony, and it is something that they prepare for all year."

In 1998, the tribe met with border officials for a series of cultural sensitivity workshops that improved relations, says Matus. "But we are braced for the ramifications of the border patrol now being part of Homeland Security as they build forces at the border and clamp down even more."

That clampdown has already affected the federally recognized Kumeyaay tribe, whose lands stretch from San Diego and Imperial counties in California to sixty miles south of the Mexican border. Four years ago, the Kumeyaay Border Task Force established a "pass/repass" plan with the U.S. Immigration and Naturalization Service (INS). It was supposed to allow the Baja Kumeyaay to apply for visas that would facilitate cross-border cultural exchanges. A year after the 9/11 attacks, the INS, without consulting the tribe, terminated the agreement, citing security reasons. So far only about three hundred Baja Kumeyaay visas have been processed, with about a thousand more to go.

Despite such obstacles, all the border nations are determined to maintain free travel within their own territories. "To us, everything is a whole; it is one piece," says Dale Phillips, the vice chairman of the Cocopah Nation, located just outside of Yuma, Arizona, about twelve miles from the border. "That line has nothing to do with us; it has to do with two foreign countries who came in and divided [the nation] in half. If it wasn't for that line, maybe we would have a lot of the elders be free to come here to tell the [traditional] stories."

45   As Ana Antone, Lavern Jose, and I approach the San Miguel Gate, vendors in t-shirts, Levis, and long-sleeved flannel shirts are

selling pop, juices, and snacks from blue and white and red ice chests. Border patrol agents wearing reflective sunglasses and military garb stare out of parked vans. Nearby, migrants wait to make their way north when darkness falls. We cross the wooden cattle guard slowly, bumping and rocking toward the dusty dirt road that will take us south.

It is late afternoon when we arrive at Pozo Verde. Set amid a cluster of small wooden buildings, Ana Antone's home is simple, clean, and comfortable. It has dirt floors and no running water. An altar in one corner holds white candles, marigolds, a buffalo skull, gourds, sage, rosaries, a cross, and an exquisite statue of the Virgen de Guadalupe. The statue has been in her family for years.

"I was born and raised here," says Antone, gazing out at the desert land. "My parents, grandparents, and other relatives are buried here. I still consider it home."

That sense of home, disrupted by a political boundary, lies at the heart of the identity of the Tohono O'odham, and all the border tribes who are intent on maintaining their traditions. "We are a broken vase," says Louie Guassac, tribal coordinator for the Kumeyaay. "There are pieces of our lifestyle and ways on both sides of the border. Preserving our culture is our priority."

Guiding Questions

1. Do you think this essay is journalism, advocacy, or both? Does Arrieta present the situation of the Tohono O'odham tribe and other "border nations" in a balanced way? Why or why not?
2. Why do you think Arrieta begins and ends the essay with her journey toward and across the border with Ana Antone and Lavern Jose, while putting the larger historical and political discussions in between?
3. Why do you think the American border policy toward Canadian-born Indians differs from the one toward Mexican-born Indians and American-born Indians coming from Mexico?

Paths for Further Exploration

1. Write about how a border you know affects your sense of place and identity, whether it is a national border, a state border, a city line, or even something as unofficial as the "lines" between neighborhoods.
2. Research the immigration issue and argue in favor of some "best practices" you think should be used to regulate the comings and goings of border tribes and nations such as the Tohono O'odham.
3. Write an analysis of the different sets of values that seem to determine where various kinds of people depicted in the essay decide to enforce borders.

The Dope on Head Shops

MATHEW DUDLEY

Mathew Dudley, an English major at Boston College, was born and raised in a small town in Fairfield County, Connecticut. A true flaneur at heart, he enjoys observing and studying city space and structures in both Boston and Tokyo, where he studied for a semester at Sophia University. In "The Dope on Head Shops" Dudley takes a unique approach to a favorite topic among student writers: marijuana laws. Rather than examining the value of laws governing the use and possession of marijuana, Dudley focuses on the sale of products related to or made of marijuana. Drawn by the inherent contrast of a hemp and paraphernalia shop (a "head shop") in one of Boston's wealthiest shopping areas, Dudley combines first-hand observation with research into the history of hemp shops and the counterculture to give a sense of how this shop has had to blend in to keep on truckin'.

✦

The head shop is an establishment of the marijuana-using subsection of America's counterculture, and first emerged in the Haight-Ashbury district of San Francisco in 1966. The creation of head shops there and then seems to have been inevitable:

> Hippie psychedelic seekers found that the books they wanted to read were scattered in occult stores, technical bookstores, and newsstands, while incense, records of Indian music and marijuana paraphernalia were still in other places. The head shop was a store that would sell anything an acid head might be interested in. (Perry, 76)

Marijuana has been a "schedule one" drug since the Substance Act of 1970 (Anderson, 237), yet this illegal drug still fuels the legal industry of head shops. Although fewer in number compared to the roaring hippie era of the 1960s, head shops can still be found in most major cities. The shops today, such as The Hempest on Newbury Street in Boston, Massachusetts, have conformed to their immediate social surroundings in order to survive increasing legal and moral conservatism. Based on the allure of the illegal cannabis plant and the products associated with its sale and use, The Hempest stands amid such stores as Chanel and

Armani in the most exclusive shopping district in Boston. No person affiliated with The Hempest whom I spoke to would actually call the store a head shop, preferring instead to call it a "hemp-clothing boutique." The Hempest, like a chameleon, thrives by blending into its surroundings.

In 1966, head shops could be extremely open about their facilitation of marijuana use and still remain open. Today, many of the products they originally sold would not be accepted in places like Newbury Street, including even those that are still legal. For this reason, The Hempest has turned to a more acceptable form of merchandise, hemp products. But don't be fooled completely—the store also contains a large number of glass pipes for sale. Obviously, they can't—and don't—advertise these as marijuana pipes. However, there is still a related, legal drug that can serve to justify the sale of these pipes, and consequently there is a big sign labeled "For Tobacco Use Only" on top of the pipe display case. Of course, the consumer does not have to sign any binding contract with the shop and is free to use the pipes in any way—and with any suitable product—he chooses, whether it be legal or not.

Without the sale of these devices The Hempest would lose a considerable profit stream, and profit, as with any business, has always been the main priority of the head shop industry. "They [head shops] were businesses. They had to deal with the same regulatory agencies and economic situations as other businessmen" (Perry, 108). The Psychedelic Shop, which was located in the heart of the Haight-Ashbury district, is thought to have been the first head shop ever established; for some members of the counterculture, that made the shop itself part of The Establishment. On January 1, 1966, the shop's opening day, a note was slipped under the front door denouncing the owners for selling out the psychedelic revolution (Hoskyns, 94). From the beginning, selling out is exactly what head shops did. The shops of the 1960s sold "basic marijuana paraphernalia such as rolling papers and roach clips" (Perry, 224) and by the 1970s shops had spread to cities like Atlanta selling "among other items, marijuana pipes designed as Star Wars space guns and comic books that introduced people to the logistics of rolling joints and snorting cocaine" (Anderson, 303). With the proliferation of head shops, prominent American subcultures were turned into a massive marketing presence that continues today in both head shops and stores like *Newbury Comics* and *Urban Outfitters* that borrow aspects of head-shop culture.

Although the genuine hippie culture of the sixties has almost completely disappeared or been appropriated, The Hempest has

no problem finding a market for its products. The store is situated in a large, popular commercial section of Boston and contains an abundance of clothes, mirroring the other stores around
it. The Hempest could sell cheap, stereotypical hippie clothes,
such as tie-dyed shirts with huge embroidered pot leaves on
them, but instead it sells articles that are trendy, simple, and
classy. The store sells both men's and women's clothing, including
hemp skirts, dresses, pants, and shoes, along with accessories like
hemp backpacks, purses, and hats. The prices are set extremely
high since the immediate neighborhood allows them to be. (The
typical Newbury Street consumer does not fret over the purchase
of a hundred-dollar shirt.) The glassware pipes are also very expensive, with prices ranging from $40 for a three-inch pipe to
$160 for a two-foot tall "bong."

5   In an interview, Jon Napoli, the owner of The Hempest,
stated that the store has been around for six years but only
started selling pipes three years ago. The store also sells, among
other things, hemp rolling papers; hemp greeting cards (with giant leaves on the cover); body care products such as skin creams,
lip balms, and shampoos; nutritional foods; and small hemp lollipops that are supposedly flavored to taste like pot. Even though
all hemp products must be imported—since the plant is illegal to
grow in the United States—hemp remains the store's foundation.
Because hemp is such a versatile plant, it can be made into a wide
variety of legal products; the more of these The Hempest can provide the more it lives up to its name and pulls in profit.

          These profits come from a diverse range of consumers. A ma-
jority of The Hempest's customers are high-school or college-aged
kids. These kids predominately buy glassware, another reason
why the price of pipes is so high. Young adults are less likely to be
frugal with their money, and will throw away a "C-note" ($100)
for a piece of glass and the opportunity to "have a little fun."
Since Boston has the greatest number of colleges or universities in
a U.S. city, there is an ample supply of students as probable customers. This demographic fact sets The Hempest on a nice, cozy
sales cushion, and there's little question of losing their main customer base in the area. The other customers are people of all
ages. These people frequent the shop for a variety of reasons, including the desire to show political and economic support for
both hemp products and for marijuana. "I don't think they should
arrest [marijuana] drug users. A lot of legal drugs are more
lethal," says Peter Wetherbee, a regular shopper quoted in a
Boston Globe article on the store. "I do believe in voting with my

dollars" (Ryan). Other customers appreciate hemp because the material does not contain pesticides. As the article reports:

> "I went through this massive spiritual revolution when I dropped out of school," says Kelly Reed of Boston, who owns three hemp sweaters, several skirts and dresses, pants, shoes, hats, socks, coin purses, and jewelry. "I became a vegetarian. I had to have veggie shoes. I had to have hemp. Hemp supports us. We should support it. So many pesticides are used in cotton," she says. (Ryan)

The Hempest seeks to appeal to this range of customers, from the legalization activist, to the vegetarian naturalist, to the counter-culturally fashionable teenager.

The store does have a very appealing layout, and is housed in the basement of one of the many historic brick buildings on Newbury Street, directly across from the Armani Café. A small garden gradually slopes down next to the black, wrought iron banister and continues to a larger flowerbed on the ground floor. The lower garden is well kept, containing small flowers like impatiens and pansies and a few sprouting tomato stalks. A set of bells jingles as someone enters, alerting the laid-back workers of incoming customers. The smells of sandalwood and lavender waft from the constantly smoldering incense stands, calming the nerves, pleasing the spirit, and perhaps covering up any unpleasant smells. Cool, mellow jazz plays softly out of the raised speakers, further enhancing the stress-free, casual atmosphere of the store. The clerks are always very polite, and never force a purchase, making The Hempest a very pleasant place to shop. The clothes are displayed neatly on the racks, separated by gender, just like any other clothing store. Cooking books adorned with marijuana leaves rest on shelves above the cash register. Surrounding the cash register area on both sides is a pair of glass cases. The first case, which is quickly seen as one enters the store, holds small jewelry, pins, rings, and earrings—all of which are socially and legally acceptable items. The more controversial merchandise, the glassware pipes and bongs, is somewhat hidden from plain view and can only be discovered by one who walks around the store. These pieces are highly protected in a case customers are warned not to lean on. If these pieces were to be accidentally broken or deftly stolen, the store would lose a considerable amount of money. Everything is set up to maximize the potential of a sale. For example, the lollipops and lip balms are located on the front counter where it is more likely for a customer to make a small impulsive buy before leaving.

Once a head shop has been able to fashion itself into a socially acceptable establishment as The Hempest has done, it is able to blend into its surroundings and reap the benefits. However, Congress has recently ratified laws altering the legality of some hemp products and many wonder if these laws will threaten the existence of places such as The Hempest.

Hemp is a huge market in the U.S. "Estimated retail sales for hemp-food and body-care products in the U.S. exceeded $25 million in 2000, up from less than $1 million in the early '90s" (Willdorf). But the Drug Enforcement Agency is now more aggressively enforcing laws that mean "all hemp . . . that contains *any* amount of THC (the main mind-altering substance in marijuana) has suddenly been classified as a Schedule 1 substance" (Willdorf). Eating a hemp nutrition bar, pretzel, or lollipop, or even drinking a hemp beer, is the same as smoking a joint, shooting heroin, or snorting cocaine. Hemp clothing, body-care products, and hemp-foods that have been certified "THC-free" will be the only products for sale from now on. However, the new laws do not ban the sale of pipes and other paraphernalia. "Somewhere in the midst of all the legalese, the slew of articles in papers across the country, and the HIA's (Hemp Industries Association) urgent appeals for action, consumers are confused, the [hemp] industry is splintering, and small businesses are hurting" (Willdorf).

10 Throughout their history, head shops have continually changed to fit new social standards and laws. Since most head shops thrive on the shadowy edges of American mainstream culture, their proprietors are largely powerless to protest governmental regulation of their livelihoods. But Newbury Street's The Hempest already sells only limited amounts of non-"THC-Free" products. Already skilled in arts of camouflage and metamorphosis, The Hempest may well survive these latest changes.

Works Cited

Anderson, Patrick. *High in America*. New York: Viking, 1981.

Hoskyns, Barney. *Beneath the Diamond Sky: Haight Ashbury, 1965–1970*. New York: Simon and Schuster, 1997.

Perry, Charles. *The Haight-Ashbury*. New York: Rolling Stone, 1984.

Ryan, Suzanne C. "High on Hemp." *Boston Globe* 13 December 1998.

Willdorf, Nina. "The War against Hemp." *Boston Phoenix* 11 April 2002: 1, 20–21.

Guiding Questions

1. How does Dudley combine interviews, first-person description, and research to give a sense of The Hempest? Does one aspect seem more important than the others?
2. What do you think Dudley's thoughts are on the morality and legality of smoking marijuana? What specific parts of the essay could you use to make a case one way or the other? What do you think Dudley's attitude is about the "For Tobacco Use Only" signs?
3. How do the student customers Dudley describes seem to match or differ from your knowledge of students in the 1960s and 1970s who might have been customers in the head shops of *their* time? Does the posh Newbury Street location attract a certain student clientele?

Paths for Further Exploration

1. Following Dudley's example, write about a specific *place* that is affected by the issues being debated on college campuses. For example, write about how a liquor store seems to be affected by drinking age laws, or how a supermarket seems to be affected by calls to label genetically altered foods, or about how a social space is affected by issues of sexual harassment and date rape.
2. Visit a store that interests you and, with the manager's permission, conduct on-site interviews with customers to get a sense of what draws them there. Analyze what seems to be working about the store and what might need improvement.
3. Examine some record stores, bookstores, clothing stores, or other kinds of establishments that have commodified aspects of the counterculture. Do you think it is possible to sell rebellion without selling out?

Someplace in Queens
IAN FRAZIER

What is it like to be in a place that is so well known in general terms that no one feels the need to be specific about it? And what if that place is also one of the most populated and diverse places on the planet? Those are the initial questions asked by humorist and reporter Ian Frazier as he examines one of New York City's most famous boroughs, a place many people simply fly over or pass through without having any detailed sense of it. Originally appearing in Double Take *magazine, "Someplace in Queens" takes a second look—and then some—at the home of everything you* think *you know about one of the Big Apple's key areas. Frazier is a former staff writer at the* New Yorker *and the* Harvard Lampoon *and is the author of* On the Rez, Great Plains, Family, Coyote v. Acme, *and* Dating Your Mom.

———————— ✦ ————————

O ff and on, I get a thing for walking in Queens. One morning, I strayed into that borough from my more usual routes in Brooklyn, and I just kept rambling. I think what drew me on was the phrase "someplace in Queens." This phrase is often used by people who live in Manhattan to describe a Queens location. They don't say the location is simply "in Queens"; they say it is "someplace in Queens," or "in Queens someplace": "All the records are stored in a warehouse someplace in Queens," "His ex-wife lives in Queens someplace." The swooning, overwhelmed quality that the word "someplace" gives to such descriptions is no doubt a result of the fact that people who don't live in Queens see it mostly from the windows of airplanes landing there, at La Guardia or Kennedy airports. They look out at the mile after mile of apparently identical row houses coming up at them and swoon back in their seats at the unknowability of it all. When I find myself among those houses, with their weightlifting trophies or floral displays in the front windows, with their green lawns and nasturtium borders and rose bushes and sidewalks stained blotchy purple by crushed berries from the overhanging mulberry trees, and a scent of curry is in the air, and a plane roars above so close I think I could almost recognize someone at a window, I am happy to be someplace in Queens.

Queens is shaped sort of like a brain. The top, or northern border, is furrowed with bays and coves and salt marshes and creeks extending inland from the East River and Long Island Sound. To the west, its frontal lobe adjoins the roughly diagonal line running southeast that separates it from Brooklyn. At its stem is the large, solid mass of Kennedy Airport, at its east the mostly flat back part that borders Nassau County, Long Island. To the south stretches the long narrow peninsula of Rockaway Beach, which does not really fit my analogy. Queens is the largest New York City borough. It has the longest and widest avenues, the most freeways, and the most crowded subway stations. It has more ethnic groups and nationalities than any other borough; observers say that it has more ethnic diversity than any other place its size on earth. Some of its schools are the city's most overcrowded. In one Queens school district, a dozen or more new pupils enroll every week during the school year, many speaking little English. Classes meet in bathrooms and on stairways; kids use stairs as desks when they practice their spelling and teachers go home hoarse every night from trying to make themselves heard. Immigrants open stores along the avenues beneath the elevated-train tracks in Queens, the way they used to under the old Second Avenue El on the Lower East Side. Queens has more miles of elevated tracks than any borough, and the streets below them teem.

I like to walk under the elevated tracks early on summer mornings, before people are up. At six-thirty, a steeply pitched shaft of sunlight falls between each pair of dark iron pillars. On down the avenue you see the shafts of light, each tinted with haze, receding after each other into the distance. Sun here is secondary, like sun in a forest or on a reef. Some of the shadows of the El on the empty pavement are solid blocks, some are sun-and-shadow plaid. Traffic lights overhang the intersections from the El's beams and run through their cycles at this hour for no one. Security gates on all the stores are down. There's a sharp tapping as an Asian man turns a corner hitting the top of a fresh pack of cigarettes against his palm. He tears off the cellophane, throws it on the ground, opens the pack, hurries up the steps to the station. Each metallic footstep is distinct. When the noise of the train comes, it's a ringing, clattering pounding that fills this space like a rioting throng. The sound pulses as if the train were bouncing on its rails, and, in fact, if you stand in the station the floor does seem to trampoline slightly beneath your feet. Then there's the hiss of the air brakes, a moment of quiet, the two notes of the signal for the closing doors, and the racket begins again. In the world under the El, speech-drowning noise comes and goes every few minutes.

Queens specializes in neighborhoods that nonresidents have heard of but could never place on a map. Long Island City, for example, is not someplace out on Long Island but on Queens's East River side, across from midtown Manhattan. High-society families had estates there when that side of the river was New York's Gold Coast. Today, it is Con Ed property, warehouses, and movie-equipment supply places. You can buy a used police car there for a third off the book price. Astoria is near La Guardia Airport, just across the river from Rikers Island, which is in the Bronx. Sunnyside is southeast of Long Island City, and below Sunnyside is Maspeth, and below Maspeth is Ridgewood, one of the most solidly blue-collar neighborhoods in the city. Springfield Gardens, in southeast Queens, has many wood-frame houses, and that general area has the city's highest fire-fatality rate. Queens used to be the city's vegetable garden and orchard, and in certain places the old farmland still bulges through the borough's concrete lacings. In Fresh Meadows, in the east middle of the borough, a cherry tree survives that was planted in about 1790. It stands on a small triangular relic of field now strewn with Chinese-restaurant flyers and abutted by the back of a beverage store, a row of small businesses, and some row houses. This year, the tree bore a crop of cherries, just as it did when it was out in the country and Lincoln was a boy.

5   In Forest Hills, in the middle of the borough, flight attendants in blue uniforms with red scarves wheel suitcase caddies up its sloping sidewalks. Woodside, on the northwest border, is the city's most integrated neighborhood. St. Albans and Cambria Heights, on the east of the borough, are almost all black and middle class. In Queens, the median black household income is higher than the median white household income—$34,300 a year compared to $34,000 a year. Howard Beach is just west of Kennedy Airport. It became famous some years ago when a white mob killed a black man there. Ozone Park, just north of it, has houses in rows so snug you can hardly see the seams between them, and each house has a lawn the size of a living room rug: some of the lawns are bordered by brick fences with statuettes of elephants raising their trunks, some are thick with flowers, some with ornamental shrubs in rows. People water in the mornings there, and get down on all fours to pick pieces of detritus from the grass. In front of 107-44 110th Street, a house with gray siding and black trim and a picture window, several men came up to the owner, Joseph Scopo, as he got out of a car one night in 1993, and they shot him a number of times. He made it across the street and died near the stone-front house at 107-35. The front yard of Mr. Scopo's former house is all cement; for many years, he was the vice president of Local 6A of the Cement and Concrete Workers of New York City.

On Kissena Boulevard, in Flushing, I passed a two-story brick row house with a dentist's office on the first floor and the sign "D. D. Dong, D.M.D." By now, my feet were hurting and my legs were chafed and I was walking oddly. At the end of a sunlit alley, a pink turban leaned under the hood of a yellow cab. A yellow-and-black butterfly flew over a muffler-repair shop. A red rose grew through coils of razor wire and chain-link fence. At a juicing machine on the street, I bought an almost-cool Styrofoam cup of sugarcane juice, grassy-tasting and sweet. Then I was among the Cold War ruins of Flushing Meadow Park, site of the 1964–65 World's Fair, which is now a mostly empty expanse coexisting with about half a dozen freeways at the borough's heart. No place I know of in America looks more like Moscow than Flushing Meadow Park: the heroic, forgotten statuary, all flexed muscle and straining toes; the littered grounds buffed by feet to smooth dirt; the vast broken fountains, with their twisted pipes and puddles of olive-colored water. I leaned on the railing of a large, unexplained concrete pool thick with floating trash and watched a sparrow on a soda can do a quick logrolling number to stay on top. No matter what, I could not get out of my mind "D. D. Dong, D.M.D."

Legally, you can buy wigs made of human hair in Queens, and two-hundred-volt appliances designed to work in the outlets in foreign countries, and T-shirts that say "If you can't get enough, get a Guyanese," and extra-extra-large bulletproof vests with side panels, and pink bikini underwear with the New York Police Department shield and "New York's Hottest" printed on the front, and pepper-spray personal-defense canisters with ultraviolet identifying dye added, and twenty-ounce bottles of Laser Malt Liquor, whose slogan is "Beam me up," and a cut-rate ten-minute phone call to just about any place on earth, and a viewing of the Indian movie *Sabse Bade Khiladi*, featuring "the hottest song of 1995, 'Muqubla Muqubla.'" Illegally, if you know how, you can buy drugs in bulk, especially cocaine. Drug enforcement officers say that Queens is one of the main entry points for cocaine in the United States, and that much of the trade is engineered by Colombians in the neighborhoods of Elmhurst and Jackson Heights, a district called Little Colombia. On the Elmhurst–Jackson Heights border, at Eighty-third Street just below the Roosevelt Avenue El, is a pocket-sized park of trees and benches called Manuel de Dios Unanue Triangle. It is named for a journalist killed in Queens in 1992 by agents of a Colombian drug cartel.

Manuel de Dios Unanue was born in Cuba, graduated from the University of Puerto Rico, and worked as a newspaper reporter in New York. In 1984, he became the editor of *El Diario–La Prensa*, the city's largest Spanish-language newspaper. At *El Diario*, he was, according to various accounts, obsessive, crusading, blindly self-righteous, possessed of a brilliant news sense, delusional, uncompromising, vain. He chain-smoked. He believed that the United States should open political discussions with Castro, a view that angered anti-Communist terrorist groups, and he printed many articles about the drug trade. He received death threats with a regularity that became a joke between him and his colleagues. Once, someone painted black zebra stripes on his white car and left a note saying he would "get it."

In the eighties and the early nineties, drug money flowed into Queens. Police said that check-cashing places and travel agencies and other businesses in Elmhurst and Jackson Heights were laundering it. Steamer trunks full of submachine guns traced to a realty company on Queens Boulevard led to the discovery of apartments with stashes of drugs and money elsewhere in the city. Colombians died by violence in Queens all the time. One year, 44 of the borough's 357 homicide victims were Colombians. Pedro Méndez, a political figure who had raised money for the 1990 campaign of Colombia's new antidrug president, was shot to death near his home in Jackson Heights the night before that president's inauguration. At a pay telephone by a florist's shop on Northern Boulevard, police arrested a man named Dandeny Muñoz-Mosquera, who they said was an assassin wanted for crimes that included the murders of at least forty police officers in Colombia. Although the authorities believed he had come to Queens to kill somebody, at his arrest they could hold him only for giving a false name to a federal officer. In prison, he requested that Manuel de Dios do an interview with him.

10   Manuel de Dios had left *El Diario* by then, fired in 1989 for reckless reporting, according to some accounts. On his own, he wrote (and published) a book called *The Secrets of the Medellín Cartel*, an antidrug exposé. He began to publish two magazines, *Cambio XXI* and *Crimen*, in which he identified alleged drug traffickers and dealers and the local places where they did business, with big photographs. In Colombia, some people—according to federal agents, José Santacruz Londono and Gilberto Rodríguez-Orejula, of the Cali drug cartel, among others—decided to have him killed. Someone hired someone and his wife, who hired someone, who hired Wilson Alejandro Mejía Vélez, a sixteen-year-old employee of a chair factory in Staten Island. One afternoon the boy put on a hood, walked into the Mesón Asturias restaurant in Queens, and shot Manuel de Dios twice in the back of the head as he finished a beer at the bar.

The *Times*, *The New Yorker*, Salman Rushdie, and others decried the murder. Police said they would solve it soon, and sixteen months after the killing, on a tip from an informant, they caught the killer and some of the conspirators, not including the higher-ups in Colombia. The killer and four others stood trial, were convicted, and went to jail. The triggerboy got life without parole. Manuel de Dios's magazines ceased publication after his death. His book cannot be found in the Spanish-language bookstores in Elmhurst, or *Books in Print*. People in Elmhurst know the name of the book, and they say the name of its author in a familiar rush, but they cannot tell you where you might find a copy. Recently, the number of local drug-related murders has gone down; people say this is because the victory of one big drug cartel over another has brought stability to the trade.

The Mesón Asturias restaurant is just across Eighty-third Street from the Manuel de Dios Unanue Triangle. On a hot July afternoon, I went into the restaurant, sat down at the bar, and had a beer. The bartender, a short, trim man with dark hair, put a bowl of peanuts by me and cut some slices of chorizo sausage. We watched Spanish TV on cable and commented on a piece about the running of the bulls at Pamplona. The bartender said that an American had been killed and that you had to know how to be with the bulls. I paid for the beer and got up to leave. I asked, "Is this where the journalist was killed?"

"Oh, yes," the bartender said.

"Were you here?"

"No, I was outside."   15

"Did you know him?"

"Yes, he was a regular."

"He must have been a brave man," I said.

The bartender stood not facing me and not facing away. He pushed the dollar I had left for a tip across the bar, and I pushed it back at him. For a while the bartender looked off toward the dim, gated window. "Well," he said, "you never know your luck."

The oldest house in Queens—perhaps in the city—is a frame   20
farmhouse built in 1661 by a man who later suffered banishment for letting Quakers meet there. His neighbors in the town of Flushing sent the Dutch governor a Remonstrance stating their belief in religious freedom not only for Quakers and other Christians but also for "Jews, Turks, and Egyptians." Today, the house, called the Bowne House, sits on a small patch of lawn between a four-story apartment building and a city playground. The theoretical Jews, Turks, and Egyptians are now real and living nearby, but nearest are the Koreans. Almost all the signs you see in downtown Flushing are in Korean, and the neighborhood has a Quaker meetinghouse, Korean Buddhist temples, and Korean Catholic and Protestant churches. At the end of the No. 7 Flushing subway line, pamphleteers for a city council person hand you fliers saying that the line is going to hell, while other people hand you fundamentalist Christian tracts saying that you are. Pentecostal churches in storefronts all over Queens have signs in the window advising, for example, "Do nothing you would not like to be doing

when Jesus comes," in Spanish and English. A multimillion-dollar Hindu temple, the largest in the city, recently went up in Flushing. Many Hindus, Buddhists, and Sikhs have recently added small celebrations of Christmas to their traditional worship calendars. Groups of Gnostics meet in Queens, and Romanian Baptists, and followers of the guru Sri Chinmoy, who sometimes express their faith by doing enough somersaults to get into the *Guinness Book of World Records*. When summer comes, big striped tents rise on outlying vacant lots with billboards advertising tent meeting revivals led by Pastor John H. Boyd.

In Douglaston, a far Queens neighborhood that still has the feel of a town, I sat on the lawn of an Episcopal church at the crest of a hill. The ancient gravestones in the churchyard leaned, the daylilies along the driveway bloomed, and the white wooden church panted discreetly in the heat through its high open windows. In Astoria, I visited St. Irene's of Chrysovalantou Greek Orthodox Church, home of the icon of Saint Irene, which witnesses say wept on the eve of the Persian Gulf War. A short woman all in black said, "Why not? Why not?" when I asked if I could see the icon, and she led me slowly up the aisle in fragrant, dusky church light. The icon, a six-by-eight-inch painting, is in a large frame made of gold bracelets, jeweled wristwatches, and rows of wedding rings donated by parishioners. On a wooden rail below it are inhalers left by asthma sufferers whose breath Saint Irene has restored. In Richmond Hill, I stopped in at Familiar Pharmacy, managed and co-owned by Mohammad Tayyab, who knows the Koran by heart. He is thirty-nine, has a neatly trimmed beard, and wears his baseball cap backward. He told me that, growing up in Multan, Pakistan, he memorized verses from the Koran almost every day, morning to night, from when he was six until he was twelve. The Koran is about the length of the New Testament. A person who knows the Koran by heart is called a *haviz*. Mohammad Tayyab recites the whole Koran once a year in a mosque during the fast of Ramadan, and reviews three chapters every night, to keep fresh. The stored-up energy of his knowledge causes him to radiate, like a person who has just been to a spa.

In Montefiore Cemetery, in another far part of Queens, the Grand Rebbe of the Lubavitcher Hasidim, Menachem Schneerson, lies in a coffin made of boards from his lectern. By the time of Rebbe Schneerson's death, in 1994, at the age of ninety-three, some of his followers had come to believe he was the Messiah. Tens of thousands of Lubavitchers from around the world have visited his grave, sometimes annoying the black families who own homes nearby. Neighbors complained that the Lubavitchers were singing loudly, drinking beer, trespassing, and asking to use their bathrooms. The sect has since bought a house near the grave for the convenience of visitors. I went to see the grave myself, on an anniversary of the Rebbe's death. Cars with out-of-state plates lined the boulevard by the cemetery gate; some cars had their doors open to the curb, and shoeless Lubavitchers lay asleep on the seats. Along the paths to the gravesite ran that orange-webbed plastic security fence in which we now routinely wrap important public events. Some of the Lubavitchers were pink-cheeked teens with blond sidecurls. Cops not much older leaned against the cemetery gate and smoked, thumbs hooked in their belts, cigarettes between their first two fingers.

Black-clad Lubavitchers in black hats were coming and going. In the patio behind the nearby Lubavitcher house, many were reciting prayers. Occasionally, an impassioned voice would rise like a firework, bursting higher than the others. A man about my age who pointed the way to the grave suggested that I remove my shoes before approaching it: "Remember, this is a holy place," he said. My running shoes looked as bright as a television ad on top of the pile of functional black brogans of many sizes already there. I ducked through a low door to an anteroom filled with candles. It led into an enclosure of walls maybe twelve feet high, and open to the sky. At the center of the enclosure was a knee-high wall around the grave itself. Men were standing at the graveside wall and praying, chanting, flipping expertly through small prayer books in their palms, rocking from side to side with the words. Heaped on top of the grave like raked-up leaves, spilling onto the smooth pebbles next to it, drifting into the anteroom, were hundreds or thousands of small square pieces of paper on which people had written prayers for special intercessions. There are so many hopes in the world. Just out of the line of sight past the higher wall, 747s descended slowly to Kennedy Airport like local elevators stopping at every floor. Across the street just out of earshot, long-legged girls jumped double-Dutch jump rope, superfast.

Guiding Questions

1. Why does Frazier begin his description of Queens with the idea that he is sometimes drawn into it by the apparently unknowable sameness of the area? Shouldn't that tend to push people away from being interested in a place?
2. How do you react to the analogy of Queens being shaped like a brain, especially when Frazier admits it does not really fit? What other kinds of biological

and organic images and metaphors show up throughout the essay? Do these surprise you in an essay about this particular place?

3. What about the humor in much of the essay? How does it affect you as a reader, and does it match up with the more serious subjects Frazier also discusses? How does he manage the balance—and does the humor make you think Queens might be a bit more fun to visit than you had previously thought?

4. Why does Frazier tell the story of Manuel de Dios Unanue in such detail? Are there other individuals who stand out as you read this essay?

5. Compare Frazier's essay with "Get Off at 161st and Transfer to the Truth" by Gian-Karlo Casimiro, an essay about the Bronx. How does each author try to change our likely assumptions about these famous New York areas?

Paths for Further Exploration

1. Write about the level of diversity (of any kind) in an area you know well (or one you investigate well). How do the various people in the area interact and shape the overall sense of the place?

2. Analyze your assumptions about a place you have often passed through (or flown over) but have not gotten to know in detail. Then do some research about the place and describe how your assumptions may have been on or off target.

3. Attend a religious service of a faith and/or ethnicity that is not your own and not familiar to you. (Be respectful, of course, and do not take notes during the service.) Write about what you discover.

King's Chapel
and Burying Ground
ROBIN DUNN

Robin Dunn is from Southington, Connecticut, and is majoring in accounting and minoring in history at Boston College. She takes great interest in travel, reading, education, writing, and of course the Boston Red Sox. Dunn hopes to one day become a CPA but also hopes to keep a pen and paper in hand and continually pursue her passion for writing. In this essay, written in response to a college writing assignment that sent students out to various interesting or historic places in Boston, Dunn places her sense of intimidation about the city next to her growing sense of awe about one of its most historically significant spaces. A reluctant observer at first, Dunn comes to recognize the unexpected pleasures of exploration and discovers connections between her studies and the place she is visiting.

---------------- ✦ ----------------

I somehow motivate myself to rise out of bed early (a college student's "early") on a Saturday morning, onto a bus (or three), and into the heart of the city of Boston to observe King's Chapel and Burying Ground. My adventure begins, well, rather slowly. Here I sit, wedged into a bus seat among a throng of college students who are heading into the city, most likely directed toward Newbury Street or the Fenway Theaters, and I'm traveling downtown as part of a homework assignment. Soon I become "deeply" involved with an *Us* magazine, still wishing that I was in bed and praying that I will find my way to the chapel without getting lost. In fact, I'm more interested in the spasmodic moth attacking the subway floodlight than the church I am soon to discover.

Sigh of relief. I make it—through the busses and the T, and with a little help from a handy pocket map my parents provided me with before we parted ways. Onto Tremont Street. It is obvious I am located within a tourist trap of Boston. I begin to feel like the nonconformist without a city map in one hand, a camera in the other, and a fanny pack around my waist. However, I proceed onward and begin to finally grasp the effects the city is having on me. I have not even reached the chapel yet when I begin to realize that waking up was well worth the effort. I pause for a moment. I will admit that the smell of subway beneath me doesn't exactly enhance the atmosphere, yet the early fall temperature, the beaming sunshine, and the sounds of the city life are almost too much to take in. Here I stand, on my own, and loving every minute of it.

The corner of Tremont Street and School Street. King's Chapel and Burying Ground sneaks up on my right. Doors open and a soothing breeze flows peacefully throughout the massive and handsome structure as if an angel were whispering secrets of its past behind every open window. An animated woman in her late fifties sits behind the front desk eager to meet and greet all those preparing to take the self-guided tour of the church. I can hardly help but strike up a conversation with this woman. Her smile alone is persuasive enough to get me to introduce myself.

Gail, as she introduces herself, tells me of myriad tales that date back to the 1600s in relation to the church and the burial grounds that lie to its side. She tells me about the Puritans,

explains the essentials of Unitarian ideals and, what interests me
most, conveys the stories of individuals who once stood where
I am currently standing.

5   I learn from Gail and from the brochure she slips into my
hand that King's Chapel was the first Anglican Church in New
England (now a Unitarian church) and was founded in 1686 by
the Royal Governor of the Province of New England. Gail tells me
this church represented all that the Puritans stood for—their
beliefs as well as their hopes to escape the religious oppression
they faced in England. I am officially bound to Gail's words when
she speaks of the thousands of Boston settlers, including many an-
choring members of Boston's seventeenth- and eighteenth-century
society, whose final resting place is within this cemetery. Among
these honorable men and women we can find John Winthrop, the
first Governor of Massachusetts Bay Colony; Hezekiah Usher, the
first book seller in Boston; Reverend John Cotton and Reverend
John Davenport; William Dawes, who rode with Paul Revere to
Lexington on April 18, 1775; Elizabeth Pain, who many believed
was the prototype for the Hester Prynne character in Hawthorne's
The Scarlet Letter; and Mayflower descendents such as Mary
Chilton, the first woman to set foot off ship in 1620.

        I am having some difficulty hinting to Gail to finish her story-
telling so I can proceed onward, yet eventually I manage to break
away from her company and begin my "self-guided tour" of
King's Chapel. Immediately I am taken aback by the hand-carved
facades on every column, the ivory color that flows throughout
the chapel, and the echoes of the other visitors who are whispering and pointing at the artifacts and monuments that line the
church walls. I am especially fascinated by the cozy booth-like
pews lined with plush red velvet seat coverings and accented with
ancient yet well preserved leather-bound books of worship and
song. The pews remain segregated from one another yet fit up to
eight people per booth. I read on to discover the pews were purchased by families of the town who would pay a certain fee to occupy a particular pew each week. Funny how a church would
separate one family from another when its beliefs promoted uni-
fying the community as a whole.

        I proceed onward. As I approach the pulpit, I notice the wine-
glass shape Gail had mentioned. I spot the hand-carved balusters
(noted by my most helpful tour book) that lead to the high pulpit
and to a suspended canopy that hovers over an area meant to am-
plify the preacher's voice. I am amazed at the design, yes, but at
this point I figure my trip is at its end and I have seen all I need to

see to write a decent descriptive analysis. Yet, as I turn around to trace my steps, I am overwhelmed by an ornate organ that rests within the choir loft. This tremendous structure is ornamented by a magnificent crown, detailed miters, and intricately designed carvings. I gaze up at it and wonder what brilliant composers and musicians once tickled its keys and imagine how wonderful the music must sound throughout the chapel's unyielding walls.

As I'm looking up, I notice the chandelier that hangs from the chapel's ceiling. It dominates the entire hall with multiple tiers of light fixtures upon light fixtures, illuminating the whole of the chapel. However, it is the embroidered leaf pattern surrounding the chandelier's fixture that catches my eye. I wonder what incredible care and continual hours of labor must have gone into the task of creating and maintaining such an elaborate piece of art.

I make a move toward the walls of the chapel and clumsily trip on a raised tile from the church floor. This stumble forces me to look to the ground and take notice of the aged, worn stone that is marbleized with a greenish tone. Again, I begin to wonder if those many names Gail ran by me once stood where I find myself positioned at this moment. I feel a chill throughout my body and I notice the hair on my arms defy the forces of gravity.

Again I believe I have absorbed enough for one day's journey and do my best to make a quick exit for the burying ground, yet I cannot seem to avoid bumping into chatty Gail once again. She refuses to let me leave until I take a look at the Bede Book that rests to the left of the Vestry. I do as she asks and take the time to glance at this small book. Anyone is invited to enter requests for prayers to be included at the upcoming weekend service. I believe the book is meant more for prayers of remembrance for those who have passed but I proceed to write a short prayer for my boyfriend who attends Fordham University. Later I'll wonder if they mentioned my prayer in the following day's service: "Here we pray for the deceased souls of Mary Smith and Joe Brown, and for Robin's boyfriend Will who is most likely having a grand old time in N.Y. at F.U." It's the thought that counts, right?

I finally slip out of the chapel (not without a quick smile from my good friend Gail), and gradually I pass through the wrought iron gates that mark the entrance to the burial grounds. I step upon an ash-colored stone path that winds its way around the graveyard, ending where it initiates, reminding me of that famous yellow brick road. I begin my journey along the bricks and take notice of the composure and order of the colorless, skeletal tomb-stones that give the graveyard its eerie spirit. Each tombstone

10

looks as if it could crumble to a million pieces with one gentle gust of wind or accidental human touch. I could easily break a piece off any one of the rock slabs as if I were picking apart peanut brittle. Like dominoes, I imagine one knocking over its neighbor if disturbed by any sudden movement such as the vibration of the subway that I now feel beneath my feet. I cannot help but wonder if such a movement is at all disturbing to those who are now laid to rest among these grounds. Here lies John Winthrop, first governor of Mass Bay, with the T riding by at forty miles per hour every ten minutes to pay its respects.

I take a moment, turn my head from left to right, and capture the site in its entirety. I am standing on one of New England's most hallowed spots yet all I hear and see beyond the gates is commercial activity at its height. I notice construction to the left of the gravesite, alongside a brick building at the graves' edge. Green ivy crawls up the sides of the wall in a fruitless effort to hide its unattractive bricks. I walk a bit farther and come across a metallic blue object. I find it to be nothing more than a crumpled Doritos bag, neatly placed among the greenery and adjacent to a sign that reads, "Please Protect Our Heritage." I force myself to believe the wind carried the bag to this resting place.

I soon approach the tombstone of Elizabeth Pain. Is this not the model for a character I had read about in one of Hawthorne's most renowned novels? I read this book, I remind myself. I have read this author's work and now I stand where his inspiration lies. I find this the most monumental moment of my travel, as if I am walking the Hollywood walk of fame and fitting my hands within those of the most talented entertainers of our time. I fantasize what greater tales and secrets this ground has held for over three hundred years. And that's just it. The church and grounds have hundreds of years on the local Starbucks. Its history will be forever preserved by all those who walk the path of faded engravings, attend the ongoing services, take the self-guided chapel tour, and treat themselves to a quick chat with Gail.

I finally make my way back to the T-station, and realize that *Us* magazine is not nearly as appealing as it had been only hours earlier. While on the T I find that everything I set my eyes on reminds me of the incredible site I have just left. The dreary and sinister stone walls that line the subway tunnels resemble the deteriorating gravestones that line the fading grass of the burial grounds. Not only am I reminded of the tombstones, but also of the olive floor tiles that I fortunately tripped on during the self-guided tour. The dim lighting of the Boylston Street T-stop is comparable to that of the light that rested on the serene altar. And finally, I stop to notice the repulsive smudge mark on the glass window to my right that immediately reminds me of where I am sitting once again.

Newton Campus. I am back within my dorm room, gathering thoughts and attempting to make something of all I have witnessed today. I reflect on my day and smile at how my morning began and how my afternoon ended. I have gained a greater interest for the beautiful and amazing aspects of city life, of its history and the endless tales that stretch back hundreds of years. I wonder what another one hundred years will do to that King's Chapel and its burial grounds, and hope that its mystery and atmosphere will be forever preserved despite all that activity the surrounding stores and restaurants provide and despite the tourists who share this sacred space with those who still use it as a site of worship. I dwell on how different times are for those who once walked those aisles and the paths of the cemetery from those who now tour in years exceeding the millennium. How remarkable a difference, yet the paths walked are one and the same.

Guiding Questions

1. Why does Dunn seem so apprehensive about going into Boston on her own. When do those feelings begin to diminish? Can you relate in some way to how she feels?
2. What techniques does Dunn use to anchor you in the scene? What attention does she pay to sensory detail? What use does she make of simile and metaphor?
3. Why do you think Dunn includes the "friendship" she strikes up with Gail, the woman at the information desk?
4. How important is Dunn's sense of history and literature to her appreciation of King's Chapel and Burying Ground?

Paths for Further Exploration

1. Dunn seems to sense the serendipity of many of her discoveries during the trip. Write about a serendipitous moment you have experienced, especially if it was on a visit to a tourist site or on vacation.
2. One of the things that Dunn notices is the close juxtaposition of this historic site with the bustle of modern urban life. Write about a place you know where a similar juxtaposition occurs.
3. Compare Dunn's essay with Mathew Dudley's "The Dope on Head Shops," which was also written as part of an assignment to explore Boston. What do

these two student essays share in their approach? How do they differ? Write
an analysis of how both Dunn and Dudley responded to the task of exploring a specific spot in a city new to them.

Punk Isn't Dead, But the Fans Just Might Kill It

SHAWN MCGRATH

*Shawn McGrath, an English major at Boston College, has lived in
both Melrose, Massachusetts, and on Cape Cod. In this essay, written in response to an assignment in a First-Year writing seminar,
McGrath implicitly widens the idea of place by explaining how members of various subgroups can occupy the same spaces (both physical and cultural) in different ways based on the divisions they
establish between themselves. Describing the various concerts he has
attended and the fans encountered, McGrath narrates his own journeys among punk's inner districts, and asks us to consider the wider
implications of all these "places" occupying the same mosh pit.*

◆

I've listened to some bad music in my lifetime.

There. I admit it. I'm not proud of it, but I'll own up to having
a copy of Puff Daddy's debut album buried somewhere in the
back of my closet in Melrose, Massachusetts. If pressed on the
matter, I'll confess that I once thought Korn was the greatest band
in the world. I'd even divulge that there is a copy of "The
Macarena Christmas" tucked away in my attic. As I've grown up,
my taste has changed. That's to be expected. It's what life is all
about. In 1998, I bought the album that would herald the beginning of that change: "Americana" by The Offspring.

Granted, that's not something I pride myself on today. On an
aesthetic timeline, that album is fixed at the end of The Offspring's decline into mediocrity. Regardless, from the moment I
first heard the catchy-as-hell guitar licks from "Pretty Fly for a
White Guy," I was hooked. Whether it was their image, their sar-
castic shots at the mainstream, or just their musical style, I'll
never know. I do know that as pop-punk and commercialized as it

is now, five years ago I felt rebellious listening to that album. I am, by genetic nature, a completist (my father is an obsessive antiques dealer) so I quickly bought the band's four other albums. I favored their earlier music, which by most standards fit securely into the punk genre. I began to seek out similar artists and soon my preference for punk had been established.

In the following years, though, my interest in punk waned. I found myself fascinated by the music put out by Rage Against the Machine. The combination of Tom Morello's stellar guitar-playing and Zach de la Rocha's passionate vocals completely won me over. Because of their lyrics and political stances, I became involved in political discussions that would have previously passed directly over my head. The fact that they had something to say really excited me. When they broke up, I was distraught and found myself attracted once again to the punk sound that the Offspring introduced me to. For the first time, I became interested enough in music to warrant going to concerts.

Boston and its surrounding areas don't strike most people as being particularly diverse. Economically, racially, and politically there *is* diversity, but the range of that diversity is fairly small, and social interaction is limited. If nothing else, though, Boston has a wide array of music scenes. On any given night, melodies find their way into the cool night air from blockbuster, sold-out pop festivals, hip-hop acts at the Fleet Center, or folk sets in one of Boston's many pubs. The harsh, driving tunes frequently filtering out of the clubs on Lansdowne Street are of yet another sort. Driving out to the Worcester Palladium yields more of the same intense and thrashing beats echoing out into the street as cigarette smoke meanders into the sky from the lit cigarettes of late-coming punks entering the venues. Lansdowne and the Palladium are the two main homes of the Massachusetts punk rock scene.

The first "punk" band I had the opportunity to see was Saves the Day. Chris Conley, the lead singer and single remaining founding member of the band, was in his mid-teens when he signed his first major record deal. Over the course of the band's career, they have produced albums with sounds ranging from vicious hardcore to catchy pop-punk to eerily melodic emo (loosely short for "emotional"). Amazingly, no single genre has been able to define their style, and their newest album, "In Reverie," has almost completely removed all traces of punk from their music. Nonetheless, my friend Adam and I were both long-term fans of the group, so we made the hour-long trek from Melrose to Worcester sparking with excitement, which even the criminally overpriced food and beverages and the intimidating, large crowd waiting for us at the Palladium couldn't dampen.

In the dim, musty environment of a concert venue, recognizing the different segments of the "punk population" is not always easy, but they're there. At the Saves the Day show, I was engrossed in my surroundings. I looked around, thinking for some reason that a shared interest in this music meant I would have other things in common with the fans around me. But I felt like an outsider, at first, because I didn't know what was expected of me in terms of fashion and appearance. My hair was too short, my pants too long, my shirt too loose. Still, the music made me feel at home. Up in the back of the venue, removed from the rest of the crowd, I could think of no subculture I'd rather be a part of. I left the show feeling refreshed, rejuvenated, and determined to fit in better visually at the next show.

One of the intriguing things about music is that there's a song or a band for every feeling in the spectrum of emotions. At this point in time, I was wrapped up in my own unhappiness stemming from being shot down romantically. Frustrated, I was faced with a choice: listen to angry music that I could relate to or try to find something to make me feel better. Indulging the extreme nature of my feelings, I immersed myself in a world of piss-poor teenage poetry and captivating guitar chops. Wrapped up in my own little bubble of frustration, I didn't see that this music was only making me worse. In my despair, I was united with my fellow concertgoers, and our mutual bond of dejection was temporarily liberating. I immersed myself more and more into the emo scene at the next few shows. My hair grew longer, my pants tighter, my outlook on life bleaker. I *loved it*. I had miserable people who could relate to me and a place where I belonged while being miserable.

I found myself adopting the demeanor of the many emo fans I interacted with, laughing scornfully at people wearing Abercrombie, mocking the fans of the same pop-punk bands I had once adored. Blind to what was happening, I was becoming just another downcast face in the crowd. The more obscure the band and disheartened the lyrics, the better the experience, the better the sense of the outsiders' community that is emo.

10   As time passed in this scene, though, I became tangentially aware of the Dropkick Murphys. I'd seen the shirts adorned with shamrocks before, which had stirred my interest, but few emo kids had good things to say about them. "Oh, there's no *depth* to their music. They're just a bunch of skinheads with no talent." On

a whim, I checked out their Web site, and discovered that their music focused on their Boston heritage and that they mixed Celtic folk traditions and hardcore street punk. Their crowd was rough. They didn't rely on marketing. They sang old Irish folk songs, American labor anthems, and songs about their experiences in the city that I called home. There was no posturing about being brilliant musicians: they just played their arses off and loved their fans. The feeling was mutual: I've never encountered such a rabid and dedicated fan base as that of the Dropkick Murphys.

About this time, I hauled myself out of the emotional pit and stopped feeling sorry for myself. The Dropkicks helped me to take class pride in the 60-hour weeks I worked in Falmouth over the summer, and I discovered a new sense of connectedness to both my city and my Irish heritage through their use of both. Buzzing with the zeal of the convert, I wrote the band a fan letter, a thank you letter, and they took the time to respond. Months later, I met bass player and vocalist Ken Casey after a concert in Connecticut, and was stunned when he showed he remembered the letter by asking after the health of an ill family member whom I'd mentioned in it. That night, replete with the odor of cheap alcohol and the ache of chapped lips caused by standing in long lines in frigid winds, was the greatest experience of my first semester of college, and absolutely cemented my love of the band. There's an amazing sense of camaraderie at Dropkicks shows that is difficult to describe, a similar but even more intense sense of community than what I'd experienced in the emo scene. But as great as that new, more intense sense of belonging was, something about it began to trouble me.

As I see it, there are three main splinter factions of punk fans in the Boston area: emo kids, street/hardcore punks, and pop-punk fans. "Emo" is a misnomer, of course, for as my friend Brad puts it, "all music can be emotional, thus emo really shouldn't be known as a genre." Nonetheless, it's found a label and a niche. Emo kids are the guys and gals decked out in their box-framed glasses, Dickies work pants, skateboarding shoes, and plug earrings that leave heinous gaping holes in their earlobes. They are generally liberal regarding politics and have a tendency to rabidly support animal rights to an almost violent degree. Of the three categories, these kids always come off like the biggest music elitists. They seem to feel that by listening to music about break-ups and emotional despair, they're somehow treading new ground. Whispering amongst themselves in the shadow-enveloped corners of venues, they love to look down on anyone whose sadness is not as apparent and extreme as their own, forgetting that the themes they're "pioneering" have been done before, and often better. While their scene thrived for the past several years, it seems to be going downhill lately, as more and more of the "indie bands" idolized by emo fans, such as Thursday, sign contracts with big-name labels.

The second group, local high school and college students who listen to the watered down, corporate-safe, bubble-gum punk music played on MTV, is a mammoth drawback to attending a concert. It's getting increasingly difficult to watch a live band without getting kicked in the teeth by an ignorant twelve-year-old girl attempting to crowd surf. I've heard eyewitness accounts of a guy who attempted to step on people's heads all the way to the stage at the Brockton Warped Tour. Garbage like that makes concert-going a chore at times. I have nothing against fun, catchy bands like The Ataris and New Found Glory, but some of the bands these fans listen to go beyond just catchy. The music of Simple Plan and Good Charlotte is poorly crafted, cliché-ridden junk. Catchy melodies are fine, but there needs to be substance under all the flash to get me interested in a band.

Relating to the street punk and hardcore fans, the third group, has become easiest for me. These fans generally have no pretenses of being trendy or cutting edge. If there is one thing that frustrates me about the current attitude of most punk fans, it's that they believe that all of the bands they listen to are amazingly inventive artists. Realistically, logically, this simply can't be the case. While The Clash were doing damn remarkable stuff in their prime, the truth is that punk music has stagnated. The argument can be made that there are a few bands whose work is progressing, like Thursday and Brand New, but the vast majority of musicians seem content to just find their style and stick with it. Street punk fans accept this fact. They don't go to hear brilliant and innovative rhythms. For them concerts are about seeing an energetic and passionate performance by a group of average guys who haven't succumbed to the "rock star" image of popular music. The teenagers and adults at these shows are more often than not conservative, working/middle-class music fans who couldn't care less about music genres and trends. Though I find them more palatable than most music fans, they've got their faults, too: I still cringe every time someone tosses out the term "emo-fag" derisively.

15   Despite that cringing, I only managed a few months ago to fully place my finger on what was bothering me most about the punk scene in Boston: the hateful division among these three groups. In myself, I saw aspects of all three kinds of punk fans. As

much as the Dropkicks had surpassed all my other favorite bands, I still enjoyed a select group of emo and pop-punk bands, and felt strange having to disguise my preferences at every other kind of show. As when I moved between Cape Cod's Falmouth and middle-class Melrose each year, I was left wondering exactly who I really was as I moved through these three different cultural places in the punk music scene.

With that realization, I gave up worrying about my punk image and allegiances altogether. I stopped caring about what haircut was in vogue with which group of concertgoers. I didn't care if my pants were too baggy or too tight, or if I wore a Dropkicks soccer jersey to a Saves the Day show. I liked what I liked, and I wasn't about to apologize for it. The clannish behavior of otherwise fascinating people frustrated me to no end. I recognized in the actions of all three groups one of the very things that I tried to escape: snobbery. Sure, this wasn't your average jock vs. geek kind of elitism, but the symptoms were there, and spreading. I gave the disease a name: "hardcore conceit."

A punk fan can self-diagnose hardcore conceit if the following apply:

a. You write people off if they aren't *emo* or *street punk* enough for you.
b. You find yourself torn over which obscure band t-shirt would be *least* trendy to wear to a show. Then you wear it.
c. You find it enjoyable to rag on anyone wearing sports jerseys or otherwise expensive looking clothes.

Take any high school or college in America today. Think of all you know about the fads, all the cliques, all the mainstream markers of the status quos. Then reverse it. In the musty, dank, tobacco-smelling recesses of a punk-venue, the rules change. Anyone wearing Abercrombie or American Eagle is out of place. Wearing a New Found Glory or Blink 182 shirt, something safely "edgy" in mainstream society, is an egregious error. Long, unkempt hair is in, tight clothes are the thing, excessive numbers of tattoos are encouraged and a facial piercing of some kind is damn near required. A genre that was founded on standing out is now guilty of the exact things that it rallied against: conformity at all costs.

That teenagers feel listening to a certain kind of music places them in an elite group is just bizarre. Somewhere along the line, *punk* stopped being an attitude and became a clique. What used to be anti-cool is now uber cool. Some punk fans have become content to simply swallow the surface meaning of the genre. Punk was never meant to be a clique or a social group—it was a contrary mindset. It was the concept of a person saying, "Hey, I don't like the way things are," and having the fortitude to do something different, but there wasn't supposed to be a *specific way* to do things differently. Popular punk. Conforming nonconformity. Outcast cliques and outcast clique outcasts. It's nonsensical. The punk genre has been turned into another corporate gimmick to cash in on the gullibility of today's youth—and on our desperate need to belong, to be part of a community.

20   All of these revelations about the genre bring me to the present reality of my life at Boston College. This is a school where "dangerous music" is an illegally downloaded and burned copy of an acoustic Nirvana album. Dave Matthews, Guster, and John Mayer are all the rage, and I can go for weeks without seeing someone wearing a T-shirt representing a band I listen to. At first, this made me feel exceedingly out of place and unwelcome. People looked at me wearing my Dropkick Murphys tour sweatshirt as if I had two heads, provoking some deeply mixed feelings in me.

On the one hand, who am I to judge other people's taste? What right do I have? If I did that, I'd be no different than the punk elitists who drove me away from the scene, just as guilty of the same attitudes that fuel hardcore conceit. Yet, at the same time, something like pride wells up in me every time I see the words "Shamrock and Roll" on the back of a t-shirt. There's no reason to believe that I'll have anything more in common with someone who wears the same shirt as me than some guy with his collar turned up wearing $80 pre-torn jeans from American Eagle. Yet, at least with the former there's a shared interest, a kind of unspoken bond already in place. Indeed, I'm finding it easier and easier to see why groups of friends so frequently resemble each other.

There are things about punk that I like . . . may be even love. Listening to "The Gauntlet" by the Dropkick Murphys, I'm filled with determination and a sense of rugged individualism. Yet, when I'm feeling down because of relationship woes, Saves the Day is waiting there for me with open arms. Listening to the latest New Found Glory album, I'm reminded of why, sometimes, it's great to have catchy tunes that just allow a person to turn the volume down on the rest of the world. The most important realization my experience with punk music has brought about is that there is a time and place in my life for each of these styles of music, and I'd only be hurting myself if I tried to deny that. The discrimination based on appearance and presumed tastes and beliefs that occurs at punk shows is atrocious and is the kind of behavior that becomes exceedingly dangerous on a larger scale. Close-mindedness could have ruined the first months of my college experience: instead, I was able to come to grips with the fact that I needed to found my friendships on something more substantial than music tees and pant styles.

Music is but one aspect of life, and punk music is but one genre of music. When taken for what it's worth, no harm is done through great enthusiasm for punk. I'm never going to forget when I pulled myself over the barricade up from beer-drenched, mohawk-sporting hooligans and stood onstage in the spotlight with Ken Casey and the rest of the Dropkicks during their rendition of "Skinhead on the MBTA." Yet, for all the excitement and elation of that experience, it was a moment: a high point to be filed away with the memories of many other things I've enjoyed. Musical taste is but one aspect of who I am, not the determining factor of my personality. It doesn't define me the way it once did, but as I get older, grow away from some friends, lose some connections to family, and move on to new stages of existence, punk music still has a significant *part* in my life.

It *isn't* my life, though, and that's an important distinction. If punk is to remain a vital part of the lives of new fans, more of us older ones might want to try to remember the difference.

Guiding Questions

1. McGrath begins with a humorous confessional about his evolving tastes in music. Given the themes of the essay, how does this approach work as an opening rhetorical gambit?

2. How does McGrath convey the sense of his growing knowledge of the punk scene from that first show at the Palladium onward? What cues you to the fact that he's learning to read the people and places he wants to be a part of? What does he do to establish himself as a credible source of information on this topic? Does it matter that he's from the Boston area?

3. Are there hints of jealousy or elitism in McGrath's initial response to the burgeoning pop-punk scene? Does he seem aware of this possibility? What finally leads him to want to avoid the "hardcore conceit" of even the subgroup he is most comfortable with, the street/hardcore contingent?

Paths for Further Exploration

1. Write about a cultural group or subgroup you are a member of, or even one you know well through observation. What sets this group apart from others? Do you inhabit places differently when you are with this group?

2. Describe a concert—of any kind—you have been to. What did it feel like? How did the sound affect you? What were people wearing? How were they acting? Are concerts and other kinds of performance spaces areas that encourage—or even require—people to act or look a certain way?
3. Write about ways you change your appearance for particular places.
4. How many of your interests and hobbies have a particular location? To what extent do your interests affect the way you interact with places, what you do in places? Describe a place in which a hobby or interest takes place. If your hobby has an online component, also write about how that online "place" changes the nature of the hobby.

The Silence of the Lambswool Cardigans

REBECCA SOLNIT

Rebecca Solnit is an art critic, activist, and museum curator, and the author of Motion Studies: Time, Space and Eadweard Muybridge, Wanderlust: A History of Walking, *and* Hollow City: The Siege of San Francisco and the Crisis of American Urbanism. *Solnit's central concerns as a writer and thinker involve the ways our sense of place is affected by—and sometimes obliterated by—the rapid pace of technology and global development. In this brief but challenging essay, which originally appeared in* Orion (www.oriononline.org), *Solnit investigates the alienation between the products we buy and the places and people who made them, often at greater costs than they will recoup. In an age when we are growing ever further away from the direct sources of what we wear, eat, and use, Solnit asks us to consider the complex stories of places and people that everyday consumer objects could tell us if we were willing to listen.*

◆

There was a time not so long ago when everything was recognizable not just as a cup or a coat, but as a cup made by so-and-so out of clay from this bank on the local river or woven by the guy in that house out of wool from the sheep visible on the hills. Then, objects were not purely material, mere commodities, but signs of processes, human and natural, pieces of a story, and the story as well as the stuff sustained life. It's as though every object spoke—some of them must have sung out—in a language everyone could hear, a language that surrounded every object in an aura of its history.

"All commodities are only definite masses of congealed labortime," said Marx, but who now could dissolve them into their constituent histories of labor and materials, into the stories that made them about the processes of the world, made them part of life even if they were iron or brick, made them come to life? For decades tales of city kids who didn't know that milk came from cows have circulated, and the inability of American teenagers to find Iraq on a map made the rounds more recently, but who among us can picture precisely where their sweater or their sugar comes from?

I've been thinking about that because a new shopping mall has opened up at the eastern foot of the Bay Bridge, in what was once, according to the newspaper, the biggest shellmound in northern California (though the town I grew up in claimed the same distinction for the Miwok mound it bulldozed without excavation for a shopping center in the 1950s). From the 1870s to the 1920s, this place was Shellmound Park, an amusement park, racetrack, dance hall, and shooting range, but Prohibition put the pleasure grounds out of business and the mound was bulldozed for industry. The remains of seven hundred Ohlone people that an archaeologist snatched from the construction site in 1924 are still at the University of California at Berkeley. Meanwhile, the industrialized site hosted paint and pesticide factories that eventually made it into a wasteland so toxic that those venturing into it wore moonsuits. It was reclaimed for shopping, and the cleanup disturbed the Ohlone remains that hadn't already been bulldozed.

The street that goes out there is still called Shellmound, but the mall itself hosts all the usual chains that make it impossible to know if you're in Phoenix or Philadelphia: Victoria's Secret, Williams-Sonoma, Express, all three versions of the Gap corporation, including Old Navy and Banana Republic, all laid out on a fake Main Street. Anti-Gap protestors haven't arrived yet, though they are frequent presences in downtown San Francisco, decrying both the Gap's reliance on sweatshop labor and the clearcutting of old-growth redwood forests in Mendocino owned by the Gap's CEO (see Gapsucks.org). But the day the mall opened, activists from the International Indian Treaty Council handed out flyers protesting the desecration of a burial ground. As a substitute for protecting the actual site, the city of Emeryville has offered a website with information about it, as if a place could be relocated to cyberspace. The mall is a distinctly modern site, a space that could be anywhere into which commodities come as if out of nowhere.

5   In *The Making of the English Working Class*, Engels recounts the crimes behind the production of everyday things—ceramics, ironware, glass, but particularly cotton cloth. He wrote in a time when objects were first becoming silent, and he asked the same thing that the activists from Gapsucks.org do, that we learn the new industrial languages of objects, that we hear the story of children worked into deformity and blindness to make lace, the story of the knifegrinders with a life expectancy of thirty-five years, or nowadays the tales of sweatshop, prison, and child labor. These industrial stories have always been environmental stories too, about factory effluents, cotton chemicals, the timber industry, the petrochemical industry.

Somewhere in the Industrial Age, objects shut up because their creation had become so remote and intricate a process that it was no longer readily knowable. Or they were silenced, because the pleasures of abundance that all the cheap goods offered were only available if those goods were mute about the scarcity and loss that lay behind their creation. Modern advertising—notably for Nike—constitutes an aggressive attempt to displace the meaning of the commodity from its makers, as though you enter into relationship with very tall athletes rather than, say, very thin Vietnamese teenagers when you buy their shoes. It is a stretch to think about Mexican prison labor while contemplating Victoria's Secret lavender lace boycut panties. The Western Shoshone rancher and landrights activist Carrie Dann, whose own family graveyard has been flooded by a goldmine pumping out groundwater to get at the gold below, once remarked to me that everyone who buys gold jewelry should have the associated spent ore delivered to their house. At Nevada's mining rates, that would mean a hundred tons of toxic tailings for every one-ounce ring or chain you buy.

The objects are pretty; their stories are hideous, so you get to choose between an alienated and ultimately meaningless world and one that makes terrible demands on you. Most consumers prefer meaningless over complicated, and therefore prefer that objects remain silent. To tell their tales is to be the bearer of bad news—imagine activists as Moses coming down from Sinai but cutting straight to Leviticus, the forty thousand prohibitions: against shrimp (see www.montererybayaquarium.org), against strawberries (methyl bromide, stoop labor), against gold (see www.greatbasinminewatch.org), and on and on. It's what makes radicals and environmentalists seem so grumpy to the would-be consumer.

Maybe the real question is what substances, objects, and products tell stories that don't make people cringe or turn away. For the past half century the process of artmaking has been part of its subject, and this making becomes a symbolic act that attempts to substitute for the silence of all the other objects. But nobody lives by art alone. There's food from the wild, from your own garden, from friends, ancient objects salvaged and flea-marketed, heirlooms and hand-me-downs, local crafts, and a few things still made with the union label, but it's not easy for anyone to stay pure of Payless and Wal-Mart. Good stories too—pricey organic and free-range and shade-grown food that is only available in the hipper stores of the fancier regions—can be a luxury.

Some of the enthusiasm for farmer's markets, which are springing up like mushrooms after rain, is of meeting objects that aren't mute, because you see the people who grew the produce and know the places they come from are not far away. This alternative economy feeds people who want to be nourished by stories and connections, and it's growing. Some farmer's markets are like boutiques with little bunches of peas or raspberries displayed and priced like jewels, but I go to an intensely multiethnic mobscene called Heart of the City Farmer's Market. The food, even some of the organic stuff, is pretty cheap and everyone is present, including the homeless who hang out in that downtown plaza all week anyway, and the locals who use the market to make up for the way supermarkets boycott poor neighborhoods. Seeing the thorn scars on the hands of the rose growers there was as big a step in knowing what constitutes my world as realizing that, in this town where it never snows, our tapwater is all Sierra snowmelt.

What bothers me about the mall is its silence, a silence we mostly live in nowadays; what cheers me are the ways people are learning to read the silent histories of objects and choosing the objects that still sing. 10

Guiding Questions

1. Do you think it is possible to return to the preindustrial world Solnit describes, one where every object told a particular story of where it was made and by whom? How would your daily habits change if you knew who made the products you buy and where these items were produced?

2. Solnit talks about the mall at what used to be Shellmound Park as "a place that could be anywhere into which commodities come as if out of

nowhere." Why do you think people design shopping areas to be uniform? In what ways do we make places the same ways we make products? Are there benefits to designing these areas to be similar, to making consumers feel that they are at once anywhere and nowhere?

Paths for Further Exploration

1. Imagine that you can hear the voice of an object you have purchased, and trace the processes by which it came to you. If you can, find out the specific areas where the raw materials of the object came from, and what kind of person or people likely worked to create it. If you want to go further, try comparing something you bought at a big chain store with a similar object bought at a local craftsperson's business. Go online and investigate the chain store at which you bought the product, looking for the countries in which the company manufactures. What do the tags on the product reveal about its history?

2. Analyze some advertising by Nike, Abercrombie & Fitch, McDonald's, or another major retailer to see whether the ads try to create a sense of connection between you and some specific place and/or people. Now think about what connections the advertising may be designed to hide or to distract you from.

3. Imagine you have been hired by a group of environmentalists and/or antiglobalization activists to assist with a PR campaign to publicize the connections between what we buy and the way places and people are treated. Your job is to help get this message across while avoiding the "grumpy" trap that Solnit describes.

Robotic Iguanas
JULIA CORBETT

Julia Corbett is an associate professor of communications at the University of Utah, specializing in environmental communication and mass media issues. Her essays have appeared in Orion *(www.oriononline.org) (where this piece first appeared) and various scholarly journals in the science and communication fields. Her book,* Green Messages: Communication and the Natural World, *is due to be published in 2005. "Robotic Iguanas" describes a place that has become familiar to many of us in urban and suburban areas, a commercial experience structured around a "natural" theme. Corbett's analysis of this peculiar restaurant may remind us of casinos or theme parks we have been to, of television shows and advertisements we watch, of books and magazines we read, and of vacations we have taken, all of which seek to put us in a close relationship with nature while letting us keep a sense of control.*

————————— ✦ —————————

On a ledge in a cliff face, a small brown iguana raises his head and says to the chartreuse iguana perched above him, "So, you wanna piece of me or what?" Soon the iguanas, joined by some toucans and macaws, burst into song: "Right here in the jungle mon, that's the life for me." Lights strobe, the toucans flap their wings, and the iguanas bob their robotic heads. On cue, waiters and waitresses join in the singing, waving strips of brightly colored fabric. A toucan shouts, "Hasta la vista baby!" as our waiter leans over and asks, "Who had the shrimp?"

Coming here was my idea. I had returned to Salt Lake City from a summer of outdoor experiences while millions of my fellow humans tuned into "Survivor" and hundreds stood in line at the new Mayan theme restaurant in the suburbs. A combination of stifling late August temperatures, unhealthy levels of smoggy ozone, and thick smoke from dozens of wildfires raging in the West left me feeling lethargic and listless. I called a colleague. "Chris," I said, "as people who teach environmental communication, we really ought to check out this restaurant with the Mayan jungle theme." To my surprise, she didn't hesitate.

Our table is on the third level of the restaurant next to a railing with a good view down to the "stage," a cliff face about two stories high adorned with tropical plants made of plastic. A gentle waterfall pours from the cliff into a large aqua pool. The rocks are molded concrete and the pool reeks of chlorine. Under clear resin, our tabletop bears a colorful design of the Mayan alphabet and calendar. Down one level to the right is an area with carpeted steps and a large video screen playing cartoons—a sideshow for children not sufficiently captivated by robotic iguanas. High above in the middle of the cliff wall is an office window, light seeping from behind closed blinds.

The house lights—already dim—grow dimmer. On the lower cliff face, steam starts pouring from holes in the rock and two red eyes begin to glow, eventually illuminating a large fiery face in the stone. A deep voice booms, "I am Copac, behold the power. . ." The message is foreboding and a bit evil, something about heat from the center of the Earth. To break the tension, one of the toucans

announces that it is about to get a lot hotter. The waiters and waitresses agree, chiming in with a chorus of, "Feeling hot, hot, hot!"
Chris and I laugh; we are seated under an air conditioning vent.
By way of contrast, I tell Chris about a Guatemalan jungle I visited,
and how even at 3 a.m. lying perfectly still, sweat would trickle from
my face into my ears and hair. As the "hot, hot, hot!" number winds
down a macaw asks for a cold towel. "I feel Mayan and I'm not even
tryin'," it squawks, instructing diners to order another drink.

The owner of the Mayan—a quirky Mormon guy with his
own little Intermountain empire of car dealerships, an NBA team,
mega movie-theater complexes, and the new theme restaurant—
said in a newspaper interview that he took great pains to give his
patrons an authentic experience. He sent his architects to Mexico
and Central America to ensure that the restaurant could recreate
the experience of visiting an ancient Mayan community. They returned with proposals for plastic banyan trees, thatched huts covering computerized cash registers, and chlorinated waterfalls.
According to a recent lawsuit, what Salt Lake's Mayan restaurant
allegedly recreated was not an ancient Mayan community but a
nearly identical Mayan theme restaurant in Denver.

The lights dim again. A disembodied female voice speaks
soothingly about standing on sacred ground, hidden in the jungle.
Two young men in loin cloths and tall, feathered headdresses
emerge on an upper cliff ledge and bang on tall drums, the slap of
their hands occasionally out of step with the drumbeat of the am-
plified soundtrack. An image of a young woman appears on the
rock wall, a water goddess of sorts with bright red lipstick. Her
name is Tecal. "The spirit of the jaguar calls and I awaken," she
says, urging us to return to a lost paradise, to the Earth, to celebrate, rejuvenate, and rebirth. As her speech crescendoes, lightning
flashes, thunder booms, and the once-placid waterfall gushes noisily into the pool, spraying the plastic ferns but not the diners beyond. People stop their conversations and turn toward the water.

Chris and I compare notes on our food (her taco salad with
iceberg lettuce is unexceptional and my shrimp are tough) and
discuss the "flood." She recalls how, in 1983, abundant mountain
snowfall and an abrupt spring melt sent City Creek roaring
through downtown, past department stores and pawn shops, a
muddy torrent of debris and fish slapping against a channel of
sandbags. Like many such floods, it was caused by a combination
of weather events and failed human attempts to control and di-
vert runoff. Both that flood and the Mayan one, I point out,
demonstrate a similar human desire for (and belief in) control of

natural elements that by their very nature are largely uncontrollable and highly unpredictable.

The warriors return, wearing only Speedos and asymmetrical face paint. The crowd has been anticipating this, the most talked-about part of the show. From the highest point on the cliff, the young men alternate fancy dives into the pool, swim around the side of the cliff, and disappear to reappear at the top for another dive.

Shortly after the restaurant opened for business, the *Salt Lake*   10
Tribune did a profile on a diver, who like all the divers was a member of a high school swim team in the valley. The diver they interviewed had immigrated from Guatemala when he was eight, and it was suggested that perhaps he had some Mayan blood in him. The story also mentioned that some restaurant patrons have asked whether the cliff divers are fake like the cliff they jump from and the lagoon they land in.

When I was a naturalist in Olympic National Park, I was frequently asked whether the deer wandering through the parking lot snarfing up Cheetos and sandwich crusts were real. Tourists also asked me what time it would rain in the coastal rainforest, as if there were a button we pressed, or as though, like Old Faithful, we could predict the rain. (Their interest was not so much in the natural patterns of a rainforest but in not getting wet.) Although the gulf between the real and artificial is vast, we have accomplished the illusion of no gulf at all, like silk flowers you must touch to determine whether chlorophyll lies within. We remake and remodel the natural world and its elements into more predictable and controllable versions, our own little themepark paradise where flowers never fade on the vine and bubbling brooks never run dry.

There is more than humor or sadness in this degree of disconnect; there is danger. We grow increasingly ignorant of the natural original and risk not valuing it—or valuing its replacement more. When Salt Lake's foothills are abloom in early spring with allium, balsamroot, vetch, and sego lilies, most residents are aware only of imported tulips and daffodils. Numerous western cities have gone so far as to codify the imports, making green grass and thirsty flowers not just a cultural imperative but a legal one.

"You wannanother margarita?" asks our waiter.

"Is that what the Mayans drank?" I ask in reply.

The skinny young man with spiky platinum hair stares   15
blankly.

"No thank you," I say.

He leaves a small, black notebook on the table and says he'll take it when we are ready.

While paying up, I wonder if my fellow diners believe they are experiencing nature or just some wholesome family entertainment that comes with a mediocre meal. Can someone who knows only censored and stylized depictions of the natural world—Disneyland, PBS, The Nature Company—ever love and understand the wonderfully complex original? Can we care deeply about the jungle or the foothills or an untamed mountain creek if we've never truly known them? The love and compassion I have for the West is rooted in decades of discovery, from brushing against a thousand sagebrush to know its potent perfume and reading the summer sky for signs of late afternoon storms. Such experiences remind me that my control is minuscule, my volition matters little, and the capacity for wonder and entertainment is infinite.

Chris and I contemplate what the Mayan has to teach us. Jungles are colorful, comfortable, and sublime. Ancient gods and goddesses—some benevolent, some not—control the weather. Nature is predictable and friendly. Animals (with human voices) are merely there to amuse us. And you can buy pieces of the jungle in the gift shop to take home. In the end, the Mayan is not so much about nature as it is about a culture that prefers plastic picket fences over wood ones, robotic animals over wild ones, reality TV over real life.

20   The lights on stage grow bright and the birds start jabbering again. One introduces herself as Margarita Macaw; another, Pierre, wears a beret and says he is from Paris. Iguanas Marvin and Harry ask the macaws if they've seen their sunglasses. A bird informs us that "it's always perfect weather" in the jungle. We leave a tip on the table; the entire show is beginning again.

Guiding Questions

1. What is the effect of Corbett's first paragraph? How does she set the scene, and what absurdities and incongruous sights does she quickly draw our attention to?
2. How does Corbett use her experiences in real jungles to explain her response to the restaurant?
3. What is Corbett's overall tone in this essay? Does she find *anything* to like about the place? Is she at all sympathetic to what drives the design of the location, the desire to control nature—or at least give the illusion of control?
4. Are there any benefits to these themed restaurants? Do they, for instance, invite some curiosity about places that might otherwise remain unknown?

Paths for Further Exploration

1. How much control over the natural world do *you* like to have in the places you go? Do you prefer at least the illusion of control, or do you prefer to experience the natural world more directly? Present an argument for or against a highly controlled encounter with nature.
2. What do you think it would be like to work at one of these nature-themed restaurants or theme parks? What would it be like to be Corbett's waiter or one of the divers? Do you think she would experience such places differently if she worked at one of them? What about commercial places structured around other themes such as history, music, or culture? How does a theme constitute a place?
3. Write about a *noncommercial* place you know that seems to make the natural world artificial. Think about places like campus greens, city parks, and even building atriums.

Becoming Native

JEFFREY A. LOCKWOOD

In "Becoming Native," a chapter from his book Prairie Soul, *entomologist Jeffrey Lockwood considers the sometimes arbitrary and shifting lines we draw between the native and the foreign. Wondering what it means to be from a particular place, and how we get to know place well enough to "become" native, Lockwood combines ecology, anthropology, and philosophy as he takes us around the world to discover surprising connections to his home place. Lockwood, a professor of natural sciences and humanities at the University of Wyoming, is also the author of* Grasshopper Dreaming *and* Locust.

---- ✦ ----

I take some pride in having devoted my scientific life to the study of the Acrididae, the "short-horned" grasshoppers. I should clarify that these insects don't really have horns. The notion here is that this group of insects has rather truncated antennae, compared to the elegant, flowing wisps that adorn their relatives, the "long-horned grasshoppers" or katydids. Being an expert on such picayune nuances of anatomy is cause for some academic arrogance. But, as Oliver Wendell Holmes reminds me, "Science is a first-rate piece of furniture for a man's upper chamber, if he has common sense on the ground floor."

And so there is a more grounded, if still somewhat obscure, basis for my pride. This source of my conceit lies in a rather unique ecological quality of the grasshoppers: they are one of the few insect families comprised entirely of native species in North America (actually in all of the Americas, as far as I can tell). These insects are, in the proud words displayed on my cereal box and yogurt tub, "all natural." The grasshoppers belong here—and we place great value on being native. Nobody wants to be an alien or to be called a stranger, outsider, barbarian, outcast, intruder, squatter, or interloper.

Fear and loathing of foreigners has resurged with the arrival of terrorism on our shores. But then, we've always had a bit of ambivalence, if not antipathy, towards newcomers. No matter what the Statue of Liberty proclaims about giving us your tired, poor, and huddled masses, the wretched refuse of the Irish shores were hardly welcomed in the 1840s and Chinese immigrants were banned in 1882. But we aren't unique in our bigotry; Australia excluded immigrants from Asia and Africa until 1965, and Europeans still struggle with accepting immigrants from these continents. Today we refer to "illegal immigrants" (a term that raises the odd matter of how a person, rather than an act, can be illegal) as aliens, as if they arrived from another planet to invade our safe and secure society. Even universities, the social bastions of free thinking, question whether there are "too many" foreign students.

Animal behaviorists, social psychologists, and anthropologists tell us that xenophobia—the fear of new things, ideas, or people—is deeply ingrained in our genetic predispositions. Like many other creatures, humans naturally avoid, even attack, unfamiliar beings. This appears to be a rather adaptive means of securing viable mates, protecting valuable territory, and avoiding dangerous predators. The logic is simple—the more someone looks like me, the more likely it is that he or she is related to me, and thus the greater the chance that helping him or her will benefit my own genetic line. But it seems that modern xenophobia, although perhaps ancient in its origins, is more complex than the evolutionary story reveals.

5   For my part, I feel an antipathy toward the strange that is motivated by the blistering pace of change in the world, a turnover of knowledge, thoughts, ideas, inventions, and creations that leave me dizzy and disoriented. I've begun to feel like each day risks leaving me a stranger in the new land of technology, terminology,

and taste. My sense of Place, an environment in which I feel grounded, is constantly eroded. As globalization homogenizes the world, I risk becoming vaguely familiar with everywhere but intimate with nowhere. The McDonald's on the Parisian street corner might be momentarily comforting but then it becomes offensive. If Paris isn't foreign and exciting, then home isn't familiar and soothing. In an odd way, I want to feel like a stranger in other lands, but I'm uncomfortable with unfamiliar people in "my" downtown coffee shop. Perhaps these two reactions reflect a realization that authentic nativity is important—and endangered.

In the 1990s I began a fight to keep the U.S. Department of Agriculture from introducing foreign fungal diseases and parasitic wasps to our rangeland in an effort to suppress native species of grasshoppers. The conflict initially appeared to be a matter of science, with battles being fought over the likelihood of these exotics establishing themselves, the potential harm to ecological processes, and the possible impacts on plants, birds, and other creatures that depend on grasshoppers. But as the war of words dragged on, the conflict became increasingly focused on values. The disagreement was distilled to a fundamental difference regarding the sense of place. The government scientists argued, "We are not particularly concerned if [the exotic wasp] tends to displace native [species], nor are we concerned if [the exotic fungus] becomes a dominant grasshopper pathogen in rangeland and crop environments . . . It is our contention that one factor that contributes to species pest status is inefficiency of the native biological control agents . . . ."

For my part, I admitted that the ultimate foundation for my concerns was that the introduction of exotic species on a continental scale assaulted my sense of Place. The insect fauna of Wyoming grasslands had become more than an object of study—it had taken root in my sense of well-being. I found my most potent ally in the writings of Eric Zencey, who maintained that scientists should "acquire a kind of dual citizenship—in the world of ideas and scholarship [as well as] in the very real world of watersheds and growing seasons and migratory pathways and food chains and dependency webs. What is needed is a class of cosmopolitan educators willing to live where they work and work where they live, a class of educators willing to take root, willing to cultivate a sense of place."

Eventually, the USDA backed down from its plans to release parasitic wasps from Australia, and the initial releases of the

Australian fungi were terminated (follow-up studies revealed no establishment). But romantic notions of people and places were noncombatants in the war. My winning argument had to do with the likelihood that one or more grasshopper species playing major roles in controlling populations of poisonous plants would be inadvertently suppressed, thereby releasing the weeds and causing widespread harm to livestock grazing on the rangelands. Without the sword of economics and the shield of enlightened self-interest, the natives would have been doomed.

If physical, mental, and spiritual health are somehow tied to a sense of being or becoming rooted or at home in a place, then it is surely essential to understand what it means to be native. In its simplest formulation, to be native is to be first to occupy a landscape. The native people are those who initially settled in a region. The term "first Americans" is at least half right; these people's ancestors were here "first," although it wasn't "America" when they arrived. Likewise, I've heard a United Nations attorney for native people refer to his clients as the "first nations," a term that may be legally compelling but imposes upon these cultures a political-legal context that seems wholly inappropriate.

10   However, I suspect that he was using the law to protect native people in the same way that I used economics to protect native species—doing the right thing for the wrong reason is a popular approach in the modern world. In any case, it is the notion of "first" that seems to matter. Unfortunately, this notion of being first becomes problematical in both practice and principle. During a fellowship in New Zealand in which I was attempting to help sort out the effects of some introduced insects, I learned a bit about the native people. Contrary to popular notions, the Maori were not the first humans on the islands. Rather, the Moriori were the original inhabitants, having eventually settled on the Chatham Islands.

They were peaceful hunter-gatherers that the later-arriving and more aggressive Maoris had no difficulty eliminating. So, the "native" people of New Zealand appear to have attained their status by virtue of genocide, a most awkward situation indeed. In principle, the "finders keepers" approach to the world seems flawed, even a bit adolescent. Surely there is more to the notion of being native than a series of largely accidental human invasions in which the first people call "dibs!" on the land. By looking backwards to define ourselves, we become locked in the conflicts of history, such as the Middle East and Eastern Europe. Søren

Kierkegaard was right, "Life is understood backwards but must be lived forwards."

In college, I had a friend who used to check the "Native American" box on various forms, although he was a European mongrel like myself. He contended that he was born here, so he was native. Technically, he was right. The term "native" is derived from the Latin "natalis," meaning "to be born." In this sense, most people in the United States are native Americans. Surely one's place of birth is important in defining and understanding oneself. Most people have heard the story about the eulogy for the fellow who died in Maine at the age of 97. The minister noted, "We'll miss Bob as 'one of our own,' even though he wasn't native to these parts, having moved here with his family when he was two years old."

But equating birth and nativity doesn't seem quite right in the modern world. Today, where you are born may have more to do with your parents' travels, the location of medical facilities, and the vagaries of employment opportunities than a meaningful tie to the land or a human community. I was born in Connecticut, but I am no more a Yankee than Edward Abbey was Pennsylvanian or John Muir was Scottish.

As I discovered in teaching a course on biodiversity at the University of Wyoming, being born in a region does not mean that one has much understanding of the land, its flora, or its fauna. For several years, my co-instructor and I conducted a survey of students, mostly freshmen and sophomore non-science majors, in which we asked them to name three plants, vertebrates, and invertebrates that were native to this state. About eighty percent of the students were from Wyoming, and given the propensity of our citizens to hunt, fish, and camp it seemed fair to expect that the students would be able to name some of their living neighbors. But I didn't have high hopes for the invertebrates, despite my passion for grasshoppers. We were reasonable in our interpretations of their answers, accepting common names such as "lodgepole pine" but not vague terms such as "pine tree." Year after year, the results were similar. About a third of the students from Wyoming could name a native plant, about a quarter could name a native vertebrate, and less than one in twenty could name a native invertebrate. Being native-by-birth seems to confer little of what we value when we refer to the virtues of being native.

Naming, whether applied to other creatures or ourselves, is a 15 powerful way of relating to the world. Sloppy language is often evidence of sloppy thinking, or so my college English professor was fond of saying. And so we ought to name our valued concepts with great care. It seems that "Native American" does not really touch on the qualities that I treasure. The essence of the underlying virtue is not that these people were the first to a new land or were born in a particular place. Ralph Waldo Emerson got close to the heart of the matter when he said, "Home is where your losses are," and this is painfully true for the Amerindians. Certainly I honor the depth of spiritual and emotional rootedness of people. But I am an ecologist, and my greatest respect is grounded in the ability of a person or a people to fit into a place, to adapt to the texture of the seasons, soils, and other life forms.

The word I seek is "indigenous." According to my dictionary, indigenousness is the quality of "having originated in and being produced, growing, living, or occurring naturally in a particular region or environment." Perhaps I am overextending this concept, but it seems to me that one can "originate in" a place without having been born there. The origins of selfhood and relationships are not necessarily a function of one's birthplace. I yearn to grow and live naturally in a place, to feel at home.

To have a home is to have special knowledge of a place that arises from first-hand experience. I began to call my house a home when it became part of my life through shared stories. Anyone could draw the floor plan, but we knew in which room our daughter and son slept on their first nights of life with us, which window was shattered by the ladder I was using while stringing Christmas lights, and which spots are favored by the cats on wintry mornings and summery afternoons. The hallway is filled with the photographic chronology of family life; the kitchen counter is stained where I cut strawberries to top the morning cereal; the bedroom carpet is faintly tinted where our son spilled paint while building his first model airplane on his own. Only we know that when the living room carpet is next peeled back and replaced, someone will find that we painted our names on the plywood floorboards in celebration of having completed an interminable remodeling project. If our house burned down, it could be rebuilt "as good as new," but the dings, scratches, and stains—the evidence of a family's memories—would be lost. It takes time to discover which corner of the house is the best sunny spot to read on a winter day (the cats providing key clues in this regard), to learn the complex lift-and-shove motion needed to open the screen door to the deck while keeping it on track, and to know when the hesitant draining in the kids' bathroom should evoke a preventive plungering of the toilet to avoid disaster.

For homes with a bit of land, a family soon learns which parts of the garden produce most reliably (plant spinach and radishes along the north side of the fence where the soil is cooler so they don't bolt in July, and plant carrots and beets near the kid's sandbox where the soil is well-drained and crumbly), where the lawn dries out first (near the blue spruce in the front yard), and where to build a good sled run from the back fence over the retaining wall and into the yard. Ethan knows just how to shoot a basketball from the corner of the driveway, arching the shot over the branch of the Russian olive and into the hoop. Erin knows where Snowball—the dwarf hamster that captured her heart and taught her about loving and dying—is buried. Just as our sphere of moral concerns begins with our family and grows to encompass an ever-widening scope of fellow humans and creatures, so our sense of place starts at our hearth, expands into our yards and neighborhoods, and then reaches into our favorite picnic spots, fishing holes, and hiking trails.

With time, devotion, and attention I have learned what a wind from the east means for the coming weather; I can anticipate the first blooms of spring; and sometimes I know which bird is in a tree without seeing the songster. There are, I would respectfully suggest, European (and Asian and African) Americans who are truly indigenous. Moreover, I accord these people the deep respect that is so often reserved for "native" Americans. Are not Edward Abbey and John Muir indigenous to their adopted homelands? These icons of the West are not, however, indigenous to my corner of Wyoming. And so, I find myself celebrating people like Larry Munn, a soil scientist in my department at the University of Wyoming who lives on a small ranch outside of town. He knows the geological story of the Laramie Valley, its fossil beds and glacial relics, its hollows and outcroppings, its grasses and shrubs, its rodents and deer, its thunderstorms and blizzards, its people and politics, and even—at least a bit—its grasshoppers. He knows much more than I do. The first people to this valley are gone, and we must not forget how this happened. But the greater tragedy would be to fail to look forward, to wallow in guilt and shame for the past without cultivating a sense of Place among those who are here now.

The grasshoppers and first Americans colonized the land as the ice sheets receded about ten thousand years ago. Together, they sculpted—and were sculpted by—the landscape. Grasshoppers co-evolved with the grasses, herbs, and shrubs. Some specialized on particular species by overcoming toxins that killed

20

other herbivores. A few discovered ways of surviving the brutal winters, so they could feast on the earliest spring growth before others even hatched. A handful of species adapted to life above timberline, taking two or more years to reach maturity in alpine meadows. Yet others became ever more elongated and green-streaked until they were nearly as thin as the grass stems and invisible to hungry birds. One species evolved into a locust, with the capacity to form migratory swarms that could eclipse the sun in their sweep across the continent. And, almost certainly, some of the early species failed to match their biology to what the land could sustain or offer and so disappeared without a trace.

Surely, the first humans also struggled to find and create their relationship with the North American steppe. Although some of the early people overexploited the large mammals which soon disappeared, others learned to use fire to create vast tracts of grasslands to nourish the bison. Some discovered that Mesoamerican plants could be cultivated and turkeys domesticated. And still others hunted and gathered, matching their movements and needs to the rhythms of the land. And so with time, these groups of humans either became indigenous or they failed, leaving ghostly traces of their mistakes on canyon walls and cave floors.

We have much to learn from these indigenous people and creatures, but their world is no longer ours. We must discover for ourselves ways of living in a land with fences, roads, and power lines. It is easy to mock the neophyte who builds his house on top of a hill with north-facing windows devoid of winter sunlight and east-facing doorways opening into the prevailing winds. In my first year in Laramie, I planted peas on a false-spring weekend in April only to have the snows return and cause the seeds to rot in the slush-soaked soil that didn't warm until early June. But my children know where to build a house and when to plant a garden.

Two hundred years after they arrived, had the first Americans discovered the limits of the herds, had they sorted out all of the edible and poisonous plants, had they mastered the materials of the land to perfect their shelters? Certainly, the costs of mistakes demanded that the first people on this land had to very rapidly become indigenous, while we have the luxury of imposing unsustainable technologies to buy time. But as reservoirs fill with silt, aquifers grow dry, soils erode, prairies are paved, and forests are cleared, we are coming to realize the limits of the land. They had wooly mammoths, we have fossil fuels—both will have disappeared in a geological moment. Ultimately, the culture arising from the second wave of immigrants has the same two choices that confronted the cultures that arose from the first wave. We can become indigenous or extinct. If we are not mindful in our pursuit of the former, our arrogance will not save us from the latter.

Guiding Questions

1. After talking about the possible evolutionary benefits of xenophobia, Lockwood further explains that part of his preference for the native is born out of a fear of the rapid pace of change in the modern world. How does he draw the distinction between these two different causes of his preference for "authentic nativity"? What examples does he use throughout the essay to do so?
2. How does Lockwood sketch out the difference between "living backwards" in a place (becoming hostage to your sense of its history, too concerned with "who came first") and having a fully informed sense of the history of the place?
3. What is the difference that Lockwood draws between nativity and birth? What about the difference between nativity and indigenousness, as he uses the latter term? How does he resolve the paradoxical idea of "becoming indigenous" to a place?
4. Why does Lockwood claim that we are poised between learning how to become indigenous or becoming extinct? Do you think he is right?

Paths for Further Exploration

1. Have you ever felt a similar preference in yourself for "natives" of a particular place, whether they were insects, animals, plants, or people? Have you ever been regarded as a "stranger, outsider, barbarian, outcast, intruder, squatter, or interloper"? Write about which natives you prefer and why, and/or about what it was like to be the outsider.
2. Write about some people you know who respond to a place because they think of themselves as having "dibs" on it. What are their reasons? How does their sense of ownership or first occupancy live itself out in the ways they inhabit the place?
3. Take Lockwood's bioregional quiz: See if you can name three plants, vertebrates, and invertebrates native to your home state, then see if you can do it for wherever you are at school if you have traveled to another state. Write about what it means to you to be able to do this or—more likely—unable to do it. (For other bioregional quizzes, see Chapter 4.)
4. Lockwood writes about how well he and his family have come to know the particular features of their home. Write something about your home that you (and your family) have only come to know by living there for some time.
5. Have you become "indigenous" to someplace? Do you think it would be easier to do this in an urban, rural, or suburban environment? Write an "action plan" for becoming indigenous somewhere.

CHAPTER 3

Where Are We Going?

Where are you going to be in five years? Ten years? Fifty years? Though you may not often ask yourselves this question so directly, it is one many of us keep in the back of our minds, a question that subtly shapes the decisions we make and our outlook on life. We might envision various answers:

- "I want to move back to the family farm in Indiana."
- "I want to be an actor living in a big city like New York."
- "I want be in medical school on the West Coast."
- "I want to be doing business in China."
- "I have no idea."

When we talk about the future, we often speak both literally (on the farm in Indiana) and metaphorically about what we will be doing then (doing business in China). Indeed, the two modes often blur together, partly because the metaphors we use to talk about time are very spatial:

- "She's really going places."
- "I'm going nowhere fast."
- "There goes the neighborhood."
- "I'm just trying to get ahead."
- "The future is out there."
- "Life is passing me by."

If it is true that *who* we are is intimately tied to *where* we are, then it makes sense that *who we become* is connected to *where we are going*.

Thinking about the future in any sense can be just as disorienting as trying to navigate a new place because the future represents change. Many of us feel uprooted for the simple reason that

149

we move so often. In 1999–2000, according to the 2000 U.S. Census Bureau, 46 million Americans moved—16 percent of the population—and one-third of people in their twenties moved. Transportation technologies allow us to get around more cheaply, and communication technologies like cell phones, e-mail, instant messaging, and the Web make geographic distance seem almost irrelevant. Such new technologies change so rapidly that we find ourselves in a constant state of relearning and retooling, always trying to keep up with the newest version of the latest device.

Even if we keep up with technological change and stay in the same physical place, we can still become dislocated in our own neighborhoods. We can wake one morning and realize that the place we thought we knew has changed dramatically—as suburbs sprawl into the country, urban neighborhoods are redeveloped seemingly overnight, a Starbucks opens on every corner, and communities struggle to deal with the various kinds of waste these rapid changes produce. Whether we move or stay put, the world keeps spinning.

So how do we get our bearings in the midst of rapid and on-going change? How do we make sense of where we are going? What we really need is a critical perspective that will allow us to make informed choices. In fact, many of us have nuanced relationships to change in which we seek a healthy balance and tension between where we have been and where we might go. The essays in this chapter assume that writing and reading about changing places give us a better chance to assess the potential gains and losses of change. In this sense, this chapter picks up where the previous two left off: before we can figure out where to go next, we have to figure out where we are and where we have been. As you read, you will begin to notice some recurring themes throughout the essays, themes that tend to bring us back to the basics:

- *Food:* Producing food is one of the most place-based activities in the world, and yet we seem to know less and less about where our food comes from and how it was grown. If we are what we eat, what do we need to know about how the food we consume changes us and the places around us? Where do we want our food to come from in the future?
- *Work:* We will spend much of our lives on the job, often in particular workplace settings. On the one hand, our jobs often affect where we live; on the other hand, where we live often determines what kind of job opportunities we have.

What do we need to know about the kinds of jobs that await us and how they will affect our quality of life?

- *Transportation:* How we get around is closely tied to the energy we consume, the jobs we have, and our sense of community. How does what we drive or how far we commute affect our future homes, neighborhoods, towns, and cities?
- *Technology:* Many products that we buy make it possible to live almost anywhere we want, while still being able to communicate with others and get work done. However, making these products nearly always creates pollution somewhere else, affecting the health of someone else's place. Do the new technologies we use help us figure out where we are going or just disorient us more?

The essays in this chapter each represent a different way of making sense of changes and trying to imagine what is coming. Eric Schlosser in "On the Range" and Erin Komada in "Auburn Renewals" both portray the impact that large cultural and economic forces are having on rural communities. In "The Orbit of Earthly Bodies," Rebecca Solnit highlights how our transportation choices affect quality of life for both individuals and environments. In "A New Geography of Hope," William McDonough and Michael Braungart offer a vision of how places and products could be designed in healthier, more sustainable ways. None of these authors claim to predict the future—clearly an impossible task; instead, they make arguments about what they think is coming and try to imagine alternatives. Because the future by definition does not exist yet, writing about what is coming always involves some measure of speculation. Sometimes mind-bending visionaries help us image the future in completely novel ways (the best science fiction often does this); more often, convincing visions of the future are grounded in close attention to what is going on right now, as well as in the insights of history.

Arguing about the future is important because we would not be where we are right now if someone had not made a persuasive case for it. For every subdivision or electronic gadget or software application, there are thousands of pages of words put to paper: memos, policy statements, legislative bills, science fiction novels, academic essays, Web sites. When thinking about what makes the future happen, it is easy to think most of it is out of our control and inevitable, unless we are the ones designing buildings and subdivisions, creating new computer technologies, or running large corporations. We may feel powerless in the face of rapid and sweeping changes. However, much of the future appears first in the words we use to imagine alternative possibilities and to persuade others to make these visions realities.

When we write about the future, it is important to view our texts as more than just leisure activities or, worse, as academic exercises designed to earn a good grade. Rather, the texts we create are statements that *do* something in the world; you are designing things that are meant to affect people. As you read the essays in this chapter, you will encounter texts designed to affect *you*. Your job is to pay attention to how they are designed, and then create your own texts, pieces of writing that not only help you make sense of the future but also attempt to persuade others to think differently about what is coming.

Ultimately, the work of imagining alternative futures is important because it forces us to think about what kind of future we are passing on to the next generation, to our children and grandchildren. As a Kenyan proverb says, "We didn't inherit the Earth from our parents; we borrowed it from our children." The ethic of sustainability involves trying to meet our current needs without crippling the ability of future generations to meet their needs— needs we cannot accurately predict. This ethic of sustainability requires us to reimagine how we live: how we make and consume things, how we design our buildings and neighborhoods, and how we communicate, travel, work, and play.

While designing a sustainable future may seem like an overwhelming project, it is a project infused with hope, hope based on the belief that human energy and inventiveness might still enable us to find a healthy way to inhabit the world. In the same spirit, the essays in this chapter express the hope that the more we read and write critically about the future, the better the chance we will know where we are when we get there—and that it will be a place worth knowing.

My Fake Job
RODNEY ROTHMAN

At age twenty-four, Rothman became the youngest head writer for The Late Show with David Letterman *and at twenty-six, gained notoriety with an essay in the* New Yorker *that described his experience*

*posing as a worker in a New York Internet start-up company. Writ-
ten at the height of the dot-com craze, "My Fake Job" is a humorous
reflection on the changing nature of work in an economy altered by
the explosive growth of the Internet.*

———————— ✦ ————————

I don't smoke, but I still take a cigarette break every day at four
o'clock. I stand there and let the cigarette burn down. I pretend
to inhale, lightly, so I don't trigger a coughing fit. The office smokers never notice; they're too busy complaining about their newly
worthless stock options, or how the latest reorg left them with a
job title they don't even understand, like "resource manager."
I never speak up, because there is a crucial difference between my
colleagues and me: I was never hired to work at this company.

I don't have stock options here. I don't have a job title here. *I
don't have a job here.* A few weeks ago, I just walked into the office.

It was the first Internet office I'd ever seen. It takes up five floors
of an old warehouse in downtown Manhattan's Silicon Alley. No one
stopped me when I came in. The sense of transience was overpower-
ing. Hundreds of employees worked at identical workstations. They
sat in thousand-dollar ergonomic office chairs, but their nameplates
were made with paper and Magic Marker. The message was clear:
the chairs could be resold; the employees were expendable.

Twenty-five-year-olds in T-shirts and cutoff fatigues pinballed
from computer monitor to coffee machine, staring at their feet.
Scattered desks were unoccupied because of April's NASDAQ im-
plosion. It struck me that somebody could easily just start showing up for work at this office. Sitting at an empty desk, minding
his own business, he would never be noticed.

DAY 1, 10:30 A.M.

I recently left a sixty-hour-a-week job so I could have more free   5
time and do freelance writing. It hasn't been going well. I have no
free time, because I'm always trying to write. I get no writing
done, because I'm always wasting time. What counts as wasting
time? How about dozing off midday while reading *InStyle*? How
about spending six hours deciding how best to spend six hours?

The building's lobby is a gray expanse of faux marble, sucking
up daylight. There's no security guard. A small group of people
wait for the elevator and sip iced coffee. Standing among them, I
feel like a CIA operative, albeit one who scares easily and is wearing Teva sandals.

I spent the early part of the morning concocting a false identity. I decided that I had just been transferred from the company's satellite office in Chicago (I'd read about it on the Web site). Then I selected a fake job title. The more I thought about it, the more I liked the sound of "junior project manager." It seemed vague, perfect for flying under the radar.

The elevator empties into an airy loft, filled with desks. In front of me, a young receptionist is talking on the telephone. I try to look distracted, as if I were junior-managing a project deep inside my mind. I see her staring at me, but her face registers no concern. She turns back to her phone conversation, and I walk in undisturbed.

I have no idea where to go. I follow everyone down a hallway and into a bustling kitchenette. The kitchenette is spacious and revolves around a large common table that nobody sits at. There is a communal refrigerator stocked with a dozen brands of soft drink, but I take a sodium-free seltzer. I have never, ever liked seltzer. Everyone loads up on caffeine and moves on. People clutch mugs that say "Omnitech" or "Digitalgroup.com" instead of those "You Want It When?" Dogbert ones.

10   I drift freely around the office. It's like a campaign headquarters without buttons. The workstations are low to the ground and clustered in fours. Everyone is on the phone. I see a man in his forties with bare feet up on his desk. I see nose studs. Nobody looks at me twice. After a few laps around the office, I decide I've worked hard enough for today. As I walk out, I turn to the receptionist and say, "See you tomorrow."

Day 2, 10:50 A.M.

There is a different receptionist today, and I walk by her too quickly to notice anything interesting. Everything feels different today, in a bad way. Back in the kitchenette, I take another repulsive sodium-free seltzer. It's now part of my office routine. Then I see a sign-up sheet posted on a bulletin board:

FEELING STRESSED? JOIN US FOR LUNCHTIME YOGA!

It's too much to resist. I sign "Mike Kramer." As I finish, I realize someone is behind me, looking over my shoulder. "You don't have to sign up, you know," she says. "Only, like, four of us go."

I turn around. She's pretty, of course, even in harsh fluorescent lighting. The collar of her blouse is charmingly askew.

I briefly imagine us doing downward dog pose on adjacent mats. Her name is Katie. (Actual names have been changed.) "Are you new here?" she asks.

"I've been here a week," I say. "I transferred from the Chicago satellite office."

I realize that employees my age probably don't use bland corporate-speak like "satellite office." "I'm a junior project manager," I add. 15

"Really?" she says. "I'm a project manager. What projects do you work on?"

It occurs to me now that I could have been more prepared. Perhaps I could have *learned what this company does*.

"I'm still finishing up Chicago projects." I begin shifting from foot to foot. Katie asks me where I live, and I tell her, "Downtown, with friends."

"No," she laughs, "where do you live *here*?"

"I, uh, don't have a desk yet," says the brilliant junior project manager, having worked for a week in an office with fifty empty desks. 20

Day 2, 10:53 a.m.

I introduce myself to the receptionist. My thinking is that if I get her on my side, I'll be able to come and go as I please. Her name is Donna. "Nice to meet you, Donna," I say. "I'm Rodney Rothman." I immediately realize my mistake and panic. I've been here for three minutes and I've managed to establish two separate false identities, one of which is technically my real identity.

"Rodney, have you met Lisa yet?" she asks, motioning to a sturdy woman in a cardigan chatting ten feet away from us.

"Yes," I lie.

"Good. So you got an ID card?"

"Yes," I lie. 25

"Good. You'll need that after six." Donna's phone is ringing, and she's not picking it up.

"Do you have an extension yet?"

"They haven't given me one."

"And that's R-o-d-n-e-y?"

"Actually . . . it's Randy." 30

"Randy Rothman?"

"Ronfman. R-o-n-f."

Donna writes my name down on a pad of paper. Donna's phone is ringing. She's not picking it up. *Pick it up. Pick it up.*

Donna extends her hand toward my sweaty palm. "Welcome to the office, Randy."

Day 3:

"Randy" is taking a much-needed personal day from fake work. I'm at an afternoon Yankee game with my friend Jay. Like many of my friends, Jay can't believe I'm really doing this; he regards me with a mixture of awe and concern. Jay was recently let go by an Internet startup. In between pitches and beers, he explains things like production tools and C++. Jay tells me that some of his former colleagues are continuing to go to work, even though they're not getting paid anymore.

35 Last night I checked out Web sites for some of the hundreds of Web consulting companies like mine. I learned about maximizing my knowledge system. I boned up on branding, decision support, and integrated E-solution deployment. Now, as I watch Tino Martinez take batting practice, I relate to his work ethic. We are strivers. We are brothers. We are improving our skill sets.

Day 4, 7 p.m.

I ride up in the elevator with a tiny West Indian security guard in a heavy wool uniform. I'd like to see him try to wrestle me to the ground. I remember too late that the office is locked after six, but it doesn't matter. The guard swipes his own card and *holds the door open for me.*

I've always liked offices during the fringe hours, early morning and in the evening. It's liberating to spend peaceful time in a place that's normally frantic. To me, the sound of a night cleaning crew is like a rolling country stream.

The office is quiet and freshly mopped. I walk around and shop for my desk. It's hard to tell which desks are unoccupied. Some people refrain entirely from decorating their workspace. That way, they can pack up and leave quickly when the axe comes down. Other desks are decorated lavishly, although I can think of harsher words to describe a green plastic M&M playing a trumpet.

I hop from desk to desk. I sit in each chair, maximizing, deploying, wanting it to feel right. I finally select a desk at the end of a large room with thirty workstations. It's well situated, facing the entire room, with nobody in back of me. It has an operational computer, perfect for taking notes. I put my feet up and close my eyes, thinking of rolling country streams.

Day 5, 10 a.m.

There's no seltzer in the kitchenette this morning. I have to take a   40
Fresca, a beverage I loathe. It's a bad omen, considering what I
have to do: sit down at my new workstation in front of an office
full of employees.

I'm purposeful as I steam through the place, steering around
bodies and desks. Nobody looks up. I reach my chair and sit
down. I wait. I let out a loud sigh. I scan the room. Everyone is
typing or on the phone. Two women in their early twenties huddle
at a desk, eating breakfast and talking: "But what if I worked six
hours on one, three on the other . . . I don't know, that's just what
they told me to do."

Whoever *they* are, I don't see them. Nobody acknowledges
me. The office has swallowed me up without a burp.

Day 5, noon

The phone rings. My imagination gets the better of me. I picture a
squadron of security guards mobilizing upstairs. ATF agents
clamber through air ducts, closing off my available exits. I wonder whether Teva sandals would cushion a twelve-story fall. I answer the phone. "This is Randy?"

"Randy. It's Donna."

I consider grabbing a spare rubber band for self-defense.   45
"Just confirming your extension."

"This is it."

"Great. Let me know if you need anything."

"Okay."

I know what I need. I need to take a break. I need to go out-   50
side and pretend to smoke a cigarette.

Day 5, 6 p.m.

Today I followed a strict schedule of affectation. Every three minutes: stare dreamily into the distance. Every five minutes: flam-
boyantly rub eyes or chin, or tap finger thoughtfully on upper lip.
Every ten minutes: make eye contact with someone across the
room and nod in empathy. Every fifteen minutes: fill cheeks with
air, then exhale while making a quiet *puh-puh-puh-puh* noise.

I take a beverage break every half-hour. Consequently, a bathroom break every hour. Establishing my own hourly bathroom
routine within the pre-established routines of my coworkers is
crucial to assimilation.

My small-talk break in the kitchenette was supposed to be every two hours, but sometimes I skipped it because of nerves. A small-talk break is a massive endeavor of strategizing. Every word is premeditated. A perfectly executed small-talk break goes like this:

ME: How crazy is this coffee machine?
WOMAN IN KITCHENETTE: Ha-ha, I know.
ME: It tastes like General Foods International Coffees.
WOMAN: Does it? Ha-ha.
ME: Ha-ha.

I've been at my desk for eight hours, and it already feels like home.

DAY 6, 8:45 A.M.

55   I came in early to beat the rush. The only other person here is a guy my age in a Mr. Bubble T-shirt. He sits under a large dry-erase board with an acronym-laden flowchart labeled "The Closed Loop Process." I'm noticing things I didn't yesterday, like the abandoned fire extinguisher on the floor next to my desk, and the office in the converted warehouse across the street, which looks nearly identical to this one. I find myself faintly bored, waiting for all the people to come in so I can act like I'm ignoring them.

DAY 6, 2 P.M.

When you work in a room with twenty other people, talking on the phone can be tricky. Every word you say can be heard and digested. It doesn't take much mental calculus for your neighbor to decipher the other end of the conversation. You learn to maximize your deployment of pronouns: "I got it . . . She said that? . . . Send me it before you do that with them there." Or you can be like the Mr. Bubble T-shirt guy and try to whisper inaudibly. His whisper was pretty audible this morning: "It's like, 'We're a news aggregator! We're a portal! We're a B2B thingy! Let's buy UPI!' *Total lack of focus!*"

My phone calls fall into three categories. Most of them are straight-up personal. I don't feel bad about this, because I believe that my colleagues would be more suspicious of me if I didn't spend half the day calling friends and family. Other phone calls relate to my real professional life: agents, other writers, etc. Because I work mostly in television, it's easy to make these calls sound Internet-related. I just use the word *network* as much as possible. My favorite phone calls are the ones that relate to my fake job. I set these up in advance by asking a few friends to call me. These calls make no sense at all, on either end, but they make me look busy.

"This is Randy."

"Randy, it's, uh, Kurt, at LogiDigiTekResources dot com, dot, uh, org."

"Hey, Kurt. The links are all crapped out. I think we need to   60
check the URL again."

"Rodney, do I talk technical on this end, too?"

"Ha-ha-ha, Kurt. Good idea. I'll check that through with client services."

"Does it even matter what I say? Blah blah blah, la la la."

"Perfect. Cc. That to me. G'bye."

It all adds to the noise: the voices, the ringing, the hum of the   65
air-conditioning, the clicking of heels on wood.

Day 7, 7 p.m.

The Girl with Long Brown Hair has bar graphs on her computer. Bar graphs! I can see her through the glass partition next to my workstation. When I go to the bathroom, she looks up and says "Hi." Dear *Penthouse:* Every so often, she leans back in frustration, and her tailored white dress shirt tightens against her chest.

I generally avoid interoffice romances, but it's different when you're a guy working at an office without an actual job. As I think about the Girl with Long Brown Hair, though, a discomfort settles in. I increasingly feel that I've taken refuge in a self-constructed crappy high-concept movie. I picture us having a secret tryst. Then my conscience gets the better of me, and I tell her about my scam. She storms out, of course. I follow her down to Tampa, to the regional meeting. I stand on the conference room table with flowers and tap shoes, singing "My Cherie Amour." Then she forgives me, we embrace, an updated version of "My Cherie Amour" by the Goo Goo Dolls kicks in, the credits roll, and we thank the Toronto Chamber of Commerce.

Enough. I pack up my laptop and go home.

Day 8, 10 a.m.

I ride up on the elevator with a fortyish-looking guy. He goes to five, I go to twelve.

"Morning," he says.   70

"Morning," I say.

Getting into the spirit of it, I add, "Hot one out there."

This is going great. He responds, "You work on twelve?"
"Yeah."
75   "What are you guys doing up there?"
"Uh . . . I have no idea."
He nods in understanding. He's been there. We hit floor five,
and he steps off.
"Have a good one," he shouts over his shoulder.

DAY 8, 11:30 A.M.

The Man in the Blue Oxford Shirt is glaring. Every time he walks
across the office, he fires a double-take at me. I have a premoni-
tion that he will be the dark agent of my downfall here. The Man
in the Blue Oxford Shirt is doughy, with thinning, shiny hair. You
get the feeling that his body type went from baby fat to middle-
aged paunch all at once. He looks so ill at ease, I wonder whether
he's a fake employee, too.
80   The Red-Haired Lady worries me even more. She's one of the
older staff members. The more silent and inoffensive I am, the
more I seem to threaten her. She probably thinks I'm an Ivy
League consultant, here to observe her and weed her out. I see
her reflection in the window whenever she creeps behind me.
We've developed a little tango, she and I. She cranes her neck to
look at my computer screen, and I lower my shoulder to block her
view of my notes. Her oversized eyeglasses make me feel like I'm
being cased by Sally Jessy Raphael.

DAY 8, 4 P.M.

While taking a cigarette break today, I meet a colleague named
Lawrence, one of what seems like five hundred guys in my office
who wear black nerd-chic eyeglasses. Lawrence says that his
office responsibilities have recently been expanded beyond what
he was hired for.
"What were you hired for?" I ask.
"Overseeing office support programs."
"What kind of programs?"
85   Lawrence takes a big drag off his cigarette. "Mostly Wellness."

DAY 9, 11:30 A.M.

Today I'm decorating my desk with whimsical junk I bought in a
Sixth Avenue Chinese variety store. I arrange it precisely on the
desk surface. On the right are two filthy pieces of rubber fruit: a
smiling orange and a frowning pineapple. On the left is a pirated
Winnie-the-Pooh figurine, for a touch of approachability. Last, I

add a plastic Virgin Mary clock, to make sure I'm not too approachable. Nothing puts people off like the promise of spontaneous sermonizing. I figure the clock alone has added three days to my stay here. At the end of the day, I put a labeled personal item in the communal fridge. Hint: it was brewed in Latrobe, PA.

DAY 10, 7 P.M.

The Girl with Long Brown Hair is working late, so I am, too. A few minutes ago her boss was down here, standing over her, pacing. I struggled to hear what he was saying, but could make out only a few phrases and an undertone of irritation:

"Are you doing all this in Photoshop? I want to do it in Quark . . . There's no dialogue happening . . . Someone should go down to Staples and get this really sticky double-sided tape . . . We have to put this out."

Before he exited, he must have sensed that he was acting like an Old Economy jerk boss, because he turned and said, "You know, you don't have to do this tonight."

"Good." She laughed. "I have dinner plans." 90

"Groovy. Bye, sweetie!"

She packs up her handbag and walks up the steps. I watch her go, and stay another hour, glad I'm not a guy who says "groovy" or "bye, sweetie."

DAY 11, NOON

When I get back from lunch, there is a meeting of at least thirty staff members in the big conference room. Why am I not part of the company's knowledge-management system?

I work the resentment out through my work: an afternoon spent devising ways to deceive the increasingly menacing Red-Haired Lady. First I open up a Microsoft Excel spreadsheet document on my computer. I've never used a spreadsheet before, but I have no problem filling it in with random numbers. Whenever I see the Red-Haired Lady's reflection in the window, I click from my word-processor file to the spreadsheet file, drumming my fingers distractedly on the mouse. My only concern is that she'll think I'm auditing her expense reports and go on the warpath.

I also draw a meaningless flowchart, labeled "Starwood 95 Project," on a legal pad, and leave it out on my desk to give me management credibility. I invent some acronyms, box them, and connect them with arrows. Then I write "August 2001" in big letters underneath, and underline it three times. This lets her know that I am very much on schedule, whatever it is that I am doing.

DAY 11, 5:30 P.M.

This afternoon, a group of middle-aged men show up in our work area and go from desk to desk talking to employees. Everyone looks terrified. I don't notice that they're approaching my desk until it's too late. "How are ya?" says one with swept-back hair. "Don't mind us, we're just taking a tour." I focus as hard as possible on my spreadsheet. My fingers dance a John Bonham solo on the mouse.

A member of the tour group speaks up: "Can I ask you a question?"

"Go right ahead."

"Is it true that there's massages on this floor?"

100   "That is true." And it is. Scattered throughout the office are fliers advertising "Back Massage by Melissa!" It's all part of chain-smoking Lawrence's Wellness empire. I've been building up the nerve to get one for days.

"Oh," the man says, already snickering. "Which floor has body piercing?"

The whole tour group explodes with laughter. I join in cautiously, then enthusiastically when I see that the tour group has begun riding the wave of hilarity to the next room.

"Take care, now," the man with the swept-back hair says, still laughing.

DAY 12, 10 A.M.

It's my twelfth day here, and the anonymity, once a pleasure, has become maddening. I feel a bubbling, reckless desire to make my existence known. Maybe that's why I've started signing my name to every sign-up sheet I see. Today I signed up for a charity walk. Yesterday I signed one labeled "May the E-Force Be with You."

DAY 12, 2 P.M.

105   This week, Lawrence and Team Wellness posted the first two pages of *Moby-Dick* by the elevator, under the heading "Elevate Your Life with Literature!" I'm not sure if they have a nine-year plan for posting the rest. I am troubled by the implication that our elevator waiting time needed to be more useful. God forbid employees stop maximizing for a few seconds.

Did anyone bother to read the first two pages of *Moby-Dick* before posting it? Ishmael takes to the open sea on a whale-hunting expedition because he is fed up with the drudgery of office life, "of week days pent up in lath and plaster—tied to counters, nailed to benches, clinched to desks." Try thinking about that on the subway home from work.

What was Ishmael so afraid of, anyway? Are scurvy, whale attack, and pirate rape so much better than working in an office? At least our office is air-conditioned. At least our complimentary Thursday morning doughnuts haven't been befouled by bilge rats. Ishmael, poor sucker, was born a hundred years too early. He could have opened "the great flood gates of the wonderworld" right here in this wonderful wave tank of an Internet office.

Day 12, 3:30 p.m.

". . . and so the universal thump is passed round, and all hands should rub each other's shoulder-blades, and be content."— Herman Melville, Chapter 1, *Moby-Dick*.

Melissa's hands are rubbing my shoulder blades. "You have a lot of tension in your neck and shoulders," she says. "You should get more massages." I couldn't agree with her more. I've been avoiding the massage room, perhaps because of a fear that Melissa would somehow sense my ruse through the deceitful flow of my lymphatic fluid. As she navigates her knuckles around my back, I meditate blissfully. Free massages. Free beverages. Companionship, flirtation, E-mail access. No disruptive phone calls, no meetings, no boss, no questions, no decisions to make. A perfect job, perfectly undisturbed by having a job.

"Sorry, Randy, back to work," Melissa says, finishing up with   110
that weird karate-chop thing. "Lots of tired backs out there. Drink water."

Day 12, 4:45 p.m.

I started the conversation, so I have only myself to blame. Laura, a friendly woman in her thirties with a broken wrist, has been working next to me all week long, and I haven't said a word to her.

"What happened to your arm?" I ask.

Laura skips the part where she got injured and just tells me her medical horror story. Andy, her "arm guy," wants to take bone from another part of her body, and she's mistrustful and scared.

"And who are you?" she adds.

"I'm Randy Ronfman."   115

"What do you do here?"

Lately, when I get this question, I lean heavily on the word *stuff*. I find it has a narcotizing effect.

"I'm here from the Chicago satellite office. I'm doing a bunch of stuff. Project managing stuff. Branding stuff."

"Branding stuff. *Really.*" Laura leans her good arm on the desk eagerly. "I'm in marketing and recruiting here. Do you mind if I pick your brain?"

120 A week ago this question might have terrified me, but now it excites me. I'm starting to believe that I actually do this for a living, that I am capable of having my brain picked about branding. Laura's question is a cataract of jargon: "Launching a B2B ... E-commerce ... inventive user experiences ... success factors ... so if you know any branding people in Chicago that could help us out with that, I'd really appreciate it."

"You don't want to work with the people there," I tell her conspiratorially. "They're not so great."

Laura's brow furrows in genuine disappointment. "Well ... maybe you could come up with some people? Do you have a few minutes?"

"Not right now," I answer. "I have a meeting at five."

This is not a lie. I do have a meeting, for a real job. Typically, I've nearly missed it. "I should be back later. When do you leave?"

125 "Six."

I make a mental note to come back at six-thirty. "Think about people you know who are very well connected," Laura calls after me as I run out. "Who could send me off into *their* network of people."

DAY 13, 5 P.M.

It's been twenty-four hours since my conversation with Laura, and I haven't seen her since. This doesn't surprise me. The office has a seizure-inducing strobe effect. People appear and disappear, switch desks, switch jobs. Today Rick, the head of the office, is walking around, asking where Lawrence is. He is informed that Lawrence has recently been "reshuffled" into a new department. Lawrence is now sitting fifteen feet from Rick's office, on the floor below us, a floor that has fewer than twenty people. *The head of the office.* And you wonder how I've been able to stay here for two weeks?

DAY 13, 8 P.M.

If it's possible to be a workaholic at a job you don't actually have, that's what I've become. The thought of going back to my apartment is loathsome, and I don't even have a family I'm trying to avoid. In this office I feel productive, even when I'm doing nothing. In my apartment, even when I'm working, I'm idle, lazy, and always a hairsbreadth away from masturbation. In her book *The Overworked American*, Juliet Schor writes about workers at an Akron tire plant who won a six-hour day. Many of them used their increased leisure time to take on second jobs. I'm beginning to think that a second, or even a third, fake job sounds like a fine idea. How tremendous it would be, traveling from fake job to fake job, taking only Fresca, leaving only flowcharts.

Day 14, 2 p.m.

To make myself feel better, I've started holding my own meetings. All day long today, friends come in, in groups of varying sizes. Sometimes I hold the meeting at my desk, in full view of the office. I like this because it gives the impression that I'm bringing in my own department. It's usually small talk and the occasional "Well, it's great to finally meet you!"

Mostly, though, we meet in the barren, glassed-in conference rooms. We close the door and gossip. For authenticity, I pace around the room and gesticulate madly. It's a Kabuki theater rendition of how I think meetings should look. At one point a woman interrupts our meeting. It turns out that we weren't in an empty conference room. We were in her office. I swear you can't tell the difference.

Day 15, 10 a.m.

Today I walk in and there's a staff-wide meeting in the conference room. Everyone is in there. My immediate concern is that they are meeting about me, preparing some form of ghastly homicidal vengeance, like locking me in the Xerox machine until I asphyxiate on toner powder.

There will always be drywall between me and them. That's the limitation of my perfect job. I can never join the inner circle. I can never become indispensable, because, no matter how hard I try, I don't really exist here.

Day 15, 4 p.m.

There's no such thing as Casual Friday in a company that's casual all week long, but don't tell that to the Man in the Blue Oxford Shirt. He's wearing a short-sleeved blue polo shirt today. Recently I found out that he's a junior project manager, like me. His name is Dennis. It's hard to maintain an adversarial relationship with a guy named Dennis, particularly one who stopped caring about me a week ago. At this point, I'm rental furniture. I haven't seen the Red-Haired Lady for days. Maybe some Ivy League consultant sent her home to New Rochelle with the rest of the forty-year-olds.

DAY **16**, **2:30** P.M.

The office smokers are abuzz today. Word is spreading that the rest of the fifth floor is going to be let go. Apparently the New York office is now officially the worst in the company. We're even lagging behind Denver, because "they're small market, but at least they control it." Each person present seems to have a compelling reason that they're the next in line for dismissal. Everyone is ticked off that most of the senior staff is conveniently on vacation and the mass firings are being handled by middle managers. Some new young guy with a patchy beard looks at me accusingly and says, "They're going after the high-salaried ones first." I don't get that. So I'm "high salaried"? Just because I happen to be the only smoker here who bothers to wear a belt?

DAY **17**, **7:45** P.M.

135   When I arrive this morning. I sense that this will be my last day at fake work. What clinches it is the new phone list. Many names are no longer on it. My name is: Randy Ronfman, with my phone extension directly beside it. I feel an intense wave of emotion, guiltless and giddy. But before too long I start thinking about the Peter Principle and decide I have been promoted past my point of competency. I know how to be a fake employee, but this is too legitimate. The only thing left for me to do is actual work, with actual coworkers who will rely on me. I've done that before. It's not as much fun.

Someday, if I'm ever a death row inmate, or a guy who sneaks into prison and pretends to be a death row inmate, I know what my last meal will be. It will be sodium-free seltzer. I like how it cleans you out. I sip one as I go from desk to desk, telling my coworkers that I'm "going back to the satellite office." Many of them have never met me before, or seen me, for that matter, but they react cordially. They assume it's their mistake, not mine.

"Lucky bastard!" one guy says.

"Your own choice, or are you 'resigning'?" another says, making quotation marks with his fingers.

"Nice working with you," the Girl with Long Brown Hair says.

I pack up my things long after everyone else is gone, savoring   140
the last of the quiet. As I leave, I stop at the dry-erase board
with the "Closed Loop Process" flowchart. I add my initials,
RMR, box them, and draw an arrow to the box. I will live on
in the office as an acronym, forever. Well, for two weeks, at least,
until someone takes down the board. That's as close as you get to
forever in this office.

Guiding Questions

1. What does Rothman have to say about work—the kinds of work we do,
   where we do it, and what counts as "real" work? What economic changes
   does he document?
2. In this piece, Rothman is an outsider who poses as an insider. What ethical
   issues arise when an outsider masquerades as an insider? What unique perspective does it offer?
3. This is a piece of creative nonfiction. However, after the *New Yorker* published this essay, it came to light that Rothman made up the incident of getting a massage and never mentioned that his mother worked at the
   company where the story takes place. The *New Yorker* issued an apology in
   the next issue, saying among other things, "The magazine does not disguise
   details or mix fact and fiction without informing the reader (not even in a
   comic piece like this one), and we sincerely regret the error." His agent defended him by arguing that he had not set out to write a piece of investigative journalism, and Rothman himself admitted to changing details of the
   office in order to disguise the identity of the company. Do you feel differently about the essay now that you know these facts?

Paths for Further Exploration

1. Write an essay that describes how an unexpected job change affected you
   or your family.
2. Write a researched essay that examines a job or field that interests you.
   How did you get interested in it? How is this type of job changing? What
   are the prospects for those attempting to find work in this field? By the end
   of your research, reflect on whether or not you think you will pursue this
   kind of employment.
3. Write an essay in which you describe the culture of a previous or current
   workplace. Describe your colleagues, the physical space, what kind of
   work you did, and your place within that community. Think about keeping
   the kind of day-to-day journal Rothman did as one possible way to write
   this essay.

Scientific Applications

SONNY FABBRI

*Sonny Fabbri, a biology major at Boston College, is from Long Is-
land, New York. The excerpt below is from a longer essay in which
he discusses what steps led him to college and what vocation he is
considering pursuing. As part of the assignment, students observed
a class in a field of their interest, discussed their observations, and
imagined themselves joining this community. Asked to consider as
well the role of writing in a particular community, Fabbri responds
by invoking the language used in the scientific world.*

———————— ✦ ————————

L ist your possible area(s) of academic concentration/major."

Filling out my college applications, I pause at this deceptively
simple question. I recognize the colleges' attempt to categorize
me, but I also recognize the question behind the question: What
do you want to do with your life? My counselor has advised me to
write something in the spaces, so I declare biology as my major.
Life processes have always intrigued me, and biology seems like a
logical choice.

With this decision made, I begin my own life processes
experiment.

Every experiment includes a system, the environment under
study. Similar to the way ecologists search for the proper area for
field research, I search for the right college in which to conduct my
experiment. My search begins at the end of my junior year when
I acquire and assemble my college applications. Although the
process requires considerable energy, my family acts as catalysts,
speeding up the process and lowering the work needed for me to
complete the job. My mother even types the personal information
sections of the applications to increase the rate of the process.

5   After extensive proofreading, each package leaves my home
and enters the processing center known as the college placement
office. The office adjusts each application and transports them
into the college environment. What happens in the next step, I
can only hypothesize.

From ten applications, only three applications will survive
the process. With three schools to choose from, I make another
crucial decision: to enroll at Boston College as a biology major.

Once I am integrated into the Boston College community, I pursue my interest in biology when I register for the required introductory science courses. Although I have conducted my initial experiments in biology, I remain uncertain about the results of my future trials.

Now, at the end of my first semester, I have given more serious thought toward my major. I realize choosing a major involves experimentation across a variety of studies.

Observation: I remain uncertain about my interests and my major.

Question: How do I ease my uncertainty?

Hypothesis: By taking advantage of the variety of courses at college, I will focus my interests into a major and career.

Experiment: I will explore the possibilities in biology and also test different areas of study.

Predicted result: I will find an interesting subject to pursue that may lead to a possible vocation.

Anatomy and Physiology, Genetics, Bacteriology, Molecular Biology, Evolution, Molecular Immunobiology. I have considered categories within the biology department, as my writing instructor requires that for our final writing assignment we investigate classes within a discipline of our choice to observe and research. With uncertainty, I pick a course from the list in the Course Offering Schedule:

BI55401 8734 3 three Physiology MW3 Higgins 265 Balkema

Phy . . . si . . . ology. What? My pre-med advisor recommends I   10
choose Dr. Grant Balkema's physiology class to visit. Remembering his advice, I click on the BI55401 link and open up into a world of . . . confusion. Well, it's not that I'm confused, but what exactly is phiseoligee? According to Dr. Balkema's course description, "This is a study of the fundamental principles and physicochemical mechanisms underlying cellular and organismal function" (BI). OK, but Dr. Balkema defines physiology too specifically, so I consult my dictionary to better understand the basic meaning of the subject. The topic appears interesting—at least to someone like me interested in "organismal function." Besides, I have only four days to finish the first draft, so Biology 554 it is.

Minutes later, I send an e-mail to Dr. Balkema, asking for permission to sit in on his class. That night, I receive a reply: "Sure." My initial excitement at his prompt response fades into a feeling of nervousness as I consider sitting in on a class filled with upperclassmen.

On Wednesday, I walk through Higgins and eventually find room 265. Escaping notice by most of the students, I slip into an empty chair. As I blend into the environment, I notice the hum of the air-conditioning vent above me and the receding peach walls of the room. The instructor enters, and I walk toward him. After I stutter my name and restate the reason for my appearance, I sit down again, and Dr. Balkema begins his lecture, tugging down the screen and powering up the projector.

The words "Regulation of Ions" stand out in black letters against the green background of the projection screen. As I stare at the screen, I catch the occasional familiar word: glucose, potassium, renal vein. But as the material accumulates, I lose focus. I try following the red dot of his laser pointer as it skirts across the projection screen, but instead I study Dr. Balkema's shorthand writing style. He presents the information with small arrows, black-and-white diagrams, and enough sentence fragments to exhaust the grammar check of a word processor. I imagine myself learning in the future how to communicate in this punctuated writing style, one so different from the language I use in the other communities in my life.

Although his projections organize the material, Dr. Balkema's teaching techniques are what make the information accessible. He relates his lecture to everyday life. For example, in his discussion of absorption in the kidney, Dr. Balkema explains the dangers associated with overuse of pain killers. He states that high concentrations of Ibuprofen in the blood can damage components of the kidneys. The students nod—everyone can relate to this example. Dr. Balkema informs his students but also engages them with questions and jokes. The atmosphere of the physiology class transforms me from visitor to student. I leave the class feeling comfortable in this community.

15   The following week I begin the next phase of the experiment, my interview with Dr. Balkema. Several minutes into the conversation, I pitch him the deeper questions: "Wh . . . uh . . . what advice would you give to a student considering biology as a major, but only considering?"

Dr. Balkema thinks and then replies, "Continue in the intro. courses, and see what happens. Take electives, and look to see which courses are exciting."

I sit back down in front of my computer to type the next draft of this experiment. "See which . . . courses . . . are exciting. . . ."

I remember the fascinating information I learned from his lecture. I remember the reasons that led me to choose biology as a major. Writing about the physiology class has allowed me to revisit my interest in biology. However, visiting Dr. Balkema's class is only one part of one experiment. His advice proves I still have more tests to complete.

That next step of the experiment includes locating other sources of information in the biology world. I decide to read the 2003 BC *BioNews* and find an article within it. A title captures my attention: "What is Postdoc? An Expanding Trend in Biomedical Science" (Roche 14). The article profiles a postdoctoral student who has earned a Ph.D. but has chosen to pursue training under the leadership of a scientist (Roche 14). The program he has joined allows scientists increased independence in the lab but also the opportunity to study under a recognized scientist. While studying biology, I have imagined a similar scenario for myself: earning a degree and then researching in a laboratory. Ultimately, I envision myself working at a cancer research center. The article makes me wonder about opportunities available to me to gain experience as a researcher.

In addition to observing a class, I have collected samples for my experiment—an interview and an article. I need one more sample from the biology world before I can complete my report. I search the Biology department Web page. As I click through the department, I notice a reference to Dr. Clare O'Connor's research in protein methylation. I read the abstract: "The goal of this research is to understand [. . .] the reactions catalyzed by a protein carboxyl methyltransferase. [. . .] oocytes are microinjected with isoaspartyl substrates." Although I am confused by the language, I connect with the words "microinjected with isoaspartyl substrates." In my current biology course, I read about genetic engineers who injected foreign DNA into cells. The work of those scientists has thus far appeared remote, but reading about the work of Dr. O'Connor changes my perspective. I realize professors at Boston College perform the processes that seemed so removed in my textbook. I might even perform those experiments someday. Although I am years away from achieving the expertise of Dr. O'Connor, I connect to her study and obtain meaningful results from this Internet research.

Although I have completed the procedures of the writing experiment, focusing my studies into a major requires further testing. Part of the continuous process involves learning from previous procedures. While the writing experiment has strengthened

20

my interest in biology, my conclusions serve only as a background. I have learned to test new areas to discover my interests. These future trials will provide the final results. With new experiments, I will test my hypothesis and reach those results.

Works Cited

Balkema, Grant. *BI 554 Physiology* (Fall: 3), 29 April 2003. Boston College WebCT. 20 Nov. 2003 <http://www.bc.edu/studentservices/acd/courses/BI/bi55400.html,700,300,csdesc)>.
———, Personal Interview. 24 Nov. 2003.
O'Connor, Clare. "Field of Interest: Protein Methylation and the Repair of Age-Damaged Proteins." 27 Aug. 2003. The Trustees of Boston College. 2 Dec. 2003 <http://www.bc.edu/schools/cas/biology/facadmin/oconnor/>.
Reynolds, Glenn H., "Nanotechnology Research Must Be Supported." 31 Oct. 2002. Fox News. 4 Dec. 2003 <http://www.foxnews.com/story/0,2933,67119,00.html>.
Roche, John, P., ed., "What Is a Postdoc? An Expanding Trend in Biomedical Science," BC *BioNews:* 2003. Chestnut Hill, 2003, p. 14.

Guiding Questions

1. The dominant metaphor of Fabbri's essay is that of scientific experiment. How does this metaphor help shape the essay? Do you think it is effective?
2. In this piece Fabbri does primary research on a topic that interests him. What counts as research and evidence in his essay?
3. What form does he decide to use to present his results? Why is it important for Fabbri to narrate the essay the way he does?
4. Fabbri finds himself disoriented in the midst of a new discourse, the unfamiliar language of biology. How does he deal with this new discourse? How does he represent the process of getting oriented?

Paths for Further Exploration

1. Why are you in college? Why did you select the college you currently attend? How does college fit into your plans for the future?
2. What major or career are you considering? Select a class in a field of your interest and contact the instructor to ask if you can observe. Once you are in the classroom, note the culture of the community: How many students are present? How big is the classroom? Does the teacher lecture, guide discussion, or both? Collect handouts, take notes, and schedule a time to interview the instructor about the class and possible career options. What other

questions might you ask? Can you picture yourself participating in this classroom or vocational community?

3. Fabbri acquires the language of a particular academic discourse. Describe the language of a particular academic community you observe, such as an economics department, a sociology class, or student art studio. What kind of writing might students need to do in this community?

4. Design and describe the ideal college classroom for any kind of course you want to select, or a room that would work well for several kinds of courses. What physical details should be in the room? What technology should the students and teacher have access to and why? What kind of lighting, sound, and textures should be there? Should it have food? Plants? Places to nap? Be creative.

On the Range
ERIC SCHLOSSER

In the following selection from his bestselling book, Fast Food Nation, *award-winning journalist Eric Schlosser examines how the forces of food production and suburban sprawl combine to impact the life of one Colorado rancher and his family. Schlosser is a correspondent for the* Atlantic Monthly *and his first book,* Fast Food Nation, *was on the* New York Times *bestseller list for over a year. His most recent book is* Reefer Madness: Sex, Drugs, and Cheap Labor in the American Black Market.

———————————— ✦ ————————————

Hank was the first person I met in Colorado Springs. He was a prominent local rancher, and I'd called him to learn how development pressures and the dictates of the fast food industry were affecting the area's cattle business. In July of 1997, he offered to give me a tour of the new subdivisions that were rising on land where cattle once roamed. We met in the lobby of my hotel. Hank was forty-two years old and handsome enough to be a Hollywood cowboy, tall and rugged, wearing blue jeans, old boots, and a big white hat. But the Dodge minivan he drove didn't quite go with that image, and he was too smart to fit any stereotype. Hank proved to be good company from the first handshake. He had strong opinions, but didn't take himself too seriously. We spent hours driving around Colorado Springs, looking at how the New West was burying the Old.

As we drove through neighborhoods like Broadmoor Oaks and Broadmoor Bluffs, amid the foothills of Cheyenne Mountain, Hank pointed out that all these big new houses on small lots sat on land that every few generations burned. The houses were surrounded by lovely pale brown grasses, tumbleweed, and scrub oak—ideal kindling. As in southern California, these hillsides could erupt in flames with the slightest spark, a cigarette tossed from a car window. The homes looked solid and prosperous, gave no hint of their vulnerability, and had wonderful views.

Hank's ranch was about twenty miles south of town. As we headed there, the landscape opened up and began to show glimpses of the true West—the wide-open countryside that draws its beauty from the absence of people, attracts people, and then slowly loses its appeal. Through leadership positions in a variety of local and statewide groups, Hank was trying to bridge the gap between ranchers and environmentalists, to establish some common ground between longtime enemies. He was not a wealthy, New Age type playing at being a cowboy. His income came from the roughly four hundred head of cattle on his ranch. He didn't care what was politically correct and had little patience for urban environmentalists who vilified the cattle industry. In his view, good ranchers did far less damage to the land than city-dwellers. "Nature isn't an abstraction for me," he said. "My family lives with it every day."

When we got to the ranch, Hank's wife, Susan, was leading her horse out of a ring. She was blond and attractive, but no pushover: tall, fit, and strong. Their daughters, Allie and Kris, aged six and eight, ran over to greet us, full of excitement that their dad was home and had brought a visitor. They scrambled into the minivan and joined us for a drive around the property. Hank wanted me to see the difference between his form of ranching and "raping the land." As we took off onto a dirt road, I looked back at his house and thought about how small it looked amid this landscape. On acreage hundreds if not thousands of times larger than the front lawns and back yards surrounding the mansions of Colorado Springs, the family lived in a modest log cabin.

5   Hank was practicing a form of range management inspired by the grazing patterns of elk and buffalo herds, animals who'd lived for millennia on this short-grass prairie. His ranch was divided into thirty-five separate pastures. His cattle spent ten or eleven days in one pasture, then were moved to the next, allowing the native plants, the blue grama and buffalo grass, time to recover. Hank stopped the minivan to show me a nearby stream. On

land that has been overgrazed, the stream banks are usually destroyed first, as cattle gather in the cool shade beside the water, eating everything in sight. Hank's stream was fenced off with barbed wire, and the banks were lush and green. Then he took me to see Fountain Creek, which ran straight through the ranch, and I realized that he'd given other guests the same tour. It had a proper sequence and a point.

Fountain Creek was a long, ugly gash about twenty yards wide and fifteen feet deep. The banks were collapsing from erosion, fallen trees and branches littered the creek bed, and a small trickle of water ran down the middle. "This was done by storm runoff from Colorado Springs," Hank said. The contrast between his impact on the land and the city's impact was hard to miss. The rapid growth of Colorado Springs had occurred without much official planning, zoning, or spending on drainage projects. As more pavement covered land within the city limits, more water flowed straight into Fountain Creek instead of being absorbed into the ground. The runoff from Colorado Springs eroded the land beside the creek, carrying silt and debris downstream all the way to Kansas. Hank literally lost part of his ranch every year. It got washed away by the city's rainwater. A nearby rancher once lost ten acres of land in a single day, thanks to runoff from a fierce storm in Colorado Springs. While Hank stood on the crumbling bank, giving an impassioned speech about the watershed protection group that he'd helped to organize, telling me about holding ponds, landscaped greenways, and the virtues of permeable parking lots covered in gravel, I lost track of his words. And I thought: "This guy's going to be governor of Colorado someday."

Toward sunset we spotted a herd of antelope and roared after them. That damn minivan bounced over the prairie like a horse at full gallop, Hank wild behind the wheel, Allie and Kris squealing in the back seat. We had a Chrysler engine, power steering, and disk brakes, but the antelope had a much superior grace, making sharp and unexpected turns, about two dozen of them, bounding effortlessly, butts held high. After a futile chase, Hank let the herd go on its way, then veered right and guided the minivan up a low hill. There was something else he wanted to show me. The girls looked intently out the window, faces flushed, searching for more wildlife. When we reached the crest of the hill, I looked down and saw an immense oval structure, shiny and brand-new. For an instant, I couldn't figure out what it was. It looked like a structure created by some alien civilization and plopped in the middle of nowhere. "Stock car racing," Hank said matter-of-factly. The grandstands around the track were enormous, and so was the parking lot. Acres of black asphalt and white lines now spread across the prairie, thousands of empty spaces waiting for cars.

The speedway was new, and races were being held there every weekend in the summer. You could hear the engines and the crowd from Hank's house. The races weren't the main problem, though. It was the practice runs that bothered Hank and Susan most. In the middle of the day, in one of America's most beautiful landscapes, they would suddenly hear the drone of stock cars going round and round. For a moment, we sat quietly on top of the hill, staring at the speedway bathed in twilight, at this oval strip of pavement, this unsettling omen. Hank stopped there long enough for me to ponder what it meant, the threat now coming his way, then drove back down the hill. The speedway was gone again, out of sight, and the girls were still happy in the back seat, chatting away, oblivious, as the sun dropped behind the mountains.

A NEW TRUST

Ranchers and cowboys have long been the central icons of the American West. Traditionalists have revered them as symbols of freedom and self-reliance. Revisionists have condemned them as racists, economic parasites, and despoilers of the land. The powerful feelings evoked by cattlemen reflect opposing views of our national identity, attempts to sustain old myths or create new ones. There is one indisputable fact, however, about American ranchers: they are rapidly disappearing. Over the last twenty years, about half a million ranchers sold off their cattle and quit the business. Many of the nation's remaining eight hundred thousand ranchers are faring poorly. They're taking second jobs. They're selling cattle at break-even prices or at a loss. The ranchers who are faring the worst run three to four hundred head of cattle, manage the ranch themselves, and live solely off the proceeds. The sort of hard-working ranchers long idealized in cowboy myths are the ones most likely to go broke today. Without receiving a fraction of the public attention given to the northwestern spotted owl, America's independent cattlemen have truly become an endangered species.

10   Ranchers currently face a host of economic problems: rising land prices, stagnant beef prices, oversupplies of cattle, increased shipments of live cattle from Canada and Mexico, development pressures, inheritance taxes, health scares about beef. On top of all that, the growth of the fast food chains has encouraged consolidation in the meatpacking industry. McDonald's is the nation's

largest purchaser of beef. In 1968, McDonald's bought ground beef from 175 local suppliers. A few years later, seeking to achieve greater product uniformity as it expanded, McDonald's reduced the number of beef suppliers to five. Much like the french fry industry, the meatpacking industry has been transformed by mergers and acquisitions over the last twenty years. Many ranchers now argue that a few large corporations have gained a stranglehold on the market, using unfair tactics to drive down the price of cattle. Anger toward the large meatpackers is growing, and a new range war threatens to erupt, one that will determine the social and economic structure of the rural West.

A century ago, American ranchers found themselves in a similar predicament. The leading sectors of the nation's economy were controlled by corporate alliances known as "trusts." There was a Sugar Trust, a Steel Trust, a Tobacco Trust—and a Beef Trust. It set the prices offered for cattle. Ranchers who spoke out against this monopoly power were often blackballed, unable to sell their cattle at any price. In 1917, at the height of the Beef Trust, the five largest meatpacking companies—Armour, Swift, Morris, Wilson, and Cudahy—controlled about 55 percent of the market. The early twentieth century had trusts, but it also had "trustbusters," progressive government officials who believed that concentrated economic power posed a grave threat to American democracy. The Sherman Antitrust Act had been passed in 1890 after a congressional investigation of price fixing in the meatpacking industry, and for the next two decades the federal government tried to break up the Beef Trust, with little success. In 1917 President Woodrow Wilson ordered the Federal Trade Commission to investigate the industry. The FTC inquiry concluded that the five major meatpacking firms had secretly fixed prices for years, had colluded to divide up markets, and had shared livestock information to guarantee that ranchers received the lowest possible price for their cattle. Afraid that an antitrust trial might end with an unfavorable verdict, the five meatpacking companies signed a consent decree in 1920 that forced them to sell off their stockyards, retail meat stores, railway interests, and livestock journals. A year later Congress created the Packers and Stockyards Administration (P&SA), a federal agency with a broad authority to prevent price-fixing and monopolistic behavior in the beef industry.

For the next fifty years, ranchers sold their cattle in a relatively competitive marketplace. The price of cattle was set through open bidding at auctions. The large meatpackers competed with hundreds of small regional firms. In 1970 the top four meatpacking firms slaughtered only 21 percent of the nation's cattle. A decade later, the Reagan administration allowed these firms to merge and combine without fear of antitrust enforcement. The Justice Department and the P&SA's successor, the Grain Inspection, Packers and Stockyards Administration (GIPSA), stood aside as the large meatpackers gained control of one local cattle market after another. Today the top four meatpacking firms—ConAgra, IBP, Excel, and National Beef—slaughter about 84 percent of the nation's cattle. Market concentration in the beef industry is now at the highest level since record-keeping began in the early twentieth century.

Today's unprecedented degree of meatpacking concentration has helped depress the prices that independent ranchers get for their cattle. Over the last twenty years, the rancher's share of every retail dollar spent on beef has fallen from 63 cents to 46 cents. The four major meatpacking companies now control about 20 percent of the live cattle in the United States through "captive supplies"— cattle that are either maintained in company-owned feedlots or purchased in advance through forward contracts. When cattle prices start to rise, the large meatpackers can flood the market with their own captive supplies, driving prices back down. They can also obtain cattle through confidential agreements with wealthy ranchers, never revealing the true price being paid. ConAgra and Excel operate their own gigantic feedlots, while IBP has private arrangements with some of America's biggest ranchers and feeders, including the Bass brothers, Paul Engler, and J. R. Simplot. Independent ranchers and feedlots now have a hard time figuring out what their cattle are actually worth, let alone finding a buyer for them at the right price. On any given day in the nation's regional cattle markets, as much as 80 percent of the cattle being exchanged are captive supplies. The prices being paid for these cattle are never disclosed.

To get a sense of what an independent rancher now faces, imagine how the New York Stock Exchange would function if large investors could keep the terms of all their stock trades secret. Ordinary investors would have no idea what their own stocks were really worth—a fact that wealthy traders could easily exploit. "A free market requires many buyers as well as many sellers, all with equal access to accurate information, all entitled to trade on the same terms, and none with a big enough share of the market to influence price," said a report by Nebraska's Center for Rural Affairs. "Nothing close to these conditions now exists in the cattle market."

15   The large meatpacking firms have thus far shown little interest in buying their own cattle ranches. "Why would they want the hassle?" Lee Pitts, the editor of *Livestock Market Digest*, told me.

"Raising cattle is a business with a high overhead, and most of the capital's tied up in the land." Instead of buying their own ranches, the meatpacking companies have been financing a handful of large feedlot owners who lease ranches and run cattle for them. "It's just another way of controlling prices through captive supply," Pitts explained. "The packers now own some of these big feeders lock, stock, and barrel, and tell them exactly what to do."

THE BREASTS OF MR. MCDONALD

Many ranchers now fear that the beef industry is deliberately being restructured along the lines of the poultry industry. They do not want to wind up like chicken growers—who in recent years have become virtually powerless, trapped by debt and by onerous contracts written by the large processors. The poultry industry was also transformed by a wave of mergers in the 1980s. Eight chicken processors now control about two-thirds of the American market. These processors have shifted almost all of their production to the rural South, where the weather tends to be mild, the workforce is poor, unions are weak, and farmers are desperate to find some way of staying on their land. Alabama, Arkansas, Georgia, and Mississippi now produce more than half the chicken raised in the United States. Although many factors helped revolutionize the poultry industry and increase the power of the large processors, one innovation played an especially important role. The Chicken McNugget turned a bird that once had to be carved at a table into something that could easily be eaten behind the wheel of a car. It turned a bulk agricultural commodity into a manufactured, value-added product. And it encouraged a system of production that has turned many chicken farmers into little more than serfs.

"I have an idea," Fred Turner, the chairman of McDonald's, told one of his suppliers in 1979. "I want a chicken finger-food without bones, about the size of your thumb. Can you do it?" The supplier, an executive at Keystone Foods, ordered a group of technicians to get to work in the lab, where they were soon joined by food scientists from McDonald's. Poultry consumption in the United States was growing, a trend with alarming implications for a fast food chain that only sold hamburgers. The nation's chicken meat had traditionally been provided by hens that were too old to lay eggs; after World War II a new poultry industry based in Delaware and Virginia lowered the cost of raising chicken, while medical research touted the health benefits of eating it. Fred Turner wanted McDonald's to sell a chicken dish that wouldn't clash with the chain's sensibility. After six months of intensive research, the Keystone lab developed new technology for the manufacture of McNuggets—small pieces of reconstituted chicken, composed mainly of white meat, that were held together by stabilizers, breaded, fried, frozen, then reheated. The initial test-marketing of McNuggets was so successful that McDonald's enlisted another company, Tyson Foods, to guarantee an adequate supply. Based in Arkansas, Tyson was one of the nation's leading chicken processors, and it soon developed a new breed of chicken to facilitate the production of McNuggets. Dubbed "Mr. McDonald," the new breed had unusually large breasts.

Chicken McNuggets were introduced nationwide in 1983. Within one month of their launch, the McDonald's Corporation had become the second-largest purchaser of chicken in the United States, surpassed only by KFC. McNuggets tasted good, they were easy to chew, and they appeared to be healthier than other items on the menu at McDonald's. After all, they were made out of chicken. But their health benefits were illusory. A chemical analysis of McNuggets by a researcher at Harvard Medical School found that their "fatty acid profile" more closely resembled beef than poultry. They were cooked in beef tallow, like McDonald's fries. The chain soon switched to vegetable oil, adding "beef extract" to McNuggets during the manufacturing process in order to retain their familiar taste. Today Chicken McNuggets are wildly popular among young children—and contain twice as much fat per ounce as a hamburger.

The McNugget helped change not only the American diet but also its system for raising and processing poultry. "The impact of McNuggets was so huge that it changed the industry," the president of ConAgra Poultry, the nation's third-largest chicken processor, later acknowledged. Twenty years ago, most chicken was sold whole; today about 90 percent of the chicken sold in the United States has been cut into pieces, cutlets, or nuggets. In 1992 American consumption of chicken for the first time surpassed the consumption of beef. Gaining the McNugget contract helped turn Tyson Foods into the world's largest chicken processor. Tyson now manufactures about half of the nation's McNuggets and sells chicken to ninety of the one hundred largest restaurant chains. It is a vertically integrated company that breeds, slaughters, and processes chicken. It does not, however, raise the birds. It leaves the capital expenditures and the financial risks of that task to thousands of "independent contractors."

A Tyson chicken grower never owns the birds in his or her   20
poultry houses. Like most of the other leading processors, Tyson
supplies its growers with one-day-old chicks. Between the day
they are born and the day they are killed, the birds spend their entire lives on the grower's property. But they belong to Tyson.
The company supplies the feed, veterinary services, and technical
support. It determines feeding schedules, demands equipment
upgrades, and employs "flock supervisors" to make sure that corporate directives are being followed. It hires the trucks that drop
off the baby chicks and return seven weeks later to pick up full-
grown chickens ready for slaughter. At the processing plant,
Tyson employees count and weigh the birds. A grower's income is
determined by a formula based upon that count, that weight, and
the amount of feed used.

The chicken grower provides the land, the labor, the poultry
houses, and the fuel. Most growers must borrow money to build
the houses, which cost about $150,000 each and hold about
25,000 birds. A 1995 survey by Louisiana Tech University found
that the typical grower had been raising chicken for fifteen years,
owned three poultry houses, remained deeply in debt, and earned
perhaps $12,000 a year. About half of the nation's chicken grow-
ers leave the business after just three years, either selling out or
losing everything. The back roads of rural Arkansas are now littered with abandoned poultry houses.

Most chicken growers cannot obtain a bank loan without already having a signed contract from a major processor. "We get the
check first," a loan officer told the *Arkansas Democrat-Gazette*. A
chicken grower who is unhappy with his or her processor has little
power to do anything about it. Poultry contracts are short-term.
Growers who complain may soon find themselves with empty poultry houses and debts that still need to be paid. Twenty-five years
ago, when the United States had dozens of poultry firms, a grower
stood a much better chance of finding a new processor and of striking a better deal. Today growers who are labeled "difficult" often
have no choice but to find a new line of work. A processor can ter-
minate a contract with a grower whenever it likes. It owns the birds.
Short of that punishment, a processor can prolong the interval between the departure of one flock and the arrival of another. Every
day that poultry houses sit empty, the grower loses money.

The large processors won't publicly disclose the terms of their
contracts. In the past, such contracts have not only required that
growers surrender all rights to file a lawsuit against the company,
but have also forbidden them from joining any association that

might link growers in a strong bargaining unit. The processors do not like the idea of chicken growers joining forces to protect their interests. "Our relationship with our growers is a one-on-one contractual relationship . . . ," a Tyson executive told a reporter in 1998. "We want to see that it remains that way."

CAPTIVES

The four large meatpacking firms claim that an oversupply of beef, not any corporate behavior, is responsible for the low prices that American ranchers are paid for their cattle. A number of studies by the U.S. Department of Agriculture (USDA) have reached the same conclusion. Annual beef consumption in the United States peaked in 1976, at about ninety-four pounds per person. Today the typical American eats about sixty-eight pounds of beef every year. Although the nation's population has grown since the 1970s, it has not grown fast enough to compensate for the decline in beef consumption. Ranchers trying to stabilize their incomes fell victim to their own fallacy of composition. They followed the advice of agribusiness firms and gave their cattle growth hormones. As a result, cattle are much bigger today; fewer cattle are sold; and most American beef cannot be exported to the European Union, where the use of bovine growth hormones has been banned.

25   The meatpacking companies claim that captive supplies and formula pricing systems are means of achieving greater efficiency, not of controlling cattle prices. Their slaughterhouses require a large and steady volume of cattle to operate profitably; captive supplies are one reliable way of sustaining that volume. The large meatpacking companies say that they've become a convenient scapegoat for ranchers, when the real problem is low poultry prices. A pound of chicken costs about half as much as a pound of beef. The long-term deals now being offered to cattlemen are portrayed as innovations that will save, not destroy, the beef industry. Responding in 1998 to a USDA investigation of captive supplies in Kansas, IBP defended such "alternative methods for selling fed cattle." The company argued that these practices were "similar to changes that have already occurred . . . for selling other agricultural commodities," such as poultry.

Many independent ranchers are convinced that captive supplies are used primarily to control the market, not to achieve greater slaughter-house efficiency. They do not oppose large-scale transactions or long-term contracts; they oppose cattle prices that are kept secret. Most of all, they do not trust the meatpacking giants. The belief that agribusiness executives secretly talk on the phone with their competitors, set prices, and divide up the worldwide market for commodities—a belief widely held among independent ranchers and farmers—may seem like a paranoid fantasy. But that is precisely what executives at Archer Daniels Midland, "supermarket to the world," did for years.

Three of Archer Daniels Midland's top officials, including Michael Andreas, its vice chairman, were sent to federal prison in 1999 for conspiring with foreign rivals to control the international market for lysine (an important feed additive). The Justice Department's investigation of this massive price-fixing scheme focused on the period between August of 1992 and December of 1995. Within that roughly three-and-a-half-year stretch, Archer Daniels Midland and its co-conspirators may have overcharged farmers by as much as $180 million. During the same period, Archer Daniels Midland executives also met with their overseas rivals to set the worldwide price for citric acid (a common food additive). At a meeting with Japanese executives that was secretly recorded, the president of Archer Daniels Midland preached the virtues of collaboration. "We have a saying at this company," he said. "Our competitors are our friends, and our customers are our enemies." Archer Daniels Midland remains the world's largest producer of lysine, as well as the world's largest processor of soybeans and corn. It is also one of the largest shareholders of IBP.

A 1996 USDA investigation of concentration in the beef industry found that many ranchers were afraid to testify against the large meatpacking companies, fearing retaliation and "economic ruin." That year Mike Callicrate, a cattleman from St. Francis, Kansas, decided to speak out against corporate behavior he thought was not just improper but criminal. "I was driving down the road one day," Callicrate told me, "and I kept thinking, when is someone going to do something about this? And I suddenly realized that maybe nobody's going to do it, and I had to give it a try." He claims that after his testimony before the USDA committee, the large meatpackers promptly stopped bidding on his cattle. "I couldn't sell my cattle," he said. "They'd drive right past my feed yard and buy cattle from a guy two hundred miles further away." His business has recovered somewhat; ConAgra and Excel now bid on his cattle. The experience has turned him into an activist. He refuses to "make the transition to slavery quietly." He has spoken at congressional hearings and has joined a dozen other cattlemen in a class-action lawsuit against IBP. The lawsuit claims that IBP has for many years violated the Packers and

Stockyards Act through a wide variety of anticompetitive tactics. According to Callicrate, the suit will demonstrate that the company's purported efficiency in production is really "an efficiency in stealing." IBP denies the charges. "It makes no sense for us to do anything to hurt cattle producers," a top IBP executive told a reporter, "when we depend upon them to supply our plants."

THE THREAT OF WEALTHY NEIGHBORS

The Colorado Cattlemen's Association filed an amicus brief in Mike Callicrate's lawsuit against IBP, demanding a competitive marketplace for cattle and a halt to any illegal buying practices being used by the large meatpacking firms. Ranchers in Colorado today, however, face threats to their livelihood that are unrelated to fluctuations in cattle prices. During the past twenty years, Colorado has lost roughly 1.5 million acres of ranchland to development. Population growth and the booming market for vacation homes have greatly driven up land costs. Some ranchland that sold for less than $200 an acre in the 1960s now sells for hundreds of times that amount. The new land prices make it impossible for ordinary ranchers to expand their operations. Each head of cattle needs about thirty acres of pasture for grazing, and until cattle start producing solid gold nuggets instead of sirloin, it's hard to sustain beef production on such expensive land. Ranching families in Colorado tend to be land-rich and cash-poor. Inheritance taxes can claim more than half of a cattle ranch's land value. Even if a family manages to operate its ranch profitably, handing it down to the next generation may require selling off large chunks of land, thereby diminishing its productive capacity.

30   Along with the ranches, Colorado is quickly losing its ranching culture. Among the students at Harrison High you see a variety of fashion statements: gangsta wannabes, skaters, stoners, goths, and punks. What you don't see—in the shadow of Pikes Peak, in the heart of the Rocky Mountain West—is anyone dressed even remotely like a cowboy. Nobody's wearing shirts with snaps or Justin boots. In 1959, eight of the nation's top ten TV shows were Westerns. The networks ran thirty-five Westerns in prime time every week, and places like Colorado, where real cowboys lived, were the stuff of youthful daydreams. That America now seems as dead and distant as the England of King Arthur. I saw hundreds of high school students in Colorado Springs, and only one of them wore a cowboy hat. His name was

Philly Favorite, he played guitar in a band called the Deadites, and his cowboy hat was made out of fake zebra fur. The median age of Colorado's ranchers and farmers is about fifty-five, and roughly half of the state's open land will change hands during the next two decades—a potential boon for real estate developers. A number of Colorado land trusts are now working to help ranchers obtain conservation easements. In return for donating future development rights to one of these trusts, a rancher receives an immediate tax break and the prospect of lower inheritance taxes. The land remains private property, but by law can never be turned into golf courses, shopping malls, or subdivisions. In 1995 the Colorado Cattlemen's Association formed the first land trust in the United States that is devoted solely to the preservation of ranchland. It has thus far protected almost 40,000 acres, a significant achievement. But ranchland in Colorado is now vanishing at the rate of about 90,000 acres a year.

Conservation easements are usually of greatest benefit to wealthy gentleman ranchers who earn large incomes from other sources. The doctors, lawyers, and stockbrokers now running cattle on some of Colorado's most beautiful land can own big ranches, preserve open space with easements, and enjoy the big tax deductions. Ranchers whose annual income comes entirely from selling cattle usually don't earn enough to benefit from that sort of tax break. And the value of their land, along with the pressure to sell it, often increases when a wealthy neighbor obtains a conservation easement, since the views in the area are more likely to remain unspoiled.

The Colorado ranchers who now face the greatest economic difficulty are the ones who run a few hundred head of cattle, who work their own land, who don't have any outside income, and who don't stand to gain anything from a big tax write-off. They have to compete with gentleman ranchers whose operations don't have to earn a profit and with part-time ranchers whose operations are kept afloat by second jobs. Indeed, the ranchers most likely to be in financial trouble today are the ones who live the life and embody the values supposedly at the heart of the American West. They are independent and self-sufficient, cherish their freedom, believe in hard work—and as a result are now paying the price.

A BROKEN LINK

Hank died in 1998. He took his own life the week before Christmas. He was forty-three.

35   When I heard the news, it made no sense to me, none at all. The man that I knew was full of fire and ready to go, the kind of person who seemed always to be throwing himself into the middle of things. He did not hide away. He got involved in the community, served on countless boards and committees. He had a fine sense of humor. He loved his family. The way he died seemed to contradict everything else about his life.

It would be wrong to say that Hank's death was caused by the consolidating and homogenizing influence of the fast food chains, by monopoly power in the meatpacking industry, by depressed prices in the cattle market, by the economic forces bankrupting independent ranchers, by the tax laws that favor wealthy ranchers, by the unrelenting push of Colorado's real estate developers. But it would not be entirely wrong. Hank was under enormous pressure at the time of his death. He was trying to find a way of gaining conservation easements that would protect his land but not sacrifice the financial security of his family. Cattle prices had fallen to their lowest point in more than a decade. And El Paso County was planning to build a new highway right through the heart of his ranch. The stress of these things and others led to sleepless nights, then to a depression that spiraled downward fast, and before long he was gone.

The suicide rate among ranchers and farmers in the United States is now about three times higher than the national average. The issue briefly received attention during the 1980s farm crisis, but has been pretty much ignored ever since. Meanwhile, across rural America, a slow and steady death toll mounts. As the rancher's traditional way of life is destroyed, so are many of the beliefs that go with it. The code of the rancher could hardly be more out of step with America's current state of mind. In Silicon Valley, entrepreneurs and venture capitalists regard failure as just a first step toward success. After three failed Internet start-ups, there's still a chance that the fourth one will succeed. What's being sold ultimately matters less than how well it sells. In ranching, a failure is much more likely to be final. The land that has been lost is not just a commodity. It has meaning that cannot be measured in dollars and cents. It is a tangible connection with the past, something that was meant to be handed down to children and never sold. As Osha Gray Davidson observes in his book *Broken Heartland* (1996), "To fail several generations of relatives . . . to see yourself as the one weak link in a strong chain . . . is a terrible, and for some, an unbearable burden."

When Hank was eight years old, he was the subject of a children's book. It combined text with photographs and told the story of a boy's first roundup. Young Hank wears blue jeans and a black hat in the book, rides a white horse, tags along with real cowboys, stares down a herd of cattle in a corral. You can see in these pictures why Hank was chosen for the part. His face is lively and expressive; he can ride; he can lasso; and he looks game, willing to jump a fence or chase after a steer ten times his size. The boy in the story starts out afraid of animals on the ranch, but in the end conquers his fear of cattle, snakes, and coyotes. There's a happy ending, and the final image echoes the last scene of a classic Hollywood Western, affirming the spirit of freedom and independence. Accompanied by an older cowhand and surrounded by a herd of cattle, young Hank rides his white horse across a vast, wide-open prairie, heading toward the horizon.

In life he did not get that sort of ending. He was buried at his ranch, in a simple wooden coffin made by friends.

Guiding Questions

1. How does this essay zoom out from the particular example of Hank to broader cultural and economic issues? How does Schlosser connect the different kinds of information he includes in the essay?
2. This essay makes its argument through several different appeals—logical, ethical, and emotional. Do these various appeals work together to create a coherent argument? Which sections are the most persuasive?
3. This is a highly researched piece. How is it similar to or different from the standard "research paper"? In what contexts would this style of argument and research be appropriate?

Paths for Further Exploration

1. Is there someone you know whose job will become extinct in the next few years? Interview that person and then conduct some research on that particular field. Write an essay in which you include parts of the interview and a discussion of this vanishing field. Now think about new jobs that have emerged in the last two decades. What jobs are they replacing? What lifestyles do they sustain?
2. Research some aspect of food production tied to land use in the United States. (You may want to consult the rest of Schlosser's *Fast Food Nation* to help you get started.) Write a persuasive paper arguing your view of "best practices" for land use and food production relative to a specific location.
3. Trace a meal you eat in a campus dining facility as best you can to its original sources, documenting how it was produced and transported to you.

The Flavor of Hope
CHIORI SANTIAGO

Chiori Santiago is a freelance writer and editor who has covered visual art, performance, music, and environmental topics in the San Francisco Bay Area since 1986. She has written a children's novel, Home to Medicine Mountain, *and she has edited two books,* Voices of Latin Rock: Music from the Streets *and* Reminiscing in Swingtime: Japanese Americans in American Popular Music 1925–1960. *In this piece, which first appeared in the September/October 2003 issue of* Orion *magazine, Santiago highlights efforts of a local organization to improve the health of an urban community by offering organic produce to local residents at affordable prices.*

◆

Every Tuesday, Farm Fresh Choice makes buying vegetables a main event in west Berkeley, California. Today, with typical flourish, Caroline Loomis, Antonio Rosano, and Karina Serna unfurl bright tablecloths, lay them over folding tables, and fill baskets with organic produce, setting up a miniature market just outside the front door of a childcare center operated by Bay Area Hispano Institute for Advancement (BAHIA). As parents arrive to pick up their children, they stop to buy yams, avocados, and eggs plucked from nests that morning.

"¿Puedo cambiarlas?" a woman asks, hoping to trade a few bruised strawberries in the basket she's selected.

"Sí, sí, señora," Rosano replies, cheerily offering plump substitutes. "You have to get good ones; the children love them," he adds, shaking the fruit into a plastic bag. "Adios, que te vayas bien," he says in farewell.

Rosano is doing more than selling a sweet treat; he may be ensuring a child's future. By bringing organic produce to neighborhoods where it's easier to buy a bottle of malt liquor than a ripe peach, the nonprofit enterprise Farm Fresh Choice encourages residents to replace fast food with the "five a day" servings of fruits and vegetables promoted by a U.S. Department of Agriculture (USDA) campaign. The three-year-old program also provides a market for local farmers of color and boosts the regional economy. And by teaching young workers to manage the business, it is planting the seeds of long-term change.

"The basic tenet that drives us is that every person has a right   5
to share the bounty of the Earth equally," says Farm Fresh Choice co-founder Joy Moore. "You can't just go to a child that's homeless and say, 'I'll feed you.' You have to empower people to help themselves; and not just that, but to share themselves."

The west and south Berkeley "flatlands" where the BAHIA center is located are less than two miles from the "gourmet ghetto" where chef Alice Waters taught America to love baby veggies. But the organic bounty hadn't spilled over into this neighborhood. In one eleven-block stretch, according to Moore, liquor stores outnumber produce markets nine to one. A 1999 Berkeley Department of Health report found that residents, predominantly African-American and Latino families, were more prone to nutrition-related ailments than people living in Berkeley's wealthier areas.

"Basically, the study showed that my grandson was likely to die sooner than a white child living in the hills," says Moore, pointing out that obesity, hypertension, and diabetes are statistically higher among African-American families that have little access to fresh, nonprocessed foods.

"American culture was eating us up," adds Martha Cueva, site supervisor of the BAHIA childcare center. "Latin people in their home countries were surrounded by fresh food, but over here we're living in apartments with no plots to farm. Everyone's working, so it's easier to grab fast food when there's no time to go to the store."

The Health Department report jolted Cueva and Moore into action. As members of the Food Policy Council, a loose coalition of local, food-related nonprofits, they were determined to improve food delivery to their neighborhoods and change eating habits in the process.

But first, the council had to identify the barriers that stood   10
between residents and healthier food. A community survey identified three main reasons locals chose Big Macs over baby beets: convenience, cost, and availability. Convenience was the biggest obstacle. Organic food generally wasn't sold in flatlands neighborhoods, and so was inaccessible to seniors or anyone without a car. Community supported agriculture farms (CSAs) could deliver preboxed organic produce to subscribers, but "you can end up with a week's worth of rutabagas you don't know how to cook," says Moore. And that's not convenient either.

Then Moore learned of a USDA grant to fund programs that spread the "five a day" message. What better place to spread that message—and offer a wide choice of fixin's—than a produce stand in front of a childcare center? The parents, Cueva reasoned, would be a captive audience, stopping by routinely with their minds on dinner. "We married our idea to [the USDA's] and came up with Farm Fresh Choice," says Moore.

The four-year grant offered seed money in increasing increments, from $37,000 in 2000 to $45,000 this past year. Local environmental institutions and Alice Waters's Chez Panisse Foundation pitched in as well. Once the BAHIA stand was established, two more produce stands were added: at the Berkeley Youth Association (BYA) and the Young Adult Project. A fourth stand is planned near a south Berkeley senior center.

The grant also removed the cost barrier. The group used the money to subsidize produce sales, offering organic veggies to the public at wholesale prices. A week's worth of "five a day" averages just seven dollars per person through Farm Fresh Choice. And shoppers can use food stamps or a Farm Fresh Choice discount punch card, issued to members in seven dollar increments. About 150 families currently have Farm Fresh Choice memberships, which are offered free of charge. Nonmembers can participate, too, but they're encouraged to sign on as members. Thirty to fifty percent of business comes from nonmember walk-up shopping, Moore estimates.

The issue of supply was resolved when Farm Fresh Choice discovered growers practically in its own backyard. Moore contracted with six farms—all operated by people of color—to provide eggs, juice, and seasonal produce. These items are picked up from the local Tuesday farmers' market in the Farm Fresh Choice van and driven to the neighborhood stands.

15   One of the program's farmers, Richard Firme, grows organic greens and beans on land worked by his Filipino father. Raised on his Mexican mother's home cooking, he believes healthy eating should be a right, not a privilege. To Firme, Farm Fresh Choice seems a good deal all around: "They help me make extra income, they get to give good food to lots of people, and they're showing young kids one way to pull away from the environment they're in, and do something else."

Farm Fresh Choice hires Berkeley Youth Association teens at twelve dollars an hour, trains them, then puts them to work for three months at the BYA stand. When their stint is up, some stay on as regular employees. Moore sees the youthful workers as the key to the project's sustainability. "We use [them] as a sounding board; as a way to come up with fresh ideas to market the program."

The young workers keep journals and attend weekly meetings, where they join in opinionated discussions about global food policy and brainstorm ways to raise the $75,000 a year needed to keep the program going after the grants expire. At the moment, they're deciding whether to charge an annual fee for membership; they decide instead to try increasing participation through a colorful brochure and door-to-door canvassing.

"You guys are doing work that goes on in corporate board, rooms," Moore says, listening and nodding as a team debates the issues.

Creativity has been key to the program's success. Martha Cueva recalls how they originally had trouble selling greens, which are a staple for many African Americans, but not as common in Latino cooking. "We started cooking classes, and now the Latinos are buying more greens," she says.

Moore, who seems to run on optimism, thinks, Farm Fresh   20
Choice is a stone cast in the middle of a pond: its influence will ripple outward to change the habits of the next generation. "I'll do whatever it takes to plant the seed in their minds," she says. "I'll use guilt, I'll cajole, I'll badger people—if that's what it takes to get them to eat real food."

Guiding Questions

1. How does the introductory paragraph quickly set the scene for this piece?
2. What kinds of research do you think this piece required?
3. How does Santiago imagine an alternate future? What kind of argument does she make?

Paths for Further Exploration

1. Is there a particular community or organization that you would want to research? What is interesting about this community? What is your connection of the community? Are you an insider or an outsider?
2. Write any essay that views a place through its food. You might describe a neighborhood, a restaurant, or a cafeteria. What does the food reveal about this place, about this particular community?
3. Santiago offers a hopeful view of the future. Do you know of other organizations contributing to a more positive vision of the future?

The Orbits of Earthly Bodies
REBECCA SOLNIT

Where we decide to live and the lifestyles we can experience and sustain in those places are intimately tied to transportation issues. Rebecca Solnit points to the profound impact automobiles have had on our sense of place in America, and offers alternative ways to think about how we get around and how we live when we arrive. Solnit is an art critic, activist, and museum curator, and the author of Motion Studies: Time, Space and Eadweard Muybridge, Wanderlust: A History of Walking, *and* Hollow City: The Siege of San Francisco and the Crisis of American Urbanism. *"The Orbits of Earthly Bodies" first appeared in the September/October 2003 issue of* Orion *magazine.*

---- ✦ ----

"I live in the city but I dream of moving to the country at least once a week." This thought is expressed in our mix of sepia-toned photos and plain-spoken text. Black text is silk-screened on a white background; the frames are black-painted wood. 14-4420873, catalog/internet only, $149.

—P. 71 OF THE POTTERY BARN HOLIDAY 2002 CATALOGUE

I've spent a month or two of each of the past several summers at a friend's small house in rural New Mexico. Every year I'd come back to the city joking that I wasn't sure I was closer to nature, but I was definitely closer to my car. Really, it depends on how you define nature. In the country, there's more wildlife to be seen—though this place surrounded by cattle ranches was not so prolifically populated as many far more suburbanized places I know, where the deer come down and eat the tulips (or, even more thrillingly, the mountain lions eat the cocker spaniels). Around the New Mexico house, coyotes sometimes howled at night, vultures, ravens, and swallows all had their appointed rites from dawn to dusk, and last summer a vivid violet bird I eventually pinned down as a male blue grosbeak arrived like a minor hallucination. Most of all, there was the changing light and sky. Without lifting my head from the pillow I could watch the summer sun rise in the northeast near where the constellation Cassiopeia made her regular nighttime appearance. I watched the transition from sunset to dusk every evening; the one time I went to a movie instead I sat there thinking. "I'm missing the show! I'm missing the show!" With views to the horizon and dark, dark nights, the sun, the moon, and the stars lived with me, or I with them, and with the lightning and wonderful cloud operas that passed by. That was glorious.

But my own life was strictly unnatural. Everything practical I did involved getting into a car, because there wasn't a newspaper, a stamp, or a bottle of milk for sale for many miles. It would have taken me a full day to walk to the nearest grocery store—and so I drove there, and to the houses of my friends, aunts, and uncles, to hikes in places less restrictive than the ranchlands, to everything. Out there in the little house on the car alarm–free prairie I had a great sense of cosmic time and a certain kind of slowing down— until it came time to hit the highway at seventy miles an hour, and that time came often.

Driving a whole hell of a lot is the unspoken foundation of most rural life in America, as well as a lot of wilderness adventuring (a backpack trip of a hundred miles begins with a single parking spot?). We talk about transportation as though the question is whether you drive a Yukon or a hybrid but the question could be whether you drive, and if so how often. I know people who really went back to the land, grew their own food, made staying home their business, ranchers whose work is really "out there," but most people who claim to be rural have just made the countryside into a suburb from which they commute to their real communities, jobs, research, and resources.

Ed Marston, publisher emeritus of the great environmental newspaper *High Country News*, once remarked that the West won't be destroyed by ranching, mining, or logging, but by ten-acre ranchettes. And those ranchettes seem to preserve the frontier individualism of every-nuclear-unit-for-itself; they're generally antithetical to the ways community and density can consolidate resources. The urbanist Mike Davis talks of "public luxury"—of the shared libraries, pools, parks, transit of urban life—as the way to sustain a decent quality of life that's not predicated on global inequality.

The "new urbanism" could be a solution if it was really about public luxury and pedestrian space, not about dressing up suburbs like Disney's Main Street USA. The old urbanism was a solution before we really had a problem. Today, most of the United States is designed to make driving a necessity, turning those who don't or can't into shut-ins, dependents, and second-class citizens. As my own neighborhood went from working-class African

American to middle-class white, it too has become much more car-dependent. A lot of people seem only to exit their houses to get into their cars, depriving themselves of the expansive sense of home pedestrian urbanism offers, or the democratic social space that's created by coexisting with strangers from, as they say, all *walks* of life. Watching this transformation taught me that urbanism and suburbia are as much the way you perceive and engage your time and space as where you live. And it made me wonder if New York City isn't, in few key respects, the most natural and democratic space in America, one where stockbrokers and janitors daily coexist in the same space and much of the travel doesn't involve any machines whatsoever.

I've had the rare luxury of living, with rustic intermissions, in the heart of a genuine pedestrian-scale city since I was a teenager, and though the house by the creek might have been natural habitat for a blue grosbeak, the city might be mine. Scratch pedestrian-scale; call it human-scale, since humans are pedestrians when not fitted with vehicular prosthetics. In this cityscape, my body is not, as it is in the country, a housepet to be exercised with scenic walks to nowhere in particular, but a workhorse that carries books back to the library and produce home from the farmers' market.

And in this city with wild edges I can and do walk to the beach and the hilltops (from which I can see the peaks of five counties, and where blackberries, miner's lettuce, and a few other wild comestibles grow). Sometimes I think that the intermittent stroll of shopping, people-watching, and errand-running is a pleasantly degenerate form of hunting and gathering, that the city with its dangers and invitations and supplies is more like a primordial wilderness than a predator-free parkland where one leaves only footprints and takes only pictures.

Really, it's about how you define nature. I think we have tended to define nature as things to look at and think we're natural when we're looking at nature, however unnatural our own circumstances at the time. If you think of yourself as species, the question of what your natural habitat is arises: it should be a place where you can forage, where your body is at home, where your scale is adequate, where your rites and sustenance are situated. And then, of course, cities host a kind of human biodiversity that delights me. San Francisco is not only one of the most multiethnic places in the world, but one of the most eclectic. The elderly Asian man in a rose-covered picture hat who strolled down my street one day rivaled the blue grosbeak when it comes to provoking amazement.

I love wilderness, wildlife, views straight to the horizon, dark   10
nights, the Milky Way, and silence, though I love my large libraries and pedestrian practices too. I wish I could have it all, all
the time. But we choose, and I think that if we changed the way
we define nature and imagined our own bodies as part of it, we
might more enthusiastically choose the places of public luxury
and human scale, not as a sacrifice but as a kind of sanity. Besides which, I saw a golden eagle in Oakland the other day.

Guiding Questions

1. Solnit's essay begins with a quote from a Pottery Barn catalogue. What role does this play in introducing the essay? How does this epigraph differ from others that you have seen?
2. This essay sets up tensions between nature and the city. What does Solnit do to create this tension, to play on expectations, to complicate common assumptions about urban and rural places?
3. Solnit wonders "if New York City isn't, in a few key respects, the most natural and democratic space In America?" How does Solnit define "nature"? How does this differ from conventional definitions?

Paths for Further Exploration

1. What are the most important "natural" places for you? What role have they played in your life?
2. Write an essay that describes your relationship to a city.
3. Write an essay that explores an important moment in your life that relates to transportation (learning to ride a bike, getting your driver's license, taking the subway).

The People's Freeway
MARCUS RENNER

Like Rebecca Solnit's "The Orbits of Earthly Bodies," Marcus Renner's
piece highlights the relationship between transportation and place, in
this case by examining the role of the freeway in his Los Angeles
neighborhood. Renner serves as Education and Community Outreach
Coordinator at the the Urban and Environmental Policy Institute
(UEPI), a community-oriented research and advocacy organization

based at Occidental College in Los Angeles. "The People's Freeway"
first appeared in the May/June 2003 issue of Orion *magazine.*

─────────── ✦ ───────────

What if we cut the fence?," Nicole Possert yelled above the
roaring traffic. On the other side of a battered chain-link
fence clogged with trash, drivers zoomed toward Los Angeles.
Nicole and I were pondering a project that would shock most Los
Angelenos: shutting down a freeway so that people could walk
and ride bikes on a road they normally experience at sixty miles
per hour.

The Historic Arroyo Seco Parkway, known to commuters as
the Pasadena or 110 Freeway, is the oldest freeway in the western
United States. Completed in 1940, it carries 120,000 cars a day
through the broad canyon of the Arroyo Seco, which runs southwest from the mountains above Pasadena toward downtown Los
Angeles. For much of its length, the parkway's six narrow lanes
wind along the concrete channel that holds what's left of the
Arroyo's stream. Together, the road and stream pass through a
dense urban landscape of pocket parks and arching bridges, leaning sycamores and historic homes.

Shutting down a freeway in Los Angeles—even for a few
hours—might seem comparable to driving a lance through a
windmill. The effort to close the parkway, however, was part of a
broader vision for the Arroyo—a dream that, if realized, could
provide a model for creating livable communities across southern
California. Such places would offer clean and convenient transportation, accessible parks and open space, and would cultivate
an appreciation of both local history and wild nature. In short,
what had drawn us to the side of the highway on this December
morning was a plan for the next Los Angeles.

The closure had a certain magical appeal. In southern California, freeways contribute to sprawl and air pollution and often
carve up communities, reinforcing and sometimes creating social
and economic divisions. Their effects are made more acute by the
fact that Los Angeles has fewer acres of open space per capita than
any other large metropolitan area in the country. Perhaps more important, freeways affect how people think about and experience the
local landscape, reducing public understanding of place and geography to origins and destinations, with nothing in between. "Freeways," said Bob Gottlieb, head of L.A.'s Urban and Environmental
Policy Institute, "are the city's biggest environmental issue."

The ad hoc group to which Nicole and I belonged was formed   5
to create a different sort of city. We viewed the act of shutting
down L.A.'s first freeway as a symbolic gesture to stimulate discussion about how to create livable urban communities.

The round cobbles of the Arroyo Seco, or "dry creek," are incorporated into garden walls, along sidewalks, in park benches
and drinking fountains, lending the Arroyo environs a different
texture than the rest of the city. In the late 1800s, this rough and
wild landscape attracted Charles Fletcher Lummis, a journalist,
historian, and archeologist of Ameican Southwest. Lummis, the
first city editor of the Los *Angeles Times*, built his own home from
stones he hauled from the river. Here Lummis hosted the artistic
and well-to-do, who celebrated the blend of city and nature they
found in the Arroyo Seco canyon. Writing for magazines such as
Land of Sunshine, Lummis and his friends crafted an image of
southern California as a place of renewal and promise with a romantic (yet fictitious) past, built around the Spanish missions
and the padres' supposedly benevolent treatment of the native
Tongva people. Packaged by chambers of commerce and railroads, echoed today in everything from the area's faux Italian gardens to Taco Bell restaurants, this image drew thousands of
immigrants to the region.

By the early 1900s the Arroyo was a center of the Arts and
Crafts movement. Rows of Craftsman bungalows arose in the
canyon. The idea that the city should blend into the landscape,
promoted by local architects, became an important part of the
Arroyo's identity. Today, streets still bend and jog around the hills
and scrub clings to the steeper slopes. Lummis's home now overlooks the freeway at Avenue 43, but his Southwest Museum—
which he built to house his collection of Native American
artifacts—still raises its distinctive adobe tower above the Arroyo.

In the process of learning how to care for her 1905 Craftsman
home, Nicole Possert became interested in this history. She began
to appreciate the central role her neighborhood had played in
southern California's development. "It was just amazing to me
that no one seemed to be aware of this area's rich history or why
it was important," she said. By 1994, she was president of the
Highland Park Heritage Trust, a local preservation group, and in
1996 she joined a state task force to address longstanding parkway issues of trash, graffiti, noise, and accidents. "My concern
was, and still is, if this is the gateway to our communities and it
looks bad, how are people going to see these historic resources?"

The original vision for the parkway—described to the Los Angeles Chamber of Commerce by landscape architects Frederick Law Olmsted, Jr. and Harland Bartholomew in 1930—was of a leisurely, scenic drive between Pasadena and downtown Los Angeles. A disorganized mix of electric trolleys, buses, and automobiles already clogged city streets; the parkway was the first in a series of modern expressways Olmsted, Bartholomew, and others proposed as part of an integrated transportation system that incorporated trains, buses, and bicycles. Following the architects' lead, engineers who designed the parkway sought to balance efficiency and aesthetics. They eschewed walls to give drivers a better view of the surrounding hills, and built arching bridges over road and stream. Broad curves followed the contours of the canyon and slowed traffic. Tawny gold sycamores leaned over the road. Wooden guardrails and garden plantings helped the parkway blend into the landscape.

10 By the 1950s, efficiency had become the primary goal of freeway architecture, and in time faster cars overwhelmed the parkway's design. Today, the road carries almost four times its rated capacity and has a much higher accident rate than other local freeways.

But in June 2002, the efforts of neighborhood activists and state officials like Possert earned the road a National Scenic Byway designation, making the parkway eligible for grants to improve safety and beautify surrounding communities. Millions of government dollars became available to revive the experience that the parkway's designers had envisioned.

Restoring the parkway to its leisurely splendor is one element of a renewed attempt to create an integrated transportation system, both for the Arroyo and the region as a whole. In 2003, the new Gold Line commuter train began running between Pasadena and Los Angeles. Proposed bus, bike, and pedestrian routes, if linked to rail stations, would allow people to travel relatively easily without a car and make the Arroyo a transportation model for the rest of Los Angeles.

The stream, too, has drawn attention from those who want to remake the city. The headwaters of the Arroyo Seco fall down a shaded staircase of pools and cascades in the San Gabriel Mountains. Downstream, the Arroyo Seco is confined to a concrete flood-control channel. So disguised, the creek flows for almost eleven miles past soccer fields, golf courses, the Rose Bowl football stadium, and pockets of seminatural, open land. It joins the parkway for the last six miles of its journey before emptying onto the broad concrete flood channel of the moribund Los Angeles River.

At the confluence of these two urban waterways is the Los Angeles River Center and Gardens, home to several environmental groups and government agencies. Every day Anne Dove, a planner with the National Park Service, drives the parkway or rides the Gold Line to work here. "There is something about the Arroyo that just resonates with people," she said. "It's something about the scale of the place, that you can see all the boundaries, all the edges within one viewshed."

For three years Anne has helped the Arroyo Seco Foundation   15
and North East Trees with a plan to restore a living stream to the canyon. In 2002, their work piqued the interest of the U.S. Army Corps of Engineers, which may remove portions of the Arroyo's concrete channel—a first for Los Angeles County. This development meshes with plans to enhance and expand existing parks and open space throughout the watershed.

Most of the land along the Arroyo's floodplain, which varies in width from fifty yards to a quarter mile, is publicly owned. By combining this land with the right-of-way that the state owns along the parkway, local environmental groups envision an eleven-mile greenway stretching from the mountains to downtown. Bit by bit, that greenway is appearing; South Pasadena is beginning construction on a four-acre nature park, and in Los Angeles, the National Audubon Society recently opened a new urban nature center overlooking the Arroyo.

The nature center lies across the Arroyo from the chain-link fence where Nicole Possert and I stood on that damp December morning in 2001. I had become involved in the effort through my employer, the Urban and Environmental Policy Institute (part of Occidental College). My colleagues and I were interested in how different Arroyo initiatives could combine to achieve the broader goal of creating more livable communities. "Working on the Arroyo gave us the opportunity to address several issues at the same time," said institute Director Bob Gottlieb. "That's really important to build the kind of diverse coalitions that you need to create an effective community movement."

We began hosting an Arroyo discussion group in 2000 for researchers, activists, and government officials to share information. When, in the spring of 2001, someone proposed a walk and bicycle ride on the parkway, everyone in the room saw an opportunity both to heighten the profile of the Arroyo and build public support for the watershed's various community projects. Soon this idea had a name—ArroyoFest—and a date: October 6, 2002. Since I was the institute's new education and outreach coordinator, my phone soon became the center of a whirlwind of activity.

A week after our scouting expedition, Nicole and I described our idea for cutting the fence to twenty people in the parlor of a Craftsman mansion at the canyon's edge. Our job had been to find the best way to get walkers and cyclists off the closed freeway and into Sycamore Grove Park, a fifteen-acre grassy parcel where we planned an all-day festival. The park is between two freeway exits. Cutting the fence was the only answer.

20   A hundred years ago, boosters extolled the Arroyo as a playground for the white upper class. The communities that share the Arroyo today—and that were represented in that meeting—present a very different face. Forty-two percent of the seven hundred thousand people sharing the Arroyo were born outside the United States. Average household incomes range from less than ten thousand dollars to more than sixty thousand dollars a year, and the varied topography has balkanized the Arroyo into a place where graffitied parks exist in the shadows of gated mansions.

During ArroyoFest's planning, people's disparate geographies began to merge; their sense of place broadened. But the task of bringing such diverse communities together to care for the shared resources of the twenty-two-mile-long Arroyo is, really, a social experiment. We began to develop an appreciation for how creating "livable communities" means more than just making the Arroyo a pretty place. Social and economic issues such as jobs, gangs, and public safety entered the conversation. For example, conversion of undeveloped open space along the Arroyo into parkland means the likely eviction of numerous people who are homeless. One important question we faced was, "Livable for whom?"

The arrival of the Gold Line train service has also sent real estate prices skyrocketing, threatening to push out low-income families and businesses. "If you talk to communities that have gone through gentrification, most will tell you that they didn't see it coming until it was too late," said Beth Steckler, who lives in Highland Park and works for Livable Places. Beth's nonprofit group is trying to get ahead of the gentrification curve in the Arroyo by converting two abandoned factories next to a light-rail stop into affordable housing. The project can't be done soon enough; the median price of a single-family home in Highland Park rose almost 70 percent in three years, topping $250,000. In many ways, success in remaking the Arroyo will depend as much on Beth's project as on restoring the stream.

It will also depend on education. Carmela Gomes has taught public school in the Arroyo for more than twenty years and sits on the Historic Highland Park Neighborhood Council. She's helped develop a weekend workshop called "A River Runs Through It" to integrate the study of the Arroyo into classrooms. "It's something that we have to pass on to our young people, this sense that this place belongs to them, this sense of home and what it means to take care of that," Carmela explained.

ArroyoFest's early meetings connected these efforts and planted seeds for a more comprehensive vision for the Arroyo's future. But the first question that everyone raised was the big one: Would the Californian Department of Transportation— Caltrans—agree to close the road? Caltrans engineers worried the closure would back up L.A.'s entire freeway system. But a detour plan and helpful letters from elected officials convinced Caltrans to let our group of starry-eyed activists have the freeway from six to ten on a Sunday morning. We turned our attention to money.

To encourage participation, we decided to allow walkers for free and to charge cyclists ten dollars. Still, we needed $250,000, and grant money was slow in coming. By March 2002, the checking account was empty and we were debating changing ArroyoFest's date to buy fundraising time. Then in June, the first of our grants came through. ArroyoFest was moving ahead.

We hired a consultant to obtain the final permits, handle logistics, and coordinate volunteers. On July 17, we had pulled together our key supporters to assign tasks when the consultant surprised everyone by saying that he didn't think we had time to prepare. He refused to do more work. Frustrated, some people stormed out; others were relieved; still others proposed a new date in the spring or summer. Everyone departed uncertain about ArroyoFest's future. After ten months of meetings, outreach, and fundraising, at the end of the night all that remained was an empty room.

The institute remained ArroyoFest's main backer, so a week later I picked up the phone to ask who wanted to stick with it, and found there was enough interest to keep going. Planning for ArroyoFest had been very informal, but our need for more structure was now obvious. Anne Dove agreed to help our diverse group devise ground rules and a decision-making process. "It was excruciating," she said. But she got it done. We soon had a regular meeting time, notebooks describing our accomplishments, and a new date: June 15, 2003. Additional grants came through, and we hired the organizers of the Los Angeles Marathon and Bike Tour to run the show. Things started to come together.

25

With Carmela Gomes's help, the institute organized workshops on the Arroyo at the Southwest Museum for more than fifty school teachers, whom we encouraged to make festival exhibits and banners. Bob Gottlieb arranged a partnership with Sweat-X, a worker-owned cooperative, to sew t-shirts for the event. Artists helped with graphic design; unions donated paper and labor for printing. Claudine Chen from the Los Angeles County Bicycle Coalition created a website. Most important, we obtained event insurance and began to receive donations from companies and public agencies that detected new energy and momentum.

In April, with two months to go, the printer delivered posters and entry forms, and we called for volunteers to distribute them. Ten people filled the small conference room for instructions. These became fifteen, then twenty, then thirty. People stood in the hallway to listen. Three hours later we shooed the last of them out the door with armloads of materials. Our plan to close the highway was in the fast lane.

30 The final weeks were a blur of phone calls, media interviews, contracts, and deadlines. Last-minute requests for booth space poured in. A final program draft went off to the printer, and a crew spruced up Sycamore Grove Park. Traffic advisories hit the airwaves, and driving, biking, and bus directions from every corner of the Southland went up on the web. A contractor cut the fence and groomed the entrance where Nicole and I had stood eighteen months before. On June 14, an article about the next day's ArroyoFest appeared in the *Los Angeles Times*. The office phone started ringing at six in the morning and didn't stop until midnight.

On the morning of June 15, Claudine Chen got up at five-thirty to bicycle to the intersection that marks the beginning of the freeway in Pasadena. "There was a lot of fog, and it was really quiet and dark," she recalled. "The first person didn't show up until six-fifteen. Then I turned around and suddenly there was this whole mob of people. They just kept coming and coming. It was pretty unreal."

At seven a horn sounded, and ArroyoFest was on. More than two thousand cyclists let out cheers as they rolled past the blue and yellow ArroyoFest banner, down the parkway, and into the mist. Ten-speeds, tandems, and tricycles hit the road as a chorus of birds and clicking bike gears supplanted roaring engines. "I always knew that parks lined the parkway, but seeing and experiencing them as I went by was magical," said one rider.

Down at Sycamore Grove Park, Anne Dove arrived a little before six and began checking in the sixty community groups that had taken booth space. Carmela Gomes was busy setting up school exhibits beneath the coast live oak trees and helping direct volunteers as they covered tables with bottled water and programs. The first cyclist rolled in at seven-thirty, and by eight the park's band shell, which once hosted John Phillip Sousa's brass band concerts, was alive with acoustic folk and Latin soul.

By eight-thirty the veil of mist had lifted for the thousands of enthusiastic walkers gathered at the parkway's ten ramps along the route. The greens and golden browns of the Arroyo seemed more vivid than usual against the bright blue sky. One volunteer brought her two teenage daughters, both of whom were less than thrilled to be awake so early. By the time the walk started, the spectacle of the event had overcome their cool reserve. One of them ran to the side of the road. "That's a passion flower!" she gasped, pointing to a delicate blossom growing on the shoulder. "I read about them in school, but I've never thought I'd actually see one."

At the other end of the canyon, in Lincoln Heights, a mostly   35
Latino crowd assembled in a postage stamp–sized park. At nine, the Nightingale Middle School band played the national anthem while three hundred children and teenagers from the Anahauk Soccer League, wearing their red and yellow jerseys, began walking a mile and a half north to Sycamore Grove Park. At Avenue 57, a giant puppet labeled "Spirit of the Arroyo" joined the procession; at Avenue 64, a lone bagpiper wearing a kilt serenaded participants. People posed for photos next to highway signs, turned cartwheels, and admired more than ninety banners made by local students and hung on fences along the road.

Freed from their cars, participants put aside their drivers' defensiveness. One schoolteacher walked four miles from Pasadena with his wife and young children. "For my daughter, it was just a big party," he told me. "It was great. You were able to see things from interesting angles that you normally miss because you're going so fast." Several people said they noticed the shape of the hills and canyon for the first time. The quiet that settled over the road drew people out of their houses. One of my former high school teachers wrote to me, "Once we reached Highland Park and you could see homes and people; it was so cool. They were taking videos and pictures, and waving and smiling."

Instead of being a means to get someplace else, the parkway became the place to be, a tree-lined plaza where residents gathered for a Sunday stroll. Neighbors sat on guardrails and chatted; people walked their dogs. Skateboarders and in-line skaters glided down the road and children raced between the lane lines.

"Walking the area was incredible," wrote another participant. "It was an amazing sight to see all the bicyclists on the Arroyo park way and all that joyous, constructive human energy in action. Without the cars along the parkway you could almost hear the trees breathe a little easier."

ArroyoFest unlocked people's imagination and demonstrated to the more than five thousand participants who took to the freeway what is possible. Nicole Possert walked down from Avenue 64. "I saw some people who had their Walkman on and were looking straight ahead, but I overheard most people saying 'Look at those trees,' or 'I never noticed that bridge before,' or 'Isn't that interesting,'" she said. "It allowed people to gain an appreciation for what a special area it is." Another participant wrote on a local listserve, "Can we open the Parkway every Sunday morning? In San Francisco and New York, they do the same with their parks (Golden Gate and Central Park). Why not here?"

By ten, Afro-Haitian dancers were performing in the band shell while a second stage hosted storytellers and a Filipino gospel choir. "The looks on people's faces when they came off that piece of pavement—just the biggest smiles," said Carmela Gomes. Children planted seedlings and had their faces painted in the park, people signed up to join community groups, and speakers like Beth Steckler talked about their projects. Several people wore fish hats, emblems for the native steelhead trout that might one day swim up a restored Arroyo stream.

40   The next day, newspapers around the country carried the headline "Thousands Snub Car Culture." From Japan to France, the press was taken with the idea of closing a Los Angeles freeway.

In the months since, Nicole and the rest of the Scenic Byway team submitted a management plan for the parkway to Caltrans. Beth Steckler's Livable Places is close to building its affordable housing. Claudine Chen organized a scouting expedition for a commuter bikeway between Pasadena and Los Angeles, and Carmela Gomes's neighborhood council is trying to create parks out of two vacant lots. The future of these and other projects in the Arroyo depends on funding, political will, and the ability to maintain and strengthen the networks created by the event, but a sense now exists that these initiatives are part of a larger, coordinated movement.

"I think it showed the community what they can do," Anne Dove said. "If people from the community can work with Caltrans to close down the freeway, just think about what else they can accomplish."

Guiding Questions

1. As people began to work together to close a portion of the highway, what issues did they encounter?
2. What effect did the event have on participants' perception of the place? What did they notice that they couldn't see before?
3. Renner puts the event in context by talking about the original plan for the highway. How do the historical plans provide a model for imagining a different future?

Paths for Further Exploration

1. Can you think of a time you have participated in an effort to bring about change in your community, perhaps in a cause linked to a particular place?
2. Describe a time when you found yourself viewing a place from a different angle or moving at a different speed than usual. What did you notice that you would not have otherwise?
3. Research a past place or technology that you think we should return to or that provides a model for addressing contemporary problems. For example, you might research a mode of transportation that is no longer used in your area, or discover the original plans for a building, park, or highway.
4. Write a proposal for an event that would raise awareness of a problem in a place you think is important.

Serious Wind

BILL MCKIBBEN

Environmental issues dramatize the importance of arguing over what is coming. Bill McKibben's op-ed piece tries to enter an ongoing political and cultural debate and add to the discussion by redefining the terms and by appealing to fellow environmentalists to think differently about this complicated issue. McKibben is the author of The End of Nature, The Age of Missing Information *and, most recently,* Enough: Staying Human in an Engineered Age. *He is currently a scholar in residence at Middlebury College in Vermont. "Serious Wind" first appeared in the July/August 2003 issue of* Orion *magazine.*

---------------- ✦ ----------------

If you want to understand how difficult it will be for our society to make the transition away from fossil fuel addiction, consider one small report that slipped out of the Department of Energy in early December of last year. It found that, despite melting poles and rising sea levels, the overall consumption of renewable energy in America fell twelve percent in 2001. Granted, this was partly due to a drought that lowered the reservoirs behind hydro dams, but the drop was also due to the fact that more solar panels were coming off houses than were going up. Equipment from the "boom years"—when Jimmy Carter was subsidizing renewable energy—is wearing out, being retired faster than it can be replaced. Solar energy use, which never accounted for even close to one percent of our energy generation, is growing smaller still. And it's not because of George Bush, not really. It's because we environmentalists never forced the political world to take renewable energy seriously.

But how seriously do we take it ourselves? If you want to understand how difficult it will be for our society to make the transition away from fossil fuel addiction, you might also want to visit a website: www.saveoursound.org. It's the home of the Alliance to Protect Nantucket Sound, and on it you will find an environmental *cri de cocur* that at first glance could be coming from any of a million citizen groups, watershed councils, river protectors, or wilderness watchdogs. Shady developers, the alliance warns, are planning a "massive power plant" that will line their pockets but endanger local fishermen, wreck property values, threaten wildlife, and "destroy the main reason people love Cape Cod: the ungoverned natural beauty, solitude, and wildness of its coasts."

Before you sign up, though, you need to know that the villains in this case plan to build windmills: 130 of them, sited well out to sea, which would provide thousands of megawatts of power annually. This is precisely the kind of renewable energy that pretty much every Earth Day speech since 1970 has demanded that we develop. Now that it's finally here, though—now that we're talking about particular windmills in particular places, not abstract and squeaky-clean "wind power"—people aren't so sure.

Opponents of the Cape Wind development protest that these windmills will be visible from shore—and they're right. How visible is a matter of debate, but on a clear day you would see their blades turning on the horizon. They point out, again correctly, that the developers are private interests, rushing to develop a resource that, in fact, they do not own, and without waiting for the government to come up with a set of rules and processes for siting such installations. The critics also insist that there's a "better" site somewhere— and again they're probably right. There's almost always a better site for anything. The whole business is messy, imperfect.

But those criticisms, however valid, are small truths. The big truths are these: Each breath of wind that blows across Nantucket Sound contains 370 parts per million of carbon dioxide, up from 275 parts per million before the Industrial Revolution, before we started burning coal and gas and oil. That CO_2 traps the sun's heat— about two watts per square meter of the planet's surface. Right now the concentration of CO_2 in the atmosphere is higher than it's been for four hundred thousand years. If we keep burning coal and gas and oil, the scientific consensus is that by the latter part of the century the planet's temperature will have risen five degrees Fahrenheit, to a level higher than we've seen for fifty million years.

And what does that mean for Cape Cod? Well, the middle-of-the-road prediction is that sea levels will rise a couple of feet this century. On a standard eastern beach sloping seaward at about one degree, a one-foot rise in sea level should bring the ocean in ninety feet. Go stand on the beach at Truro and make your own calculation.

Big truths have to trump small ones. It becomes a caricature of environmentalism to object that windmills kill birds or fish—in fact, new windmills kill very few birds compared with the original models. In fact, says Greenpeace, offshore windmill platforms in Europe have often turned into artificial reefs providing prime spawning ground for fish. But even if windmills did kill some birds, that's a small truth—the big truth is that rising temperatures seem likely to trigger an extinction spasm comparable to the one that occurred when the last big asteroids struck the planet. Already polar bears are dying as their ice empire shrinks; already coral reefs are disappearing as rising sea temperatures bleach them, and by some accounts, they may be gone altogether before the century ends.

The choice, in other words, is not between windmills and untouched nature. It's between windmills and the destruction of the planet's biology on a scale we can barely begin to imagine. Charles Komanoff, an independent energy consultant in New York, calculates that Cape Wind's windmills could produce as much as 1.5 billion kilowatt-hours annually. Or, looked at another way, if they aren't built, twenty thousand tons of carbon will be emitted each week as coal and oil and gas are burned to produce the same amount of energy. The windmills won't provide all the power for the Cape, but they might provide something like half, which is a lot.

In the real world, the one where the molecular structure of CO_2 inconveniently traps solar radiation, you don't get to argue for perfection. You can say, as opponents of the Cape Wind project have said, that we'd do more to fight global warming by improving gas mileage in our cars. You can say that we should insulate our homes and build better refrigerators. You can say that we should plant more trees and have fewer kids. And you would be right, just as every Earth Day speech is "right." But I've given my share of Earth Day speeches, and seen the effect they had. Sooner or later you've got to *do* something. And if we're to have any chance of heading off catastrophic temperature increase, we have to do *everything* we can imagine. Hybrid cars *and* planting trees *and* a new president with the foresight of Jimmy Carter. And windmills, all the hell over the place. Right now renewable energy in America is at six percent and falling.

10   Which is not to say it's going to be easy. The plans to build big turbines provoke mixed feelings in me too. I live in the mountains above Lake Champlain, where the wind blows strong along the ridgelines. I'll battle to keep windmills out of designated wilderness if that ever comes up, but right now I'm joining those who are battling to get them built on the ridgeline nearest our home. And battling to see them not as industrial eyesores, but as part of a new aesthetic. The wind made visible. The slow, steady turning that blows us into a future less hopeless than the future we're steaming toward now.

Guiding Questions

1. Why does McKibben choose to address the disagreement over windmills on Cape Cod? Why is this a useful controversy for him?
2. In the essay, McKibben addresses a sympathetic audience of fellow environmentalists (the readers of *Orion* magazine), but he tries to persuade some of them to think differently. How does this intent affect the way he argues? How does he develop credibility and address objections when disagreeing with people who would agree with him on most other issues?
3. Toward the end of the essay, McKibben asserts a different set of choices for how we could address the future. Why does he choose to restate the choices the way he does? Do you think his method is persuasive?

Paths for Further Exploration

1. Describe a debate in a community you know well where people disagree over how place should be developed or preserved. What are the terms of debate? If the dispute was resolved, how did it happen? How did this argument affect you?

2. Examine a controversial issue linked to place, such as drilling for oil in wildlife refuges, building student housing near an existing residential neighborhood, or creating an office park in an empty suburban field. Write an essay that tries to redefine the terms of the debate, as McKibben's does, in order to more effectively present an argument for what should be done.

Auburn Renewals
ERIN KOMADA

Erin Komada is a sophomore at St. John's University in Queens, New York. In this place portrait, Komada takes us on a walking tour of her hometown in rural Pennsylvania and the surrounding communities. As she describes the distinctive qualities of this rural area, she reflects on the challenges and choices these communities will face in the future in order to preserve their past.

◆

Whenever I hear the word "neighborhood" my thoughts flash immediately to an intersecting line of townhouses, each complete with immaculate lawns and flowers in every window. But that is not my neighborhood. My so-called neighborhood is located in the coal region of Pennsylvania, nestled on the side of a mini-mountain called Sculps Hill. Sculps Hill can best be described as a group of homes randomly scattered along a twisting road, which makes trick-or-treating a difficult task. A quarter of a mile from the main road sits my house, my home. It is secluded, but cozy, and provides the privacy many want but cannot find.

I love my house! I have lived there ever since I was an infant. In fact, my birth was the reason my parents relocated from their small house in Macungie, a town close to the New Jersey border. Our growing family led to the decision that they wanted to have a bigger home in a nicer part of Pennsylvania. To me, my house is beautiful and full of rustic charm. It is a two-story white house with a basement, bathrooms on each floor, kitchen, two offices, three bedrooms, and a living room. The hardwood floors make the interior feel snug and each room contains at least one window to let in sunlight. Our front lawn is enormous, and at the top of the lawn is located a vegetable garden (also known as my mother's hobby). Adjacent to our house is our three car garage which we had constructed in 1999 because our snowy winters tend to damage our cars. Our meadow, dappled with different varieties of trees, borders our driveway. At the top of our driveway stands our above ground pool, only four feet deep but still perfect for cooling yourself in the summer.

If I were to walk the distance from my house to the road, I would find myself in a dirt lane canopied by cherry, maple, magnolia, oak, and pine trees and enclosed on the left side by sumac shrubs. This dirt lane, believe it or not, is my driveway. As I walk, I might see rabbits or hear cicadas and bees; on a rare occasion I will cross paths with a deer. I look at the meadow and relive the countless picnics of the summer and the joys of sledding down the hill in the wintertime. In my eighteen years living here, my greatest (and probably only) fear was that I was going to chip a tooth by crashing my sled or my bike.

Finally, after that downhill trek to the road, I would turn and walk around a sharp curve in order to reach the next driveway, which extends to a house that I have never seen, occupied by neighbors I have never met. These neighbors, however, own the cornfield that borders our property, and each autumn I awoke to the sound of their tractor harvesting the cornstalks. A little further down the road, there is a muddy swamp that was intended to be a pond, but the project was abandoned before taking any tangible form. Now both the owners and the bulldozers are gone, leaving behind a massive muddy puddle, unfit for fish—a manufactured eyesore. Now there is little hope that anyone will buy the property and finish the project. The puddle will continue freezing in January and thawing to an algae-green in the spring.

5   On the opposite side of the road are split-level houses, that try (and fail) to pose as a miniature housing development, each one having a lawn too big for its house. They look odd and out of place, especially with several rolling hills of cropland as their backdrop. At this point in the tour, I would have seen no one, neither on the street nor in their car nor at the window. Everything is quiet except for the chirping of sparrows and flutter of grasshopper wings.

After walking nearly half a mile without seeing any notable landmarks—a pond here, a driveway there, a school bus shelter nearby—I would come to the best example of the simplicity and loveliness of my neighborhood. The house has wooden siding and a natural charm, and in the back are gardens and greenhouses which serve as the nursery for the occupants' business: growing and selling herbs. I remember coming here with my parents to visit for an afternoon. While they talked, my sister and I played for hours with the various animals they kept. We passed the time chasing chickens, feeding geese, and caressing cats. The house reflects the same natural, easy-going attitude of the occupants. Because they live for the simplicity of life, little things like the first flower blossom of the season make them most happy. The entire estate appears chaotic, with plants spread well beyond their pots, and yet in that chaos one finds a pacifying freedom: the plants mirror the owners, both doing whatever pleases them most.

I wish that everyone in my neighborhood could see the beauty and the charm of the area. Unfortunately, many do not; they only see boredom and the misery that emanates from despair. I don't blame those who focus on the bad parts of the area; I often do the same. The towns have so many shortcomings and not nearly enough advantages to make up for these failings. Though beautiful, pastoral life can be extremely dull.

Taking the highway is necessary in order to reach any town in the vicinity of my house. To the left is Auburn, the town which my address claims is my home. I thank God day and night that I never had to grow up within the town of Auburn. The town feels like a coma as no one ever ventures out of their house. The main street is dead. Passing through the town, one might question whether it is in fact inhabited or whether it was just forgotten and left to fade into memory. The homes are ill-kept and run down; paint flakes off the siding of nearly all the residences. I do have to give Auburn a little credit, though, for trying to develop some characteristics of a town. First of all, it has a church: *the* Church of Auburn, which is a little red building plopped in the middle of main street. Second, there is a scout lodge for boy and girl scouts, which I must admit I am partial to because every Tuesday when I was a child I attended Brownie meetings in that hall. Finally, it claims a post office, bank and pizza parlor. The bank is really more of a drive-through ATM and the pizza parlor is family run, but to Auburn these are huge achievements.

If you would go in the opposite direction of Auburn, you would find a town on a completely different side of the spectrum: Orwigsburg, a town that is kept pristine and sanitary. Here you can see people walking up and down the streets and even spot a few shops (mostly florists) and restaurants. Again, there are not many activities available for young people, but there is a real sense of pride in the townspeople. Blue Mountain, the school I attended and which is thought of as the best school in my county, is

located in Orwigsburg. In fact, Orwigsburg is so nice that my
grandmother decided to move from the city of Pottstown to
Orwigsburg, purely because she loved the little town's charm.

10   Despite the efforts of these little towns, the economy still remains dead. Hardly any new business opportunities move in and
most decent jobs can only be found outside of the county's borders.
Many find themselves unwilling or unable to make the drive out of
Schuylkill County every day, and those who stay must resign themselves to working for minimum wage. This stagnant economy creates a real problem with poverty in the area, and a large class
division. Doctors and the higher-paid citizens live in Orwigsburg's
housing developments, the middle class lives in town, and the poor
live in trailer parks or dilapidated houses. An increasing number of
lawns are littered with rusted refrigerators and cars, the trademark
sign of resignation and poverty. I can see the signs of unemployment and despair everywhere in my county as nothing moves in
and stores are constantly going out of business.

          This dead economy has another downside—*boredom*—an es-
pecially troubling issue for the youth in my area. There is absolutely nothing to do; all we have is time and space. There are
really only two legal activities to participate in if you don't want
to drive for nearly an hour: bowling and miniature golf, which get
old quickly. The result of this lack of activities is a high percent-
age of underage drinking, with most kids beginning at the age of
thirteen. Eventually they progress to marijuana, sex, adrenaline
rushes (endangering stunts and driving well over the speed limit
on winding roads, for example), and ecstasy. Some even begin
taking really hard drugs. All of these things can lead to crime, and
with Reading, the sixth most dangerous city nationwide with a
population between 75,000 and 99,000, less than an hour away,
the entire area may be socially destroyed within a decade.

          I see my area at a crossroads, and it is up to the citizens to
decide which route to take. Will they sit back and watch as a
lovely area is destroyed both socially and physically? Can they
just allow businesses to pave meadows and set up shop only to
move out within a year, leaving behind little but a paved lot? Will
they let their laziness get the better of them and decide to just sit
back and watch the area dissipate, to surrender as they have always done? Or will decide they have had enough and that they
will not let go of their little community?

          The local communities can choose to come together to bring
life back to the area. Local people can franchise popular businesses in already erected buildings. These franchises will bring

revenue back into the towns. Once people see the benefits of keeping money in their area, they will begin to lend greater support to local businesses. Residents need to think long-term, to support some franchises without selling the soul of the town. If a business wants to buy some land, the town should analyze whether a new business is worth the cost of losing valuable green space. Sometimes new stores are just what a dead economy needs, but a new lot is not always necessary.

Once the economy is revived, the social life of the area will awaken. By having cultural programs suitable and interesting for all ages, the free time of the townspeople will be devoted to improvement rather than crime. Movie nights and community events strengthen ties between residents, which makes it easier to deal with problems as they arise. If there are plenty of things to do, then drugs will be less attractive for young people.

My native area is not weak. After all, the citizens of this place   15
have beaten back the drug lords from Reading (at least for now). These communities continue to exist, though perhaps not thrive, and the mere fact that they are still around proves the determination of the towns. There are many places like this in America— quiet nowhere towns. Perhaps their silence is the reason they still exist but maybe their camouflage is the reason why they have not progressed. Either way it is time for a decision. I have plenty of hope for my area. If the residents love it as much as I do, they will make the right choices. I don't think anyone would want to see the area further dissipate, and at the same time I feel at ease knowing that others value the area's beauty as if it were a part of themselves. The towns have the power to reclaim the area, to reform it and turn it into a thriving community. All they need is motivation.

I am now walking back up my driveway, and in the distance I see the tower that Verizon constructed in May—another image that makes me sad because it destroys what I consider my neighborhood. I understand the need for progress and agree we need more business in my area; but I would still like the peace of my neighborhood to be preserved. I want development, not urbanization; businesses, not warehouses; progress, not destruction. Whatever route the area decides to take, I hope that the little piece of land I call my neighborhood will not be erased or ruined. I want to be able to return as an adult and walk down the lanes uninterrupted by traffic, to keep a tiny piece of what's left of rural America, to preserve the pristine beauty of nature. I see portions of my past slipping away, but I know that at least my memories can never be fully destroyed.

Guiding Questions

1. Komada creates a verbal portrait of her hometown. What are the techniques she uses to create this description for the reader?
2. The essay contrasts the towns of Auburn and Orwigsburg, both places familiar to the author. How do these places differ in Komada's experience? What problems do residents of rural areas face?
3. At the conclusion of the essay, Komada expresses a desire for both preservation and development in the places she calls home. How does she negotiate between these seemingly contradictory forces?

Paths for Further Exploration

1. Describe a place important to you that is changing in disturbing ways. What is causing the change? What could be done to impede the change, and by whom? Do people have different views of this place and how it should change? Write a persuasive essay in which you provide a historical context for the issue, provide evidence and support for both sides, and offer possible solutions.

Virtual Vermont: The Rise of the Global and the Decline of the Local

STEPHEN DOHENY-FARINA

In his book The Wired Neighborhood, *Stephen Doheny-Farina explores the relationship between our lives online and our lives in physical places—the local communities in which we are situated. Though this book was written when the Internet was first gaining popularity, the issues he raises are still relevant, especially as the online environments we inhabit increasingly influence the way we interact with physical places. In "Virtual Vermont," Doheny-Farina examines the Internet's economic and social effect on local communities, and he encourages us reflect on whether or not the time we spend online keeps us from investing in our place-based communities in meaningful ways. Doheny-Farina is a professor in the technical communications department at Clarkson University in*

Potsdam, New York, where he teaches courses in creative nonfiction writing, communications and community development, social implications of new communication/media technologies, and rhetoric.

——————————— ✦ ———————————

It's fall. You are driving along the back roads of Vermont, winding around mountains and through colonial villages amid gusts of copper leaves. As you descend into an open river valley, you see the patchwork of small farms and silos and the occasional church steeple, just like the Vermont pictured in the brochures sent by the state tourism bureau. Up ahead you spot a farm stand, and you slow down. The stand is an old wooden structure, solidly built but listing a bit to the northeast, battered from years of winter storms whipping up this valley from the south. To the right of the structure a few rows of dried corn stalks—some still intact, some broken and toppled—are brittle evidence of the past summer's crop. To the left, sits a white wooden clapboard house, and beyond that, several faded red barns. Just past the house lies a leafy pumpkin patch. Already a farmhand has been harvesting orange pumpkins and laying them in rows across the front lawn of the house. Another couple of rows line the front of the stand. You pull off the road and get out of your car.

Three thousand miles away, a woman in Oregon sits in front of her computer screen. She is exploring the World Wide Web through her Mosaic-style interface, which allows her to follow a path of never-ending hypertext links. But in this case she is armed with an address—http://www.cybermalls.com—for an online business service called CyberMalls. Once connected, she can point and click her way to a number of businesses organized in groups. After scanning the possibilities, she chooses *CyberMont*, and a page appears with the following heading:

> CyberMalls' CyberMont Home Page
>   Welcome to CyberMont, CyberMalls' showcase of Vermont Products and Services.

She scans the options in CyberMont and chooses *Storefronts and other Products*. When she is presented with a page-long list of hypertext links to Vermont companies and services, she chooses *Cold Hollow Cider Mill*, where she can follow the company's links

234 Stephen Doheny-Farina

to see a variety of its products and ordering information. The first link she takes introduces her to the company:

Welcome to the Cold Hollow Cider Mill
Dear Friends,
   Fall in New England is a glorious time of the year. The spectacular color of the leaves, the cool crisp fresh air, and the harvesting of summer crops all combine to create the look and feel of times gone by. Here in Vermont we cherish old-fashioned values and purity of products. The Cold Hollow Cider Mill specializes in the finest Vermont foods, made with the freshest ingredients.
   We invite you to enjoy this on-line catalog and fill your pantry with an assortment of apple products, maple syrup, jams, jellies and much more. We also offer a wide selection of gift packs featuring these same fine products. If you have any questions, or would like some advice on putting together your own combination, please do not hesitate to call us. Our staff is available daily from 8:00 A.M. until 6:00 P.M. EST for your convenience. Please take advantage of our toll-free 1-800-327-7537 number. On-line ordering is available through our CyberShop Menu.
   Remember, it's not too early to start thinking about your holiday needs.
Sincerely,
Eric & Francine Chittenden

After exploring all of Cold Hollow's links, she decides to purchase a box of Vermont Macintosh apples grown in the Champlain Valley. Later she checks out a Vermont health food store that sells premium apricots from Turkey. She pays for it all with Ecash, an electronic form of currency that enables her to use credit without revealing her Visa card number.

While those transactions are spanning the continent, you bite into one of the apples you've just purchased at the farm stand. You love the taste, the snap and tang of this local Macintosh apple. But you probably don't realize that the apple was grown thousands of miles from Vermont. Indeed, if you had stopped here and bought spinach on May 1 or lettuce in early June, cucumbers and corn before July 4, cantaloupes in mid-July, or grapes, oranges, and peaches anytime, you would not have bought produce grown on this farm. In fact, you would have bought produce grown neither in Vermont nor in New England. You might have had some New Jersey corn and some South Carolina peaches, but it is far more likely that everything you would have bought would have come from California or Florida.

As you stand by the side of the road eating your apple, you   5
are consuming not Vermont produce but Vermont. Where the apple comes from doesn't matter. What is grown on this farm, if
anything, doesn't matter. All that matters is that you see, feel,
hear, and taste something that seems to be Vermont. Likewise,
the customer in Oregon who buys Vermont apples or Vermont
health food, fudge, smoked meat, and so on, is purchasing the image of Vermont simplicity and rectitude—the clean, rural, solid,
and unspoiled feel of Made-in-Vermont. And this thing, this Vermont, the legacy of a way of life long since passed, is constructed
in ever more powerful and pervasive ways by electronic communication technologies.

Food distribution in Vermont is an example of globalizing opportunities enabled by advanced electronic communications. The
result is the creation of an image of Vermont constructed on a
system that supports mass-produced, centralized food production
and—notwithstanding Cold Hill Farm and others that sell produce grown in Vermont—inhibits local food production.

There are three kinds of farm stands in Vermont. In the first,
the farmers sell only what they grow, either at stands adjacent to
their farms or out of the backs of trucks parked along a road.
Fewer and fewer farmers do this. Many more buy produce from a
Vermont produce distributor so that they can begin selling a variety of attractive fruits and vegetables as soon as the spring weather
allows. As their growing seasons progress, these farmers will replace remotely grown produce with the harvests from their own
fields, so, for example, by the third week in July they may stop selling New Jersey sweet corn and start selling their own.

But many farmers are discovering that it doesn't pay to grow
their own produce. They can sell their own corn for, say, eight to
ten dollars a bushel after putting seven dollars' worth of work
into the production of that bushel; or they can buy remotely
grown corn from the distributor for seven dollars, put no money
into production, and still sell each bushel for eight to ten dollars.
Further, when locally grown produce is plentiful, the farmers'
ability to profit by growing their own produce drops precipi-
tously. In August they can buy remotely grown tomatoes, summer
squash, zucchini, and peppers for less than it costs to grow them.

The smart farmers buy all their produce from the distributors, leaving their farms as a front. One farmer, for example, cut
back his production and upped his purchases year by year, and
now he merely grows a few rows of corn and some pumpkins by
the road. The rest of his many acres are mowed. Another farmer

asked the distributors not to deliver during the day so that his front would not be compromised. These places are no longer farms; they just simulate farms.

10   How can it be more profitable to buy wholesale produce grown thousands of miles away than to grow your own and sell it next to the fields in which it grew? Most people would assume that this is the result of developments in farming science and technologies and of changes in government regulations and sub-sidies. But the key to this system is the revolution in electronic communication technologies. Local food distributors, such as those in Vermont, are linked through communication networks with independent food brokers, the big corporate growers, and the large trucking firms to bring the centralized, mass-produced food to local markers.

The brokers lie at the heart of this network. They buy pro-duce from the big growers to fill the orders that come in from the local distributors. They also select the trucking firms to carry the orders to their destinations. The brokers are constantly in cellular connection to all parties—the growers, the truckers, and, in this case, the Vermont distributors—as they go from the fields to the warehouses to their offices. Further, they move their operations frequently (depending on what produce is being harvested where), so their business is completely enabled by mobile cellular communications.

The trucking companies can track their trucks via satellite to ensure that each load reaches its destination as efficiently as pos-sible. The satellite connection also makes possible two-way com-munication between truckers and dispatchers to monitor the status of the shipments and handle problems. The Vermont dis-tributor can plan its warehousing and distribution by tracking the continual influx of out-of-state trucks carrying produce that will be sold and shipped to purchasers throughout Vermont.

The key to this dynamic is for all parties to continue to in-crease the efficiency of the distribution system: from the brokers' cellular connections to the truckers' route and load management to the distributors' delivery schedules, the entire process is a com-plex communication system in which knowledge about the cur-rent and future states of the produce, the market, and the transportation are analyzed and acted upon.

As the system is fine-tuned, the local Vermont farmers have more difficulty competing, and most find it impossible. Some Vermont food distributors have adopted a buy-Vermont-first pol-icy to help keep local farmers in business. But trading with twenty-five Vermont producers or farmers on a given summer's day is less efficient than dealing with the two or three alliances of big growers, brokers, and truckers. So the state depends on the will of the Vermont food distributors to purchase whatever local produce is still available in order to keep Vermont looking and feeling like Vermont. This is a virtualization on a grand scale. Rural Vermont is undermined, but it is the rural image that drives the state economy. If Vermont loses that image, what is Vermont?

This question was raised in June 1993 when the National Trust for Historic Preservation released a report that put Vermont on its list of the eleven most endangered historic places. The Trust attempted to publicize the threat that commercial and technological development posed to the state's image.

This tension between the supposedly real Vermont and its image was treated on an episode of the television show *Good Morning America* on April 26, 1994. The report featured the work of a well-known Vermont artist whose prints often depict Vermont buildings and landscapes. This is art rooted in a sense of place, said the reporter, who was shown driving his car through the countryside and who assured us of his authentic knowledge of Vermont by noting that he went to college at Dartmouth, just over the New Hampshire border. In one segment of his report, the camera would show a picturesque shot of, say, a church—an image designed to make a viewer think "That's a classic New England scene"—and then would dissolve into the artist's conception of that scene. The dissolve showed how seemingly faithful the artist was to the place—how the artwork represented a real place and thus was somehow authentic.

But of course that artwork is not a photograph; the medium, a type of printing technology, enables the representation to take on an idealized form. The lines are crisp, the colors bright, the shadows straight. The simplicity and rectitude of the church is shown clearly in the print. But based on *Good Morning America*, you might say that the "real place," the image you see on the screen, had that same simplicity and rectitude.

The trick is that the video image is also an idealized construction. In neither the artist's view not the video camera's do we see the Mobil Mini Mart on one corner of the adjacent crossroad. In neither view do we see the condominiums built in a faux New England style on the side of the nearby mountain. But those developments are not hidden. Indeed, they are what fuels concerns like those expressed by the National Trust for Historic Preservation. And people who agree with such concerns usually respond by voting to enact strict environmental and historic preservation standards that regulate development and land use. Vermont has many such measures in place, and yet the quality of its Vermont-ness is declining. Local life is actually being undermined by means far more insidious than development of strip malls and condos. Indeed, few of us understand how vast technological-economic engines fueled by electronic communication networks replace local life with the image of local life.

More important, we forget about the hooks that pull us in and bind us to the globalized life. As a typical consumer, I have come to expect fresh vegetables to be available year-round. I think I am healthier and I know I'm happier always having a range of vegetables to consume. If my local food stores took away my grapes or red and yellow peppers in January, I would be one of the many complainers lined up at the courtesy desk. And yet I live in a remote region with a short growing season.

20   Just as local food production has been supplanted by mass food production, local culture and community are being sup-planted by mass culture and the image of virtual community. That hook has been embedded since the rise of the early mass-communication technologies and is now nearly impossible to re-move. Not only do I need sweet seedless red grapes from Chile all year, I also need a never-ending stream of increasingly compelling entertainment and intellectual stimulation, much of which dis-tracts me further from my local social and physical world.

My distraction has a variety of sources, each of which has been offered as the answer to the question, What is, or will be, the Information Superhighway? Some say that this Infobahn is the Internet, the vast computer network of networks that we gain ac-cess to through companies like Netcom Communications, Perfor-mance Systems International, and UUnet. These companies sell such services as the ability to connect to remote computer servers around the world (through telnet), to search and retrieve infor-mation stored at remote sites (through file transfer protocol, gopher, or the World Wide Web), to send and receive e-mail, to engage in synchronous chat with others around the world (through MUDS or Internet Relay Chat), and to participate in asyn-chronous discussion forums (such as Usenet or listservs).

Others will say that the information highway is composed of both the Internet and the networks supplied by what I like to call the BANC—the Big American Net Companies, like America Online, Prodigy, CompuServe, and the Microsoft Network. Although these companies offer access to the Internet, their primary service has been to create microcosms of the Internet, each with a national reach. That is, a subscriber to one of these networks can communicate with other subscribers around the nation through asynchronous discussion forums and synchronous chat sessions, and can conduct research through information search-and-retrieval services.

But the most likely manifestation of the information highway will be whatever network is created by the broadband communications giants. These are the evolving mega-corporations that control an ever-shifting combination of media among telephony, cable and broadcast television networks, movie and television studios, cellular and satellite communications, and computer hardware and software. (The communications giants for the most part encompass the Internet access providers and the BANC, but they do not, nor does anyone else, control the Internet.) Add to this mix a myriad of small and large companies engaged in virtual reality development, CD-ROM companies, and the computer game industry, dominated by giants like Sega and Nintendo. Collectively, these entities will offer us a range of products and services from the much-ballyhooed and little-needed movies-on-demand to interactive multimedia networks offering games, home shopping, and information retrieval to immersive networked VR geared primarily toward entertainment and advertising.

The source of my distraction—and the essence of the information infrastructure—is, most simply, all these entities, all at once, all the time. These are the alliances of growers, brokers, truckers, and distributors that produce, sell, and deliver mass culture. Their collective force sustains us.

Within this environment the most powerful distraction engines are networks in any of their forms. And the most compelling dynamic within any network is the individual interacting with others. Networks currently offer primarily text-based interactions, but as they evolve toward multimedia and immersive VR (recall the Personal Virtual Workspaces), their attraction and our distraction grow.

The networks present the attractive possibility of finding new places that transcend the mundane physical spaces restricting our daily lives. We therefore become concerned with developing and maintaining remote, disembodied relationships. Says Stephen M. Case, the founder of America Online, "Our goal is to build a strong sense of community. . . . People are more mobile than they used to be. The vision 50 years ago in which you grew up in a town and spent your life there and knew everybody is now the exception, not the rule. I think people have a thirst for community. Interactive technology is not the be-all and end-all. But in a small way a service like AOL can help bring people together to discuss issues they care about. It's a core part of this medium and something, I think, that the larger companies looking to get into the market don't appreciate. It's not just about video-on-demand and interactive shopping."[1] According to Case, you need not be concerned about reintegrating your life into your surroundings, you need only subscribe to any of a number of national or global communities.

But what kind of community is possible on such a large scale? The entities that Case and others label virtual communities resemble entities we all encounter in our offline lives. They do not constitute communities—online or offline—but they often feel like communities. Robert Bellah and his colleagues have called these collectives "lifestyle enclaves."[2]

In *Habits of the Heart* Bellah and his co-authors note that *community* has many meanings, and the term is often used in connection with a way of life—the skiing community, the show dog community, the criminal justice community, the truck driver community. But a true community is a collective (evolving and dynamic) in which the public and private lives of its members are moving toward interdependency regardless of the significant differences among those members. In contrast, lifestyle enclaves are segmental because they describe only parts of their members' private lives—usually their behaviors of leisure and consumption—and celebrate the "narcissism of similarity" through the common lifestyles of their members. Anyone different is "irrelevant or invisible in terms of one's own lifestyle enclave."[3]

Lifestyle enclaves flourish where individuals need not depend on others for much beyond companionship in their leisure lives. As individuals rely more on national and global ties than on local ties, the need for complex, integrated communities—collectivities of interdependent public and private lives—is replaced by the need for isolated individuals to bond through lifestyle enclaves, which provide only the *sense* of community.

30   This is my life. Think back for a moment to the ephemeral moment of social bonding that I experienced at the local movie theater. Look at the anecdotal evidence I used to lay claim to community. I said I saw "many familiar faces: college students and faculty, some local joggers—people I knew from Frozen Foote, a series of winter road races in a neighboring town—and a few members of the local bicycle club and the local chapter of the Adirondack Mountain Club." To me that group was the convergence of different enclaves

of interest in which I participate. To someone else that group could have been configured very differently. What's worse, many people may have considered that group not as a configuration at all but as just a collection of individuals out to the movies. Why these diverse possible viewpoints? Because despite the way I want to interpret that event, there was no *public* in that theater; there was no gathering of a people with a common interdependence based on the social, psychological, economic, and environmental necessities of a particular place and time. We were merely an aggregation of individual consumers.[4]

Our public lives are shaped by economies that focus our attentions on national and global matters. The regional economy where I live, for example, is dominated by four colleges, several multinational manufacturers, logging, tourism, and farming. Farming—as in Vermont—is in decline, and the remaining industries focus nearly all their energy on competing on a national and global scale. The locally owned retail businesses have gradually disappeared after losing their customers to the national chains in outlying shopping centers. The universities require their employees, from custodians to presidents, to work toward two goals: to develop wide-scale (regional, national, international) renown for the institution, and to provide education for the students, nearly all of whom come here for four years and then return to homes all over the world. . . . The manufacturers and loggers can survive only by exceeding industry standards established in a global market, while the regional tourism industry is manufacturing and broadcasting images designed to persuade consumers worldwide to come and interact with those images for a week's vacation. For most of us in this economy our public lives thus concern issues external to our localities.

Further, one kind of local public space has largely disappeared: the places for public discourse about the issues, problems, and celebrations that affect a locality as a whole. Life in American cities and suburbs is notorious for having eliminated public space for public discourse. When we combine the belief that our economies have relieved us of the need to rely on our neighbors for our economic well-being, the hostile environments that plague our cities and isolate our suburbs, and decades of urban and suburban planning that have inhibited the creation and maintenance of spaces in which individuals can easily interact, we come to believe that public life beyond work is either nonexistent or so remote it is irrelevant to daily life. The planners, as noted by Ray Oldenburg in *The Great Good Place*, rarely consider such public spaces—"third places," he calls them—important anymore.[5] In spite of this, however, the romantic notion persists that small-town life includes public discourse and engenders an interdependency among co-located townspeople. This way of life, I'm afraid, is lost, too.

To me this loss is best illustrated by the charade that journalists and politicians play every election cycle when they go in search of "real people" congregating naturally in public places throughout small-town America. In cities journalists can stand on streets and shove microphones into the faces of harried, vaguely fearful, or resentful passersby. In the suburbs the only thing that passes for public space is the shopping mall—hardly a site of local public discourse on the local public good. But where in rural America, in which public space supposedly still exists, can journalists go to find a public? They go to one of the only remaining icons of public gathering that seems not wholly compromised by ideology or some special-interest group. They go to the coffee shop.

But, of course, there is no public there. Reporters and politicians may find a slice of the local populace—retired men, the unemployed, the few locals left who actually work on Main Street (all of whom typically fall on the conservative end of the political spectrum)—but that locale is no more likely to reveal a public than would a Catholic Church service, a Masonic Temple meeting, a Macintosh user's group, or a meeting of a regional chapter of the People for the Ethical Treatment of Animals. Still, politicians go to the coffee shop to appear to be in touch with real people; journalists go there either because they're lazy or because they realize they can probably obtain quotes from people who speak with regional accents or who don't use proper grammar—both of which provide authenticity to the journalists' reports. The entire enterprise is futile, because the heart of a community is no longer located anywhere.

35   If reporters or politicians came looking for what passes as public space in my town, they would have to interact with locals' personal lives. Their best chance of garnering a cross-section of the town would be to spend a weekend between November and March shivering in one of our three ice arenas to watch hours of youth, high school, and college hockey and figure skating.

Recently my town was the site for what was billed as a community celebration to honor a local woman who had won a gold medal in the Winter Olympics. School children were bussed to one of the large college hockey arenas. Town officials, religious leaders, college administrators, state and federal representatives, and the "general public" filled the arena for what turned out to be a pleasant event of great goodwill. Certainly, the Olympic athlete deserved congratulations for her outstanding performance under the kind of intense pressure that few of us ever have to experience. Those who organized the event were right to do it and did a fine job. Unfortunately, I felt at this event something like the tourist at the Vermont farm stand consuming the image of Vermont.

The Olympian had moved to the area a few years before and as a result of the demands of training and performing had not spent a lot of time actually living here (although she had devoted much of that time to community service in the schools). During the ceremony we were shown excerpts from a cbs television interview with the Olympian, and later we witnessed the unveiling of a mixed-media rendering of the athlete in action, a piece done by an artist from another part of the country who was creating a series of Olympic art and who had shipped the piece north just for this event. Several speakers said that they hoped the Olympian had plans to stay in the area and make it her home. We all engaged in the images of community celebration, but the event felt at best like a genuinely affectionate welcome to and celebration of a relative newcomer from a lot of people who really didn't know each other (many of whom, like myself and other college people, had not lived here all that long themselves), and at worst it felt like a play about community bonding.

With such large-scale events rare, the closest things we have to public discourse are meetings of the school board and the town board, but those are primarily the sites of special-interest debates: somebody wants a tax variance to build a new hydro-dam; an informal group of parents wants to take action regarding a new school bus schedule. Although such deliberation is important, it rarely involves a common public debating the common good.

Here, as in most places, our sense of community arises out of interest-group interactions like these. Local community is the aggregation of enclaves of interest and occurs, most significantly, where those enclaves intersect. And accordingly, much of what we may think of as public discourse occurs in our private lives. Few clear lines between public and private exist in such communities.[6]

Overall, the largest area of intersection among enclaves in my   40
town involves child-rearing: school functions, the Parent-Teacher Association, school sports, school board meetings, community youth associations, and other mostly leisure- and consumer-related activities. Recognizing this, one town in the region has

raised a sign near the main road bearing a version of an African cultural proverb: "It takes a whole village to raise a child." This is a powerful idea. But in practice, what it winds up meaning is that it takes an active and well-rounded mix of interacting co-located interest groups to raise a child.

An entity we call a community is sustainable when it comprises a critical mass of interest groups tending to its social, psychological, economic, and environmental needs. Because most of the work of a community does not occur in public space, it must occur through this range of interest enclaves. Communities are in danger when the viability and range of those groups are undermined.

The net can either enhance communities by enabling a new kind of local public space or it can undermine communities by pulling people away from local enclaves and toward global, virtual ones. The second trend is in ascendancy. Much of the net is a Byzantine amalgamation of fragmented, isolating, solipsistic enclaves of interest based on a collectivity of assent (regardless of the minor dissents—"flames"—that occur within them; indeed, the much-discussed phenomenon of flaming is merely a symptom of the lack of real community amid this impoverished thing called virtual community).

Examine again the words of Stephen Case: through the net people can build a "strong sense of community" because community based on place is gone. Come with me, he says, and find online what we've lost everywhere else.

Endnotes

1. Schwartz, Evan, "Linking the Information Superhighway to Main Street," *New York Times* (October 9, 1994): sec. 3, 10.
2. Bellah, Robert N., Richard Madsen, William M. Sullivan, Ann Swidler, and Steven M. Tipton, *Habits of the Heart: Individualism and Commitment in American Life* (New York: Harper and Row, 1985), 72.
3. Bellah et al., 72.
4. Kemmis, Daniel, *Community and the Politics of Place* (Norman: University of Oklahoma Press, 1990), 4–8.
5. Oldenburg, Ray, *The Great Good Place* (New York: Paragon House, 1989).
6. For a discussion of the distinctions between public and private life, distinctions both real and false, see Mouffe, Chantal, "Democratic Citizenship and the Political Community," in *Community at Loose Ends*, ed. Miami Theory Collective (Minneapolis: University of Minnesota Press, 1991), 70–82.

Guiding Questions

1. This essay was written almost ten years ago. Does it feel dated? In what ways do you think the issues he raises are still relevant? What has changed since the beginnings of the Internet?
2. Doheny-Farina cites the distinction Robert Bella makes between communities and "lifestyle enclaves." What role do these definitions play in the author's argument?
3. According to Doheny-Farina, "the net can either enhance communities by enabling a new kind of local public space or it can undermine communities by pulling people away from local enclaves and toward global, virtual ones." What examples can you think that reflect both of these possibilities?

Paths for Further Exploration

1. Describe an online community you participate in and examine the way it functions as a community. How are these relationships different from the other kinds of relationships you have?
2. Analyze a Web site related to a locale. How does this site connect people to that place? How could it be improved to strengthen this particular community?
3. Create a Web site that acts as a guide to a place. For example, you could design a site that guides visitors to under-twenty-one clubs near your university, to the best bird-watching spots in the area, or to resources for international students who have just arrived in your community.

A New Geography of Hope:
Landscape, Design, and the
Renewal of Ecological Intelligence
WILLIAM MCDONOUGH AND MICHAEL BRAUNGART

According to William McDonough and Michael Braungart, authors of Cradle to Cradle: Remaking the Way We Make Things, *the serious environmental problems we face today are ultimately a result of bad design. In their view, it is not enough to consume less and recycle more; we need nothing short of a second Industrial Revolution, one patterned on the effective designs exhibited by nature. In the essay that follows, McDonough and Braungart argue that if we use nature as our model for designing the places where we live and the products we consume, it is possible that human beings can have a positive, regenerative effect on the world rather than a wasteful, destructive one. William McDonough is an architect who has served as the dean of University of Virginia School of Architecture and is the founding partner of a firm committed to sustainable design. Michael Braungart is a chemist who lectures around the world on critical new concepts for ecological chemistry.*

───────────── ✦ ─────────────

Imagine seeking revelations on the weedy edge of a Kmart parking lot. It may sound absurd on the face of it, but there is a long tradition of meditating on landscapes extremely antagonistic to life in order to understand life itself. In the biblical tradition, the pilgrimage to the desert wilderness is seen as a journey to a barren, forbidding place that nonetheless offers a vision of renewal. "Going to the mountain" has become parlance for having something serious to think about. The inhospitable places of the contemporary world—brownfields, landfills, abandoned neighborhoods—are the work of human hands, but they too are natural landscapes with a revelatory power all their own. The expanse of asphalt surrounding a strip mall may express ignorance of the living Earth, but it is nonetheless a shaping of land by earthly creatures. Like a beaver dam or an anthill, it is rich with information and metaphor about the relation between the laws of nature and the design of the world we inhabit. A lot of this information may be negative feedback— the asphalt heating up in the noonday sun, for example—but to ignore the signals of human presence is to miss an opportunity to engage the extremities of the landscapes we have created and, by design, to lay the foundation for their renewal.

Seeing hope in the extremities of the human world begins with our perception of landscape. For North Americans the landscapes most often associated with renewal are the iconic images of the sublime and distant wilderness. Wallace Stegner captured this sense of the wild in his "Wilderness Letter" of 1960. When Stegner wrote his famous plea for wild country, the daily lives of most Americans were so remote from the landscapes of mountain, forest, and tallgrass prairie, he was obliged to appeal for the preservation of the idea of wilderness. If the wild was no longer the landscape against which we took our measure, or even a place we knew, he wrote, "the reminder and the reassurance that it is still there is good for our spiritual health even if we never once in ten years set foot in it."

"We simply need that wild country available to us," he continued, "even if we never do more than drive to its edge and look in. For it can be a means of reassuring ourselves of our sanity as creatures, a part of the geography of hope."

He was right, of course. Wild places are sacred, and even infrequent pilgrimages to see them can inspire a sense of wonder and a reverence for life. But perhaps we have taken Stegner too literally. Perhaps a distant wilderness, an idea of wild country, positions nature too far from our daily lives. Stegner himself was intimate with his surroundings yet North Americans tend to think that true nature can only be found on the pristine, remote extremities of civilization and that these places have little to do with the everyday human world. Culture is here, nature far away. The trouble is not the idea of protecting and preserving wilderness. It's that the design of the world we inhabit—our communities, our workplaces, our economy—is so impermeable to nature, it is all too easy to leave our reverence in the parking lots of national parks.

This separation from natural landscapes, our sense of looking   5
in from the edge, is reinforced by the picturesque, the sense of the land as a static backdrop. But landscape has more lively meanings, too. Tracing the word's deeper roots, the landscape architect Anne Whiston Spirn finds meanings that suggest that landscape is in every sense our home. In Danish, German, and Old English, she writes, "landscape associates people and place." *Land* "means both a place and the people living there," and the roots of *-scape* suggest an active, sensual, aesthetic partnership with other life.

Indeed, writes Spirn, "all living things share the same space, all make landscape." For humans, to dwell in a place, to cultivate soil or build a town, is to be a "co-author" of landscape with trees, wind, water, plants, and animals. A deep knowledge of the dynamics of these connections—the language of landscape—can create fluent dialogues with place. Absent contact with the natural world, however, the language of landscape is easily forgotten.

We live in a time when our dialogues with place are not very fluent. The discordant strains, some subtle, some ghastly, are written on the landscape. They may be unnoticeable, without a sense of history, as in the enclosing of the central lawn of the University of Virginia in 1890, which compromised the openness of Thomas Jefferson's design and obscured the school's relationship to the surrounding countryside and the nearby Blue Ridge Mountains. In Jefferson's original plan, notes Spirn, the open lawn "linked two sources of knowledge: books and nature." Notes of discord may also be produced by an absence, as on the naked streets of cities where to plant a tree or to garden is to enter a Byzantine world of regulations designed to keep nature at bay. These are the more subtle expressions of dissonance. Others scream. There are, for example, the extremities of the worlds we protect and those we burden with waste: the majesty of Rocky Mountain National Park and Yucca Mountain, the proposed site of a future nuclear waste dump on sacred Shoshone land; the astonishing heights of Denali and the equally astonishing Fresh Kills, the 2,000-acre landfill on the marshlands of Staten Island, a mountain of trash so big it is the highest point on the eastern seaboard. And sometimes these landscapes are one, as on the hallowed slopes of Mount Everest, where sherpas last year hauled out from a high-elevation Base Camp more than four tons of discarded oxygen bottles, garbage, and human waste.

None of us need look too far to see some element of these extremities; contemporary architecture recapitulates them in the built environment. Designers, architects, landscape architects, and engineers, after all, mediate the boundary between people and nature. Working with mass, membrane, and transparency, the designs of buildings and grounds are either responsive to place— which tends to engage people and materials in dialogues with the natural world—or exist in stark isolation from their surroundings. The latter is the industrial norm. Many architects today, for example, no longer rely on the sun to heat or illuminate buildings, and consequently few know how to find true south, let alone converse with landscape. And so we find in our homes, cities, and workplaces the disconnection between culture and nature.

At its most extreme, this disconnection yields artifacts like Biosphere 2, a landscape co-authored not with the surrounding Sonoran Desert, but with a dream of outer space, a fantasy marriage between the worlds of EPCOT (Experimental Prototypical Community of Tomorrow) and ecology. Conceived to test the feasibility of a self-sustaining space colony, the glass-and-aluminum domes of the three-acre Biosphere 2 were built to re-create the Earth's natural systems in a completely sealed-off, human-made world. As reported in the *New York Times*, "the aim was to have human inhabitants thrive in a miniature world made of sea, savanna, mangrove swamp, rain forest, desert and farm, the areas and atmospheres interacting to form a totally independent life-support system."

10   In September 1991, the first crew of eight Biospherians was sealed inside the structure; as their first year drew to a close, recalled the *Times* report, things began to go awry. Air temperatures

soared. Oxygen and carbon dioxide levels fluctuated wildly. Brittle tree limbs collapsed and desert became chaparral. All the pollinators died, as did 19 of 25 vertebrate species. The only insects to survive were katydids, cockroaches, and an exotic species of ant known as *Paratrechina longicornus*—the crazy ant—which swarmed over every ecosystem in the enclosure. During the second year of the crew's stay, the complex needed to be regularly resuscitated with oxygen, and by 1994 attempts at self-sufficient living were abandoned. Despite annual energy inputs costing up to $1 million, the regulation of biogeochemical cycles in a closed ecosystem proved to be more complex than imagined.

While the designers of Biosphere 2 hoped to create a hermetically sealed building—that was the purpose of their experiment—we can find this an instructive cautionary tale. In some imaginations the fantasy of Biosphere 2 suggests that we are actually capable of reinventing and controlling the natural systems that have evolved over billions of years to create life on Earth. Such a view treats us as little more than machines, which need only regulated nutrient flows to survive, but don't need an unobstructed view of the sky, or the feel of a natural breeze on the skin, or the taste of fresh fruit from a nearby tree rooted in the deep, inimitable microcosmos of the Earth's soil.

This is not to gainsay technology or scientific inquiry; both are crucial to the human prospect. But in these technologically marvelous times we would do well to consider what we intend with our technical innovations. The unexamined innovations of the industrial revolution gave us a civilization that uses technology to overcome the rules of the natural world, and, along with astonishing wealth, we got a century of extraordinary ecological decline. Indeed, the enthusiasts of space colonies need only travel to the copper mines of Chile or the nickel mines of Ontario to find a landscape devoid of earthly life. Sadly, we don't need to go so far to see the world's unraveling.

Barren landscapes, however, are not the inevitable outcome of the human presence in the world. They are instead the result of design failures that express just how little we know of our place on Earth. But design can also express ecological intelligence, which is rooted in the intention to understand the nature of interdependence rather than the application of brute force. Attuned to the flow of natural processes, ecologically intelligent design, we could say, is the practice of the language of landscape, the performance of fluent dialogues with place. An ecologically intelligent designer, rather than shutting the world out, attends to the way nature works, seeking information from the unique characteristics of locale. The availability of sunlight, shade, and water; the subtleties of climate and terrain; the health of local birds, flowers, and grasses all become fundamental to design. And when the making of a broad spectrum of things—from buildings and energy systems to cities and regional plans—is informed by a mindfulness to the particularities of place, we might begin to experience nature's reemergence in our everyday lives and see the landscape anew.

Exploring the use of mass, membrane, and transparency in architecture reveals how design can participate in landscape. Biosphere 2 is an extreme example of an impermeable membrane, but it is really only the logical extension of the controlled environment of a Phoenix high-rise, which uses glass to create the illusion of transparency. The windows provide distant views but don't open; people are trapped indoors while the heat of the sun pours in and air conditioning creates a habitable interior world. But there is a signal of a new design strategy in another way of living in the desert, practiced by a culture that has perfected the art of permeability—the Bedouin.

15   *Bedu* is the Arabic word for "inhabitant of the desert." For centuries the Bedouin tribes migrated from oasis to oasis in the deserts of Arabia and the Sinai. They moved about in a land in which every element of survival—food, water, soil, energy—was devastatingly rare. And yet the culture that emerged from these extremities could hardly be called arid. Instead, from a deep understanding of the harsh realities of the land grew both a fierce protectiveness of territory and a rich tradition of music, poetry, hospitality, and elegant design.

The Bedouin tent, for example, shows how simple and elegant—how suited to locale—good design can be. On the move in their migratory rounds, the Bedouin needed shelter that was both portable and reliable in a variety of conditions. On the plains of the Sinai, temperatures often rise above 120°F. There is neither shade nor breeze. But the black Bedouin tent of coarsely woven goat hair provides a breathing membrane. The black surface creates a deep shade while the coarse weave diffuses the sunlight, creating a beautifully illuminated interior. As the sun heats the dark fabric, hot air rises above the tent and air from inside is drawn out, in effect creating a cooling breeze. When it rains—as even in the desert it sometimes does—the woven fibers swell, the tiny holes in the fabric close, and the structure becomes tight. The tent is lightweight and portable and can be easily repaired; the fabric factory—the goats—followed the Bedouin around, providing valuable wool while transforming the botany of the desert into horn, skins, meat, milk, butter, and cheese. When the tent wears out, it can be composted, returning nutrients to the precious soil of a river valley oasis. This ingenious design, locally relevant and culturally rich, makes the desert skyscraper's stark separation from local material and energy flows look downright primitive.

Most Western buildings, like high-rises of glass and steel, are designed without a thought for locale. There is, however, a vernacular tradition that can still be drawn on to begin to reconnect the human habitat with the natural world. Vernacular architecture is often thought to be the poor country cousin of "real" architecture—the happenstance outcome of local tinkering rightfully overshadowed by the world's great buildings. As Nicholas Pevsner famously said, "A bicycle shed is a building; a cathedral is architecture." But while we venerate the beauty of our soaring cathedrals and museums, we might also begin to think of vernacular architecture as a rich and evolving aesthetic tradition in its own right, an art that elegantly expresses "the native language of the region."

In the vernacular tradition, good design springs from what fits. In New England, for example, the traditional saltbox house provided shelter from the extremities of the northern winter by responding to what nature allowed and offered. The house was built with a high south wall with many windows to take full advantage of the light of the sun. A steep roof shed driving rain. The hearth was placed in the center of the house so that the warmth radiating from the heated mass of the chimney would not be stolen by bitter winds buffeting the outer walls. On the north side of the house evergreens were planted to further protect it from harsh winter weather. And on the southwest, a maple tree provided shade in the summer and sugar in the spring. The trees became an essential part of the house and the house a part of the landscape. If human artifice is seen as an artifact of nature, they are one.

Working with educator David Orr at Oberlin College, we designed a new environmental studies center that is not only sensitive to locale, but is itself like a tree: a building enmeshed in local energy flows that accrues solar energy, purifies water, and provides habitat for native species. The energy of the sun is collected with rooftop solar cells and pours through southwest-facing windows into a two-story atrium, lighting the public gathering areas. Wastewater is purified by a constructed marshlike ecosystem that breaks down and digests organic material and releases clean, safe water. An earthen berm protects the north side of the center from harsh weather, as do the young trees in the newly planted forest grove, which has begun the long process of reestablishing the habitat of the building's northern Ohio location. And even though the interior feels much like an outdoor classroom—it's lit by the sun and refreshed with fragrant breezes—the students spend much of their time outside tending the garden and orchard. The building offers students and teachers ongoing participation in natural processes.

20   Perhaps the most moving lesson imparted by the building is that the human presence in the landscape can be regenerative. Not simply benign or less bad, but positive, vital, and good. This is not a rhetorical lesson. At Oberlin, habits of mind grow out of daily interactions with wind, water, soil, and trees; they become the skills and knowledge that inform intelligent design. Those skills can be carried many places, allowing an engagement with the living presence not just of the picturesque or the pastoral but also of a mosaic of extreme landscapes in need of restoration: landfills, crumbling neighborhoods, industrial sites, old cities rent by superhighways. This is the new geography of hope.

On Fifth Avenue in Manhattan, if you look north or south from around 74th Street, you may see sailing over the uptown traffic an enormous red-tailed hawk. Red-tails have been living on the 12th-story ledge of a building on the east side of Fifth Avenue for nearly a decade now, and their nest, a big, shapely tangle of sticks, is visible from the street. If you're lucky, or just patient, you may see the hawks perched on a balcony railing or gliding from the nest on airborne hunts for pigeons and songbirds in nearby Central Park.

It's not what most people expect to find in New York—in fact, it's miraculous to behold—but the hawks are hardly alone in reclaiming a perch in the city. Peregrine falcons, once nearly extinct, nest on skyscrapers and bridges. Egrets, herons, and bitterns have returned to the islands of the East River and New York Harbor. Snowy owls, notes Anne Matthews, a chronicler of wild New York, hunt rabbits along the runways of JFK International Airport. And along with the locals, "migrating birds fly over Manhattan nearly every night of the year."

The presence of wild birds in New York is just the most visible evidence that the city is a complex, evolving ecosystem. A 40-island archipelago where the surge of tidal currents has never ceased, where sea air drifts down Brooklyn subway steps, New York is an organism embedded in nature. Still, the return of wild creatures is a striking reminder. North American cities have always been most strongly connected to the wild and the rural by the flow of raw materials, goods, and waste. As the historian William Cronon tells it, the story of cities is the story of the economic and ecological relationships between a metropolis and its rural hinterland. Typically, a city's economic life transforms the landscape in ways that are not terribly friendly to wild animals, whether they live within urban borders or in the far-off landscapes that are the source of metropolitan wealth. In most cases, the animals aren't moving in, they're moving out.

Consider 19th-century Chicago. In *Nature's Metropolis*, Cronon traces how Chicago's grain, meat, and timber markets transformed the landscape of the West. Railroads, grain elevators, cow pastures, stockyards, feedlots, and wheat farms stretching from Illinois to the Rocky Mountains all emerged in relation to Chicago's markets. All of these landscapes of production created a "gritty web of material connections" that fed, clothed, and sheltered the people of Chicago and its hinterland, many of whom enjoyed the benefits of a thriving culture. But not without cost. The harvest of commodities also created a bevy of "ghost landscapes" on both ends of the rails that carried nature to market. On one end, the overcut white pine forests of Wisconsin, the plowed-under tallgrass prairie, and the slaughter of the bison. On the other, the hovering dark cloud of coal smoke, the stench of meatpacking, the sorrow of tenement dwellings in the Great Gray City. All of which is to say that landscapes rural, urban, wild, and industrial share a common fate: To do well by one, we must do well by all.

We'd like to suggest that each of these landscapes can be a   25
healthy, generative place, a place that allows people and nature to fruitfully co-exist. The industrial revolution is not the model by which we gauge our hopes. The conflicts between nature and industry evident in Chicago's story—the same conflicts that have yielded ghost landscapes all over the world—were not the result of a grand, carefully conceived plan. Instead, they took place gradually as industrialists, engineers, and designers tried to solve problems and take immediate advantage of what they considered to be opportunities in a period of massive and rapid change. Few foresaw the exhaustion of the Earth's resources or appreciated the true beneficence of its natural systems. The ways in which natural resources were used to produce goods reflected the spirit of the day—and yielded a host of unintended, yet tragic consequences. Today, design can reflect our growing knowledge of the living Earth, allowing participation in landscape that not only renews our engagement with the natural world, but restores the land itself.

Conception of place is the foundation of ecological intelligence. With Earth in mind, our relation to the landscapes we use changes dramatically. Consider, for example, the Menomonee of Wisconsin, a tribe that has been harvesting wood for generations using a method of logging that allows forests to thrive. Conventional logging operations, like those that cut timber during Chicago's boom years, are focused on the single-purpose, utilitarian goal of producing a certain amount of wood pulp. Little attention is given to nesting birds, the diversity of microorganisms in the soil, or the headwater streams that emerge in the shadows of the forest canopy. The result is a clear-cut landscape devoid of the rich diversity of life. The Menomonee, on the other hand, principally cut only the weaker trees, leaving the strong mother trees and preserving connectivity in the upper canopy for birds and arboreal animals. On the ground, the living system of the forest also remains intact. There is sunlight and shade, the nutrient cycles are uninterrupted, and water flows from the land as it has for generations. The forest remains a forest, a celebration of abundance and biota, shadow and life.

This strategy has been enormously productive. In the 1870s, the Menomonee identified 1.3 billion standing board feet of timber—what, in the timber industry, is tellingly known as stumpage—on a 235,000-acre reservation. Over the years they have harvested 2.25 billion board feet and there are 1.7 billion standing. One might say they have figured out what the forest can productively offer them.

Industry, too, can be a regenerative force. When designers employ the intelligence of natural systems—the abundance of the sun's energy, the effectiveness of nutrient cycling—both factories and manufactured products can nourish rather than deplete the world. We are currently leading a team restoring an industrial site, for example, that at one time would have been abandoned. Built more than 75 years ago, the site was one of the most productive in the world. By the end of the 20th century, however, it had become a brownfield, a sprawling wasteland of dilapidated buildings, leaky pipes, and old equipment. The land was contaminated, bare of all but the most persistent vegetation, and a nearby river was badly polluted. The company could have fenced off the site and built a new factory where land and labor are cheap. Instead, it decided to transform it into a healthy, productive, life-supporting place.

The new plant we're designing will feature skylights for daylighting the factory floor and a roof covered with growing plants. The "living roof" will provide habitat for birds, insects, and microorganisms and, in concert with porous paving and a series of constructed wetlands and swales, will control and filter storm water runoff. Native grasses and other plants will be used to rid the soil of contaminants, and thousands of trees will be planted to create habitat for songbirds and aid in the bio-remediation. It is a landscape of renewal.

No gesture of restoration is trivial. Yet renewing the industrial 30 landscape is certainly deepened when all the ways in which we use energy and materials are in harmony with the larger patterns of life. That's why we've begun to create products designed with the same care as the ecologically intelligent factories that manufacture them, products made with materials that, like the blossoms of a fruit tree, provide nourishment for something new after each useful life. The carpeting used in the Oberlin College building, for example, is leased from a manufacturer that will retrieve and reuse the materials for new, high-quality carpets. The upholstery fabric used for the auditorium chairs is biodegradable; when the fabric needs to be replaced it is removed from the frame of the chair and becomes food for the garden. We call these discrete material loops the "technical metabolism" and the "biological metabolism" and their elements, biological and technical "nutrients." When all manufactured products and materials are designed as nutrients that flow in these closed-loop cycles, we will be able to celebrate, rather than lament, the human ecological footprint.

Imagine the fruits of such a shift on a large scale. Imagine a garden metropolis, a city of buildings like trees. To begin, even a single building like a tree in an urban neighborhood could spark a meaningful transformation. In communities with an industrial past, such as Brooklyn's Red Hook and Gowanus neighborhoods, a building designed to be part of nature provides a place for residents to experience firsthand the natural processes that sustain life.

In the 19th century Red Hook and Gowanus, like old Chicago, nature came to market. In the 1850s, in fact, the warehouses on the Brooklyn waterfront stored for shipment to foreign markets the grain grown in Chicago's hinterland and shipped east via the Erie Canal. In Brooklyn, the grain barges traveled the Gowanus Canal, formerly a creek that meandered through the wetlands of the Red Hook peninsula. Markets and fortunes changed, but the neighborhoods have nearly always been both a hardscrabble town and an industrial vortex, drawing refineries, factories, shipyards, and Robert Moses' elevated freeways. It's not an easy place to garden.

Yet, as in Manhattan, there is an emerging sense that nature has a place here. The sprawling rooftops of the old warehouses are wonderful places to invite her return. Blue crabs and pink jellyfish have already returned to the beleaguered canal, the first living creatures seen in the Gowanus in decades. People are returning to the docks, not only to work in new commercial ventures, but to fish, stroll, and watch the waters of Upper New York Bay. A conventional developer might see this landscape as empty, ripe for taking and making; an ecologist might see that it is full of life and possibility. Why not enhance the local web of life? Why not cultivate an urban agricultural district on the rooftops of Red Hook and Gowanus, a network of public gardens that makes visible the vital connections between water, soil, food, and human culture?

The residents of Gowanus have already begun to do so. An old soap factory a couple of blocks from the canal has been converted into a thriving arts center, and plans call for ongoing renovations to the building that will make it even more of a community hub. A rooftop garden will be planted with wildflowers, herbs, and vegetables. Neighbors will tend the garden, producing food for their families and for the children who attend after-school dance classes in the studio housed below, where the windows open wide and the air is sometimes touched with the scent of the sea. While solar panels harvest the power of the sun, cisterns will collect rainwater. Even the building's wastewater will flow in cycles; it will be purified by an indoor botanical garden on the ground floor and reused to water the garden, a profoundly meaningful process in a neighborhood that once flushed its sewage into the canal. Over a day, over a year, over a lifetime, sense and gesture in this small garden world will reveal the living layers of landscape.

35   It may be years before buildings like trees, rooftop gardens, and the return of birds and wildflowers, block by block, reshape the urban landscape. Years, too, before intelligence and attention and the work of our hands heal our rivers, forests, farmlands, and small towns. But the renewal of an old conversation with the natural world has begun. By our own intentions and by grace we will grow more fluent. This is the work and the pleasure of generations to come. Through it we will find our way home and realize, as we grow ever more aware of our place in the landscape, that we have been home all along.

Guiding Questions

1. McDonough and Braungart contrast two building designs: the Biosphere 2 project and the Bedouin tent. What point do they attempt to make by examining these two very different approaches to design?

2. To what audience do you think this article was addressed? On what basis can you make this judgment?

3. The essay introduces specialized language—"vernacular architecture," "technical metabolism," "biological metabolism." How did this affect your reading experience? Do the authors make their essay accessible to readers who may be unfamiliar with such terms?

Paths for Further Exploration

1. Describe something that you have designed (or redesigned). What was this process like? Describe the finished product: What did it do? Was it successful?
2. Throughout this essay, the authors ask you to imagine places that have been designed in more sustainable ways. Based on the design concepts and examples they outline, write a proposal for how to redesign a particular place.

CHAPTER 4

Tools for Getting Places

This chapter offers a toolkit of exercises and resources to guide your exploration of places, including brainstorming exercises, tips for interviewing, observation techniques and helpful online resources. The toolkit is arranged in eleven subsections: (1) getting oriented, (2) interviewing, (3) taking notes as you observe, (4) responding to classmates' Essays on Place, (5) locating aerial and topographical photos, (6) bioregional quizzes, (7) accessing webcams, (8) letterboxing, (9) neighborhood writing groups, (10) chambers of commerce, historical societies, and college or university archives, and (11) online databases.

GETTING ORIENTED

The following brainstorming exercises will help you start thinking about places and hone your descriptive and analytical skills.

1. Find a photograph of a place important to you. Study the image and then begin writing about it:
   - What place is captured in the picture? Where is it? Why is it important?
   - Describe the physical aspects of the place.
   - Describe your emotions, both during the time the photograph was taken and as you study it.
   - Who took the photograph? Who, if anyone, is in the photograph?

   Are there specific answers from this list that you can develop into an essay? As you begin writing about this photograph, remember to concentrate on the details and try to contextualize—not merely retell—a story of this place.

2. Explore your campus and select a persuasive text—a flyer, e-mail petition, party invitation, advertisement, editorial, "roommate wanted" ad, etc. Where did you find the text? What kind of persuasive methods does it use to appeal to its audience? Think about the community that generated this text and the community that received it—are they the same? What does this text indicate about this particular place and its communities?

3. Find a copy of your school's catalog/application package and study the photographs, statistics, and student testimonies. Determine how your college is "selling" itself; think about its persuasive techniques and its audience. Now log on to your school's Web site and compare the information, format, and audience. Do you feel the institution's representation of itself resonates with your understanding of the place?

4. Choose a restaurant and "read" it: Start with the specifics (location, interior, music, arrangement of tables) then step back and analyze why this place exists, and what it reflects about society. Reread Julia Corbett's "Robotic Iguanas" and think about how the function and purpose of restaurants has changed in the last few decades and what those changes reflect about society.

5. On a sheet of paper, draw a map of your hometown, current location, or where you imagine you will be in the future. Draw the places that are most significant to you: your house, apartment, or dorm and those of your friends, a favorite hangout, your high school, and so forth. Spend ten minutes or so drawing, then choose one of the places on your map and write about it. Describe it in as much detail as you can, from the physical description of the place to the emotional attachment you have to it. Why is this place on your map? How does it connect to the other places? If you were to write a research paper about this place, what angle might you take? Who do you associate with this place?

INTERVIEWING

Locating Interview Subjects

Talking to other people is a great resource for exploring places. Here are some tips to get you started.

- People you already know (parents, neighbors, roommates, coworkers) can be great sources of information. Consider the place you are writing about and what kind of information you seek. If you are experiencing a new place, can you interview an "insider," someone who knows the place, its culture, and patterns well? If you are an insider, perhaps you would like to interview a newcomer, someone who can notice customs and details that have become commonplace to you.

- If you are hoping to interview someone you do not know well, what should you consider regarding asking permission and requesting that person's time? What does it require to be a good and respectful questioner and listener?

Asking the Right Questions

- **Tell me about . . . :** The broadest question. Might get your interviewee to talk widely and explore aspects of a place you would not consider. Good opener.
- **Who, What, When, How, Where, Why:** More directed questions but still open-ended. Good for getting specific but broad information.
- **Yes/No Questions:** Narrow questions that clarify a point, obtain specific information. Good for follow-ups or seeking out details.

Recording an Interview

There is no right way to record an interview; decide the advantages and disadvantages for yourself:

- *Tape or digital recorder:* Allows you to focus on the discussion without struggling to write it all down. You will need to have and be able to use the technology. Requires transcribing later, which can be time-consuming, but you will have the exact words. Some people may feel inhibited when being recorded, and you should always receive permission first.
- *Note-taking:* Many of the world's best interviewers do not record but listen and converse, writing down important words or phrases as the person talks. Immediately after the interview, they add to those notes to make up a transcript.
- *E-mail:* E-mail and instant messaging allow for text-based interviews, which can be useful if interviewing someone at a distance; plus, the transcript comes ready-made. It is more work for the interviewees, however, and you do not get to hear their tone or sense their emotions and physical presence from working solely in print.

What to Do with Interview Information

There are several possibilities:

1. *Summarize* (with no quoting): Best used to convey information that might not be all that interesting to read in a quote.

   - *Example:* Kaitlin told me about how working here has helped her meet more people around town and understand how the community works together. Certain town organizations want tickets to their upcoming events to be available at the Gourmet because of the large volume of people passing through. Currently, the PTA asked the shop to sell the Annual Wine Tasting tickets to customers.

2. *Quote a key word or phrase:* Best used to capture the flavor or uniqueness of the speaker's tone.

   - *Example:* Dennis asserted that the weekdays were filled with "business people and school teachers" bustling to get to work.

3. *Integrate a quote into part of a sentence:* Best used to fit in the speaker's words as a grammatical part of a sentence.

   - *Example:* Martha quickly asserted, "this place wouldn't work as a chain." Too many people feel this atmosphere is better than an "impersonal store like a CVS."

4. *Quote complete sentences:* Best used when a speaker's sentence can't be paraphrased without losing something important.

   - *Example:* If Wal-Marts and Starbucks are replacing mom-and-pop stores, could these sweeps affect the Gourmet? "Definitely not," he said without hesitation. "There exists a certain ritualism here. Everyone has their own niche."

5. *Quote a longer block of text:* Best used to allow the speaker's voice to really be heard by your readers in an extended manner.

   - *Example:* Tom remembers the early days of the Gourmet:

   When this place opened, you could buy a coffee for 59 cents. A bagel was 75. Everyone knew everyone. The postman, boy, he was a crabby man, but he always took his break here and sat in that corner warming up on cold mornings. There were no Starbucks back then.

Exercise: Working with an Interview Transcript

Questions to Consider

1. What kind of angle or approach to place do you draw from the interview transcript below. What is the most interesting idea or aspect of this place, according to the interviewee?
2. Underline the five best or most useful phrases or sentences in the transcript.
3. Write one sentence incorporating some part of this transcript in a way that you might do so if you were writing an essay.

Paula Mathieu, November 2, 2004:

What I like about Old Cambridge Baptist Church is that its looks are deceiving. From the outside, it seems like a stately, old, and maybe even stodgy New England Church. I mean, it's right next door to the Harvard Inn. But then when you step inside, you see a whole different world, way more eclectic and funky, way more connected to the world, you know? I mean, step in the vestibule and you might see ballet dancers from the Jose Matteo Dance Company preparing for their evening performance. Kids from the neighborhood can take dance lessons there too. But the ballet company shares space with Irv's Sunday morning Church service. It's not a stodgy, high-church place at all. It's worn looking—could use good paint job. And then the basement, wow, it's like a beehive of activity. I remember the first day I walked down the stairs there. Had to duck my head so I wouldn't hit it on the hanging pipes. The place was so dark, with narrow passages. I didn't think too much at the time. I dunno, it's funny how things change when you've been going for a while and then you look back and boy they were different than before, do you know what I'm saying? Anyhow, the basement houses so many different charity and activist organizations—Spare Change News, which is a newspaper sold by homeless people as a positive alternative to begging; Bread and Jams, a homeless day shelter; Solutions at Work, a jobs program and furniture bank. Those are the groups I know the most about. But then there's also the Gay and Lesbian Task Force and the Ethiopian Women's Group. But the whole place is a network of important activity, of real life, where people can go and get help if they need it. To me that's what makes OCBC a great Church—it really is of its community and plays an active role in it. Homeless people, dancers, churchgoers, gays and lesbians, Ethiopian women all can find a home there. It's not just a Sunday operation, but it caters to its "flock" seven days a week in a variety of ways.

How to List Interviews in Your Works Cited

Mathieu, Paula. Personal Interview. 2 November, 2004.

TAKING NOTES AS YOU OBSERVE A PLACE

Here is an exercise to help you practice and hone your observational skills. Find a place on campus and plan to spend at least 30 minutes observing and taking notes. Evenly divide a sheet of paper vertically into two columns. In the right column, perhaps using bullets to denote each observation, write down everything you observe: the smells of a place, the people around you, etc. Be as observant of your surroundings as possible, even if the place is familiar to you. Write down everything you can, but also take time to pause and look around.

Later, when you return to your room, sit down with these pages of observations and carefully review each item. Try to make some connections and analytical observations and to ask some questions. In the left column, write down these connections. Follow the example below—some observations and conclusions about a student athletic complex:

Conclusions	Observations
Some students describe the "plex" as one of the most intimidating places on campus.	It's 12:00 and the place is very crowded.
	Many female students are using the Stairmaster.
Women who are exercising on these machines are called the Elliptical Nazis.	
	Instructors work out early in the morning.
	Athletes use the facility throughout the day.
How much does this place contribute to the eating disorders epidemic on campus?	Mostly women are using the facility.
What other campus spaces are popular with faculty and students outside of the classroom?	
Are these facilities safe?	Some of the equipment looks dated.

I wish I had noticed the number of
females versus males; I'll notice
this detail the next time I visit.

Who can I talk to about plans for
renovating the complex?

Some of the connections in the left column could lead to a number of interesting essays. As you review your observations, continue making connections and thinking in broader terms about your place. The left column will help you determine what details you can enhance, summarize, or leave out completely. You will want your descriptive essays to be a balance of concrete observations and abstract connections and conclusions—in other words, a balance of information from both columns.

RESPONDING TO CLASSMATES' ESSAYS ON PLACE

The questions below can help you respond to classmates' place writing. Write at least a few sentences addressing each of the following topic areas.

Angle

Has the writer crafted a clear angle or interesting hook that interests the reader in the piece? What is the angle? What could the writer do to engage the audience right from the beginning?

Observational Writing Skills

Has the writer clearly evoked the place or culture he or she wants to write about? Is the place clearly described, with interesting details that point to significant things or help to say something significant about it? Does this writing appeal to your senses as a reader? Is there enough description? Too much? What could help you understand and experience the place more fully?

Inside Versus Outside Knowledge and Audience Awareness

How is the writer's status as insider, outsider, or both treated? If the writer is an insider, does he or she provide enough background for readers who are outsiders? What additional information would be useful? If the writer is an outsider, does he or she convey enthusiasm and curiosity about the topic? What additional information would be useful? As a reader, is there anything (terms, concepts, places) you do not fully understand or want to know more about? What additional research or information would you find useful?

Interviews

What role do the interviews play? Has the writer interviewed one or more interesting informants about the place or culture? Would more questions for that informant or questions of other informants help clarify or expand the piece? What central questions have been answered through the use of the interviews? What questions do you wish the writer might have asked? Is enough material quoted directly from the interviews—or was there too much? Do you get a vivid sense of the interviewees? What could the writer do to give a clearer sense of the informant(s)?

Tone and Writing Style

Does the piece have any humor in it? At what points in the paper do you think humor might be appropriate? Are the overall tone and writing style concise, engaging, and a pleasure to read? What revisions should the writer consider regarding writing style and tone?

For the Reader

What aspects of this paper might be useful to readers in revising their own papers?

LOCATING AERIAL AND TOPOGRAPHICAL PHOTOS

Looking at your hometown, campus, house, or residence hall from above can enrich your sense of a place you already know well, and the topographic maps can give you a stronger sense of how the environmental features of any given place affect how those who live there experience it. You can locate aerial and topographical photos through TerraServer (http://terraserver-usa.com/), which is sponsored by the U.S. Geological Survey in partnership with Microsoft Corporation and others. This service provides users with the ability to view USGS aerial imagery and topographic maps of nearly any address they might want to view.

BIOREGIONAL QUIZZES

Bioregional quizzes test how much you know about the environment around you, and can be prompts for research and discovery. "Where You At?" is a well-known bioregional quiz and is currently hosted on the Web site of the Association for the Study of Literature and Environment (ASLE) at http://www.asle.umn.edu/archive/readings/quiz.html. Students from rural areas are more likely to do well on this quiz, but even they will be challenged by it, as most of us (unless we are already committed environmentalists and observers of place) know very few of the answers to these questions.

Where You At? A Bioregional Quiz

Developed by Leonard Charles, Jim Dodge, Lynn Milliman, and Victoria Stockley. First appeared in *Coevolution Quarterly* 32 (Winter 1981): 1.

1. Trace the water you drink from precipitation to tap.
2. How many days until the moon is full? (Slack of two days allowed.)
3. What soil series are you standing on?
4. What was the total rainfall in your area last year (July–June)? (Slack: 1 inch for every 20 inches.)
5. When was the last time a fire burned in your area?
6. What were the primary subsistence techniques of the culture that lived in your area before you?
7. Name five edible plants in your region and their season(s) of availability.
8. From what direction do winter storms generally come in your region?
9. Where does your garbage go?
10. How long is the growing season where you live?
11. On what day of the year are the shadows the shortest where you live?
12. When do the deer rut in your region, and when are the young born?
13. Name five grasses in your area. Are any of them native?
14. Name five resident and five migratory birds in your area.
15. What is the land use history of your region?
16. What primary ecological event/process influenced the landform where you live? (Bonus special: What's the evidence?)
17. What species have become extinct in your area?
18. What are the major plant associations in your region?

19. From where you're reading this, point north.
20. What spring wildflower is consistently among the first to bloom where you live?

Scoring

0–3: You have your head up your ass.

4–7: It's hard to be in two places at once when you're not anywhere at all.

8–12: A firm grasp of the obvious.

13–16: You're paying attention.

17–19: You know where you're at.

20: You not only know where you're at, you know where it's at.

Here are some supplemental bioregional activities and questions:

1. Trace the flow of water (especially runoff from storms and watering lawns) from your home to an ocean or a large underground aquifer.
2. Choose a favorite meal and trace the ingredients backward as far as you can go, noting how many states or countries are involved.
3. Trace the path of the energy that powers your home or residence hall from its source to you. What pollutants are released along this pathway and by what processes?
4. What are three environmental issues facing your home area and/or your school's area?
5. What is the elevation above sea level where you live now?
6. Name seven trees common in your area.
7. Name seven mammals common in your area.
8. Name seven birds common in your area. Which are year-round residents? Which are summer residents, and where do they migrate to in the winter?
9. Name the three major waterways or bodies of water in your region.
10. How many full constellations can you see on moonless nights in your area?

ACCESSING WEBCAMS

Webcams are great resources for viewing public places at a distance, and for prompting research into how different modes of surveillance (and our awareness of them) change our relationships to place. Many city centers, campuses, and historic locations have webcams that let remote viewers get a sense of the daily ebb and flow of people and activities. More specialized webcams allow browsers to track the progress of storms, volcanoes, various animal species, and even traffic. The Worldwide Webcam Directory, a collection of links to public webcams, can be found at http://www.leonardsworlds.com/camera.html.

LETTERBOXING

Letterboxing (http://www.letterboxing.org/) is an activity that began some years ago in the United Kingdom and has now spread to North America. It provides creative opportunities for exploring an area or place. Letterboxes lead each other on elaborate scavenger hunts, leaving personalized clues in small, homemade boxes for each other to follow in a search through an evolving variety of public places. A place-based writing class might want to consider a letterboxing campaign on or near campus.

NEIGHBORHOOD WRITING GROUPS

Groups like the Chicago Neighborhood Writing Alliance (http://www.jot.org/index.html), sponsors of the *Journal of Ordinary Thought*, and others like them throughout the United States encourage writers from all walks of life to write about what is important to them. Often, these writers engage concepts of place in provocative ways, coming from perspectives not always found in a college setting. Check community Web sites in your own area to find similar writing communities.

CHAMBERS OF COMMERCE, HISTORICAL SOCIETIES, AND COLLEGE OR UNIVERSITY ARCHIVES

Local chambers of commerce and historical societies (most have Web sites) can be good resources (along with the reference materials in your campus library) for research into local places. Architectural records, zoning laws, historical development statistics, land use histories, and much more can be found through these organizations. Most colleges and universities also have archive collections of materials deemed important to the history of a school (and often of the surrounding areas). These collections often include valuable records of the physical and cultural history of a school, and academic archivists are usually thrilled to talk to students and help them with research projects. Talk to a professor or a reference librarian about getting access to these materials.

ONLINE DATABASES

Many search engines, including general ones like Google, will lead you to a variety of Web sites that might assist you in your research of particular places. Online databases like Expanded Academic Index or LexisNexis, usually available through your campus library, are good places to start your research.

Arrieta, Rose. "A Nation Divided," from *Orion* (Vol. 22, No. 4, July/Aug. 2003, pp. 34–41). Reprinted by permission of George Washington Williams Fellowship.

Black, Catherine. "The Joy of Mud," from *Re-Generation*. Edited by Jennifer Karlin & Amelia Borofsky, copyright © 2003 by Jennifer Karlin & Amelia Borofsky. Used by permission of Jeremy P. Tarcher, an imprint of Penguin Group (USA) Inc.

Casassa, Andrea J. "The Coffee Shop." By permission of the author.

Casimiro, Gian-Karlo. "Get Off at 161st and Transfer to the Truth." By permission of the author.

Corbett, Julia. "Robotic Iguanus," from *Orion* (Sept./Oct. 2003). Reprinted by permission of the author and *Orion*.

de la Huerta, Gabriela. "In My Kitchen" is reprinted with the permission of the author. Originally published by the Neighborhood Writing Alliance in the *Journal of Ordinary Thought* (Fall 2002).

Di Tata, Virginia. "A Bridge Between Two Cultures." By permission of the author.

Doheny-Farina, Stephen. "Virtual Vermont: The Rise of the Global and the Decline of the Local," from *The Wired Neighborhood* (1996), pp. 41–55. Reprinted by permission of Yale University Press.

Dudley, Mathew. "The Dope on Head Shops." By permission of the author.

Dunn, Robin E. "King's Chapel and Burying Ground." By permission of the author.

Fabbri, Salvatore M. "Scientific Applications." By permission of the author.

Fletcher, Ron. "By Dawn's Early Light," from *Boston Daily Globe*. Copyright © 2003 by Globe Newspaper Co. (MA). Reproduced with permission of Globe Newspaper Co. (MA) in the format Textbook via Copyright Clearance Center.

Frazier, Ian. "Someplace in Queens." Originally appeared in *Double Take Magazine* (Summer 1997). Reprinted by permission of the author.

Gonzalez, Ray. "Hazardous Cargo," from *Milkweed's: The Colors of Nature*. Copyright © Ray Gonzalez. Used by permission of the author.

Harden, Blaine. "A History in Concrete," from *Preservation Magazine* (Nov./Dec. 1996). Courtesy of Blaine Harden.